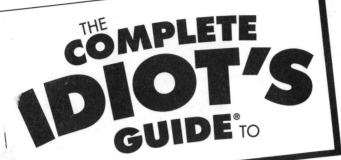

THE COMPLETE IDIOT'S GUIDE® TO

Slow Cooker Cooking

by Ellen Brown

A member of Penguin Group (USA) Inc.

*This book is dedicated to my family—Nancy, Walter, Ariela, Jesse, Josh, and Ilan—with
gratitude for their love and support during the many changes in my life.*

International Standard Book Number: 1-59257-136-0
Library of Congress Catalog Card Number: 2003108346

05   04   8   7   6   5   4   3

Interpretation of the printing code: The rightmost number of the first series of numbers is the year of the
book's printing; the rightmost number of the second series of numbers is the number of the book's printing.
For example, a printing code of 03-1 shows that the first printing occurred in 2003.

Printed in the United States of America

Publisher: *Marie Butler-Knight*
Product Manager: *Phil Kitchel*
Senior Managing Editor: *Jennifer Chisholm*
Senior Acquisitions Editor: *Renee Wilmeth*
Development Editor/Senior Production Editor: *Christy Wagner*
Copy Editor: *Nancy Wagner*
Illustrator: *Chris Eliopoulos*
Cover/Book Designer: *Trina Wurst*
Indexer: *Brad Herriman*
Layout/Proofreading: *Donna Martin, Ayanna Lacey*

Contents at a Glance

Contents

Foreword

Anyone who has gotten married since the early 1970s probably has at least one slow cooker around the house. If yours is like mine, it's still in pretty good shape, although a bit dusty, because you just don't use it very much. And that's a shame.

Slow cooking, also known as braising or stewing, is actually one of the most ancient and well-respected cooking techniques known. Unfortunately, too many people think "slow cooking" is just a tough cut of meat and a couple cans of stuff left to simmer while they're at the office. Convenient? Sure, but appetizing? Hardly! So when I was first approached about writing this forward, I feared this would be yet another book of "can-opener cuisine." Happily, I was wrong.

As soon as the manuscript arrived I started reading, then I dusted off the ol' slow cooker and went into the kitchen. Frankly, although I work with food every day as a culinary arts instructor, I almost never use a slow cooker. It's such an easy technique that it seems like cheating. I never thought about using a slow cooker as being "real" cooking. The final results of my recipe tests were real, however—real good food.

Drawing on years of experience as a recipe developer, cook, and writer, Ellen Brown has produced a new collection of slow cooked dishes destined to become classics. Ellen's straightforward approach to slow cooking and easy-to-follow recipes explain how to get the most from your slow cooker without sacrificing quality and flavor. As you'll see, slow cooking techniques can be used to produce hearty soups and stews, vegetarian entrées, party treats, comforting desserts, and much more. With a properly stocked pantry and a little pre-planning, you can soon be enjoying healthy, gourmet food without spending a minute more than necessary in the kitchen.

Sure, slow cookers can make meals convenient, easy, and economical, but what we all *really* want is nutritious food that tastes great. This book takes slow cooking from quick convenience to gourmet cuisine. It includes dishes you'd expect to find— Sunday Pot Roast, Stuffed Peppers, Spinach and Artichoke Dip, and Chicken and Dumplings, for example. But Ellen also brings slow cooking techniques to gourmet endeavors such as Duck Confit (why didn't I think of that?!), Coq au Vin, Veal Marsala, Butternut Squash Bisque, and Lobster Bread Pudding.

Ethnic cuisines are also well represented. Recipes such as Cassoulet, Paella, Moussaka, Chinese Red Cooked Chicken, and Steamed Pork Dumplings make international cuisine doable even on a busy Tuesday night.

Ellen makes it clear that this is real food meant to be produced by and for real people. Let her show you what can be created when the "ancient" art of slow cooking meets the modern slow cooker.

Bon appétit,

Sarah R. Labensky

Sarah R. Labensky, CCP, is founding director of the Culinary Arts Institute at Mississippi University for Women, where she teaches cooking and administers MUW's four-year Baccalaureate degree program in culinary arts. She is also the co-author of eight culinary reference and text books, including the best-selling *On Cooking: A Textbook of Culinary Fundamentals* and *Webster's New World Dictionary of Culinary Arts*.

Introduction

It's really easy to make great food in a slow cooker. You fill it up, plug it in, turn it on, and walk away. Then voilà! You walk into the house hours later to be greeted by the luxurious aroma of the delicious, homemade dinner that awaits you. It's not magic, but it sure seems like it if you're harried and stressed at the end of a busy workday.

Or for those times when you have an enjoyable day of leisure, now you don't have to feel tied to the stove or feel guilty that your pleasure precluded a home-cooked meal for your family. With the slow cooker, neither work nor play requires sacrificing a nutritious dinner.

There's no question about it: Slow cooking has a role in our fast-paced lives. As time has become such a precious commodity, our dinner tables are increasingly filled with cardboard boxes from nutritionally bankrupt fast-food chains. Slow cooking provides the alternative. It does take some advance planning, but that becomes almost second nature once you've started using this simple electric appliance.

The recipes in this book are "real food." They're not made with convenience products that list more chemicals on their labels than words recognizable as foods. A slow cooker doesn't need modern magic. The principles of slow cooking go back centuries.

Economy is another benefit of slow cooking. It's the less tender and less expensive cuts of meat that are best suited to low heat. They become incredibly tender after a few hours in the slow cooker. And foods like dried beans, the basis for a treasure-trove of dishes, are just pennies per serving.

Slow cooking is also easy, and this book assumes only the most basic cooking skills. Many of the recipes take no more than 15 minutes of "hands-on" preparation time, and there are many tips for how to accomplish most, if not all, of the work the night before you cook the food. Because there are few cooking skills required, readying food for the slow cooker can even be a job parceled out to young family members—and why not make meal prep family time?

The slow cooker solves another of the societal quandaries we face today. On nights the family does not eat together, dinner can become a catch-as-catch-can feeding frenzy rather than a well-balanced meal. Problem solved with the slow cooker. Once the slow cooker has completed its work, the food can stay hot for a few hours. That means one member of the family can eat before a sports practice and another can enjoy the same quality of food after a movie.

The slow cooker is not a miracle machine. It can't do everything. It will never produce a crispy french fry or a fluffy angel food cake. But once you know what it can do—and learn that what it does, it does very well—the slow cooker will become part of your cooking regimen.

How This Book Is Organized

The book is divided into seven parts:

Part 1, "A Fast Course in Slow Cooking," will teach you all you need to know before turning on a slow cooker for the first time. There are sections explaining how slow cooking works, giving facts about food safety, and detailing what foods to stock in your pantry so you're always in the Express Lane at the supermarket. Another chapter tells you what foods work in slow cookers and how to modify your favorite recipes for slow cooking. When you finish this part, you're really cookin'.

Part 2, "Enticing Appetizers," showcases one of the slow cooker's many strengths—making delicious hot dips for parties. You'll also learn the range of other hors d'oeuvres the slow cooker can create, from crunchy nuts to satiny spreads.

Part 3, "Satisfying Soups," will convince you that soup is food for the soul. The recipes in this part run the gamut from a wide range of small vegetarian and bean soups to meals in a bowl made with poultry and meats.

The title of **Part 4, "Stews to Savor,"** says it all. The chapters in this part contain recipes for poultry and all sorts of meats. The last chapter sheds new light on an old favorite, chili, and its many variations.

Part 5, "Crock Around the Clock: Main Courses for All Times of Day," will demonstrate the slow cooker's versatility in creating delicious main dishes. The recipes in this part are for whole poultry pieces, roasts, and chops. There are also one-dish meals that come from many countries, and completing the section are dishes that are appropriate for breakfasts and brunches.

Part 6, "Healthful but Homey," encompasses many types of nutritious foods. One chapter showcases fish and seafood soups, stews, and main courses. Then there are several chapters devoted to categories of side dishes—vegetables, beans, and carbohydrates. These are recipes that become the star when your entrée is a simple food that has had a trip to the broiler or grill.

Part 7, "Grand Finales," includes dozens of homey desserts. There are recipes for healthful fruit dishes that glorify the best of the produce department, and there are also decadent chocolate and other rich concoctions that will satisfy even the most demanding sweet tooth.

After the dessert chapters you'll find some useful appendixes. There's a glossary to add to your knowledge of cooking lingo, and a chart to aid in converting measurements to the metric system.

Extras

In every chapter you'll find many boxes that give you extra information which is either helpful or just interesting.

Cooker Caveats

It's always a good idea to be alerted to potential problems in advance. Cooker Caveats boxes provide just such a warning, either about cooking in general or the recipe in particular.

Crock Tales

Check out these boxes for tidbits of food history and amusing quotes about food. They're fun to read and share with friends, and they'll make you sound like a real gourmet.

Ellen on Edibles

Cooking has a language all its own, and some of the terms and ingredients can be intimidating if you don't know what they mean. Look to these boxes for technique and ingredient definitions if you don't want to flip to the glossary.

Slow Savvy

Slow Savvy boxes are full of cooking tips. Some are specific to the recipe they accompany; others will boost your general cooking skills or give you ideas for food presentation. These tips are meant to make your life easier and your time in the kitchen more pleasurable.

Acknowledgments

Writing a book is a solitary endeavor, but its publication is always a team effort. My thanks go to …

Renee Wilmeth of Alpha Books and Gene Brissie of James Peters Associates for proposing the project.

Christy Wagner and Nancy Wagner for their expert and eagle-eyed editing.

Karen Berman for her expert advice and valuable culinary insights.

Tigger-Cat Brown, my furry companion who kept me company for endless hours at the computer—and ate all the mistakes.

Special Thanks to the Technical Reviewer

The technical reviewer for *The Complete Idiot's Guide to Slow Cooker Cooking* was Karen Berman, a Connecticut-based writer and editor who specializes in food and culture. She is a contributing editor to *Wine Enthusiast* magazine, and her work has appeared in magazines, newspapers, and newsletters. She is the author of an illustrated history book, *American Indian Traditions and Ceremonies,* and has worked in various editorial capacities on numerous cookbooks.

Trademarks

All terms mentioned in this book that are known to be or are suspected of being trademarks or service marks have been appropriately capitalized. Alpha Books and Penguin Group (USA) Inc. cannot attest to the accuracy of this information. Use of a term in this book should not be regarded as affecting the validity of any trademark or service mark.

Part 1

A Fast Course in Slow Cooking

Dishes made in a slow cooker deliver the same great taste as those cooked on top of the stove or in the oven. But there are fundamental differences in how those dishes get from mere ingredients to finished dish. In Part 1, you will learn about slow cookers and how to use them to become a slow cooking connoisseur.

After you become familiar with your slow cooker and its potential, you'll probably want to adapt your favorite recipes to cook in "slow mode." There's a section in this part to help you accomplish just that.

Gearing Up for Great Food

In This Chapter

◆ Slow cookers and how they work

◆ Choosing the slow cooker that's right for you

◆ Slow cooker food safety

◆ Foods to keep on hand in the kitchen

◆ Equipment that will speed preparation

◆ Recipes for homemade stocks

Turning a piece of meat over an open flame was prehistoric man's first culinary technique. This incendiary school of cookery was the only act in town for more than a millennium. Then it was complemented by slow cooking. The first slow cooking was done in pottery, as it is still today. By the fifth century B.C.E., iron pots holding simmering food were left to cook all day and night in the fire's embers.

Although slow cooking was a necessity in the past, today it's a choice. With some advance preparation, busy people can enjoy a delicious, home-made meal that cooked without anyone around to watch it—thanks to the slow cooker!

Anticipatory Aromas

The mouthwatering aroma that greets you when you walk into your home at the end of the day is the first benefit of a slow cooker. Although the food is barely simmering, it's been cooking for long enough that the innate flavors of all the ingredients have blended together and filled the air. By the time a dish is ready, it has been simmering for some time. Like a puff of smoke coming up from a genie's bottle, it lures you right to the kitchen.

Slow cooking continues to grow in popularity. *Appliance* magazine's annual survey of households showed that by 2001, slow cookers were present in 65 percent of American homes. That figure was up from 58.7 percent in 1994. The Rival company, the maker of the first slow cooker, the Crock-Pot®, places the figure even higher, at 69 percent.

> **Crock Tales**
>
> Rival introduced the first slow cooker, the Crock-Pot®, in 1971, and the introductory slogan remains true more than 30 years later: It "cooks all day while the cook's away." Crock-Pots® were originally produced in colors popular for appliances at the time—avocado and harvest gold. Rival now estimates that more than 80 million Crock-Pots® have been sold.

Slow Cooking Science

Slow cookers operate by cooking food using indirect heat at a low temperature for an extended period of time. Direct heat is the power of a stove burner underneath a pot; indirect heat is the overall heat that surrounds food in the oven. Think of it this way: If you're standing on a hot sidewalk, you're feeling direct heat, but the heat you feel when you're lounging on the beach under the sun and your whole body is warm is indirect heat.

Success Is the Sum of Its Parts

Slow cookers are not rocket science. They are simple, uncomplicated electric devices that are also energy efficient. A slow cooker uses about as much power as a 60-watt bulb. Here are its parts:

- A glass or plastic cover so you can see if the food is simmering without raising the lid.

- A crockery insert that holds the food and insulates it from contact with the heating elements. Once the food has cooked, the pottery holds the heat and keeps the food warm.

♦ A wrap-around heating element encased between the slow cooker's outer and inner layers of metal that never directly touches the crockery insert. As the element heats, it gently warms the air between the two layers of metal. The hot air heats the inner metal casing that touches the crockery. This construction method eliminates the need for stirring because no part of the pot gets hotter than any other.

♦ And last but not least, there is the control knob. All slow cookers have Low and High settings. Some also have a Stay Warm position. Some new machines have a programmable option that enables you to start food on High and then the slow cooker automatically reduces the heat to Low after a programmed time. The Low setting for most appliances is about 180°F, and the High setting is about 300°F.

Cooker Caveats

There are appliances on the market now called slow cookers but really are not. These machines have a different assembly structure not consistent with the way true slow cookers operate. They have metal inserts and sit on a base that cooks by direct heat. Unless food is stirred frequently, it will burn on the bottom.

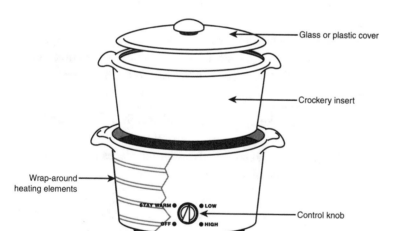

Each part of the slow cooker has a purpose that, when combined with the others, helps produce the even, low heat needed for long cooking times.

Reasons to Believe

One obvious reason to use a slow cooker is the flexibility it provides, especially for people who work outside the home during the day. Slowly cooked dinners can replace the nutrient-poor fast-food option and most often are healthier for you, too. Here are some other slow cooker advantages:

- The slow cooker's long cooking time tenderizes less-expensive cuts of meat, stretching your food budget.

- Foods such as thick stews and bean dishes that tend to stick to the bottom of a pan placed over direct heat don't stick in a slow cooker.

- Slow cookers provide a third hand for party prep. Use a slow cooker to free up the oven for food that needs higher heat. Plus, a slow cooker can be left alone while you're tending to food in pans on the stove.

- Slow cookers are forgiving. A dish can cook for an extra hour or two, especially on Low, without the risk of it burning.

- Slow cookers don't heat up the kitchen—perfect for summer cooking.

- Slow cookers keep food warm so family members can eat at different times, if necessary, and the food will remain hot.

Picking Your Pot

Shape and size are the two criteria to consider when buying a slow cooker. The tiny 1-quart models are a great party pal and hold dips warm for hours, but they are not very versatile. If you're going to have only one slow cooker, it should have a $3^1/_2$- or 4-quart capacity. These sizes hold enough food for four to six servings. The 6-quart models are good for larger families or for cooks who like to make large batches of food and freeze some for future meals.

Slow Savvy
Unless otherwise specified, all the recipes in this book were cooked in a 4-quart slow cooker.

Cookers come in round and oval shapes, and both cook equally well. I prefer the oval shape because it accommodates larger pieces of meat better and it seems better for making desserts.

Safety First

Cooking with a slow cooker is not only easy, it's also safe. The Food Safety and Inspection Service of the U.S. Department of Agriculture approves slow cooking as a method of safe food preparation. The lengthy cooking and the steam created within the tightly covered pot combine to destroy any bacteria that might be present in the food.

Although slow cooking is innately safe, it's up to you as the cook to make sure this translates to the food in your pot. A slow cooker should always be at least half-full so it can generate the necessary steam. A smaller quantity of food will not produce the steam needed to kill bacteria.

Banishing Bacteria

Fruits and vegetables can contain some bacteria, but it's far more likely that the culprits will grow on meat, poultry, and seafood. Store these foods on the bottom shelves of your refrigerator so their juices cannot accidentally fall on other foods. And keep these foods refrigerated until just before they go into the slow cooker. Bacteria multiply at room temperature.

It's not wise to cook whole chickens or cuts of meat larger than those specified in the recipes in this book because during slow cooking, these large items stay too long in the bacterial "danger zone"—between 40° and 140°F. It is important that food reaches the higher temperature in less than 2 hours and remains at more than 140°F for at least 30 minutes.

Cooker Caveats

If you're dusting off a slow cooker that's been in the basement for years, it's a good idea to test it to make sure it still has the power to heat food sufficiently. Leave 2 quarts water at room temperature overnight, then pour the water into the slow cooker in the morning. Heat it on Low for 8 hours. The temperature should be 185°F after 8 hours. Use an instant read thermometer to judge it. If it is lower, any food you cook in this cooker might not pass through the danger zone rapidly enough.

If you want to cook large roasts, brown them in a skillet on top of the stove over direct heat before you place them into the slow cooker. This will help the chilled meat heat up faster as well as produce a dish that is more visually appealing.

A Safe Head Start

Because mornings can be frantic times in a household, you might want to prepare the dish you're cooking for the next day the night before. If you cut meat or vegetables in advance, store them separately in the refrigerator and layer them in the slow cooker in the morning. Always defrost meats and poultry before placing them in the slow cooker. Frozen foods cool the contents of the slow cooker and prolong the time period spent in the danger zone.

Do not store the cooker insert in the refrigerator because that will also increase the amount of time it takes to heat the food to a temperature that kills bacteria.

Also, do not preheat the empty insert while you're preparing the food because the insert could crack when you add the cold food.

High Heat Boost

If at all possible, start the slow cooker on High for the first hour of cooking time to boost it through the bacterial danger zone. If you're running out of the house and won't be home to turn the heat to Low after an hour, don't worry. Remember that 1 hour of cooking on High is equal to 2 hours of cooking on Low, so calculate accordingly.

Appliance manufacturers say that slow cookers can be left on either High or Low unattended, but use your own judgment. If you're going to be out of the house all day, it's advisable to cook food on Low. If, on the other hand, you're going to be gone for just a few hours, the food will be safe on High.

Watch the Juice

Even though slow cookers do not require a lot of power to operate, they are electrical appliances, and the same safety rules apply as with any electrical appliance. Be careful that the cord is not frayed in any way, and plug the slow cooker into an outlet that is not near the sink. Never immerse the metal housing into water, even if the slow cooker is not plugged in, and never puncture the metal casing. Clean the metal casing with a soapy sponge only when the slow cooker is disconnected from the outlet.

Slow Savvy
Slow cooker lids are transparent so you can see what's happening in the pot without letting out heat and steam. If there's condensation on the lid, rather than lifting it to see inside, jiggle the lid and the condensation will dribble into the food so you can see what's going on.

Don't Peek

It's always tempting to pick up that lid and see what's happening in the pot. But resist the temptation. Every time you peek, you let out some heat and steam, so you will need to add some cooking time to the total. If cooking on Low, add 15 minutes. If cooking on High, add 10 minutes. That's why slow cookers all have transparent lids, so you can see what's going on without lifting the lid.

Post-Dinner Drill

Here's the good news: As long as the temperature remains 140°F or higher, food will stay safe for many hours once it's done cooking in the slow cooker.

Leftovers should never be refrigerated in the crockery insert. Freeze or refrigerate leftovers in shallow containers within two hours after a dish has finished cooking. Also, food should never be reheated in the slow cooker because it takes too long for chilled food to pass through the danger zone. Once it has been reheated on the stove or in the microwave, it can be kept warm in the slow cooker until serving time.

Slow Savvy _____
Cooking in glazed pottery and at low temperatures means that food rarely sticks. To ensure easy cleanup, spray the inside of the insert with vegetable oil spray before adding the food. If food does stick, which rarely happens, soak the insert in hot soapy water and then wash it clean.

Worst-Case Worries

A slow cooker needs electricity to cook, so the lack thereof is about the biggest food safety worry you have with a slow cooker. If you've been cooking in your slow cooker and can tell from your electric clocks that the power has been off, throw away the food in the slow cooker, even if it looks done. You have no idea if the power outage occurred before the food passed through the danger zone.

If you're home when the electricity goes off, finish cooking the food by another method. If you have a gas stove, transfer the dish to a pot and finish it that way. You can also place it in a metal pot on a charcoal or gas grill. Or call a friend who might have power and rush your slow cooker right over.

Larder Largesse

A well-stocked pantry and refrigerator will keep you in the supermarket's express lane, because all you'll need is a few ingredients to complete any dish. The best way to make sure your pantry is full is to create a master list of its contents. Once you use an item, check it on the page and review your list when penning your shopping list for the next foray to the supermarket. Another option is to mount a dry-erase board on the pantry closet door and log in your list of needed supplies.

Packing the Pantry

Almost all slow cooked recipes rely on some sort of liquid to *braise* the food. Keep a large supply of the following in your pantry:

Ellen on Edibles _____
The official term for what we might call stewing or boiling is braising. **Braising** is a cooking method that cooks food in liquid in a covered pan at a low temperature. The resulting food is always tender because the long cooking breaks down the fibers. Almost all slow cooked dishes are braised.

- Canned chicken and beef stock
- Chicken, beef, and vegetable bouillon cubes
- Canned diced tomatoes
- Tomato sauce
- Tomato paste
- Dried and canned beans of all types
- Small pastas such as macaroni, orzo, and penne
- Rice, both long-grain converted and arborio

Slow cooked recipes use very little oil, but you should keep some on hand:

- Olive oil
- Vegetable oil
- Nonflavored vegetable oil spray

Slow Savvy _____
Markets today are drowning in olive oils. They range in price from a few dollars to the equivalent of the gross national product of a third-world nation. The expensive stuff is a condiment and is meant to be drizzled on salads. The cheap stuff is for frying foods before they're placed in the slow cooker. Not only is it a waste of money to use expensive oil, but it also doesn't work as well.

The following dried ingredients are used in the recipes in this book from time to time and are good to have on hand in your pantry:

- Cornstarch (used for thickening gravies)
- All-purpose flour
- Granulated sugar
- Dark brown sugar

Dairy products are not treated kindly by the slow cooker, but these natural canned dairy products work well in many recipes:

- Evaporated milk
- Condensed sweetened evaporated milk

Your Flavorful Friend Herb

Dried herbs and spices work very well in slow cooked dishes. Because the cooking time is long, it's best to use whole leaves rather than ground for herbs such as oregano and basil. The ground form of spices like cinnamon and cumin work fine, though. Although many dishes are seasoned with salt and pepper at the end of the cooking time, herbs should be added at the beginning so you don't have to remove the lid from the slow cooker during the cooking process.

Here's a basic list of herbs and spices used extensively in the recipes in this book:

- Basil
- Ground cinnamon
- Ground coriander
- Ground cumin
- Herbes de Provence
- Oregano
- Sage
- Thyme

I'm also fond of Old Bay Seasoning. It was initially intended for seafood dishes, but it's really versatile and gives food a complex flavor because of the large number of spices in the mixture. The Bay in question is the Chesapeake, and the mixture contains celery salt, mustard, red and black pepper, ginger, mace, cinnamon, and paprika.

Slow Savvy

Storing your dried herbs and spices in pretty clear-glass bottles in a rack over the stove is about the worst place to keep them, because both heat and light are foes of these foods. Keep them in a cool, dark place to preserve their potency. The best test for freshness and potency is to smell the contents. If there is not a strong aroma, you need a new bottle.

The Chilled Collection

Now that the shelf-stable stuff is accounted for, there are some basic foods you will need that you probably have on hand in the refrigerator at all times anyway:

- One quart whole milk
- One pint half-and-half
- One half-pint heavy cream
- One dozen eggs
- One pound butter

Slow Savvy
You can rinse a bunch of parsley, trim off the stems, then wrap it in bundles and freeze it. When you need some, you can "chop" it with the handle of a knife. It will chop easily when frozen.

Some grated cheeses round out the list:

- Parmesan
- Cheddar
- Swiss

Carrots, celery, garlic, and onions are the vegetables used most frequently in these dishes. In addition, keep a bunch of fresh parsley on hand.

The Pot's Pals

You don't need a large collection of pots and pans to make these recipes because the slow cooker does most of the work. Your food processor is the best friend you can have for most dishes destined for the slow cooker. You'll frequently need to chop vegetables very fine so they'll reach the finish line at the same time as the meat, and there's no better way to accomplish this than the on-and-off pulsing action of a food processor. Food processors are also much better to *purée* soups than a blender. A blender tends to give all foods the texture of a milk shake. Plus, a blender's small capacity means you'll need more time to purée many batches.

In addition to a food processor, all you need in terms of cooking equipment are the following:

- A few plastic cutting boards
- A few skillets
- Mixing bowls
- A broiler pan

Ellen on Edibles
Purée is a French term that means to process until you have a thick and totally smooth liquid, instead of a thinner liquid containing solid pieces of foods. This can be done in a food processor fitted with a steel blade, in a blender, or by pushing foods through a food mill.

And in the gadget department:

- Some long-handled cooking spoons
- A slotted spoon
- A soup ladle
- A garlic press
- A vegetable peeler
- An instant-read meat thermometer

Then there are your knives:

- ◆ At least one paring knife
- ◆ A chef's knife
- ◆ A boning knife
- ◆ A carving knife

People cut themselves with poorly sharpened knives much more often than with sharp knives, and dull knives make the job of cutting harder and can detract from the appearance of the food, so make sure you've got some way of keeping knives sharp. A steel rod or sharpening stone is much less expensive than the electric gizmos and serves the same function with the aid of a little elbow grease.

Stocking Up

In a pinch it's great to have a can of stock to open, but nothing compares with the rich flavor homemade stocks add to soups, stews, and all braised dishes. Making stock is about as difficult as boiling water, and they're great made in the slow cooker. You'll notice that none of these stocks is salted so you can add just the right amount of salt to a dish.

Slow Savvy _____
Do you have some vegetables like carrots and celery stalks that have gotten a little limp in the refrigerator? Why not save them for stock? Wrap the vegetables and place them in the freezer, then defrost them before they go into the slow cooker to make the stocks.

Chicken Stock

Prep time: less than 15 minutes • Minimum cooking time: 5 hours • Makes 2 quarts

2 quarts water

2 lb. chicken pieces (bones, skin, wing tips, etc.)

1 carrot, scrubbed, trimmed, and cut into ½-inch chunks

1 medium onion, peeled and sliced

1 celery stalk, trimmed and sliced

6 black peppercorns

3 sprigs fresh parsley

3 sprigs fresh thyme or 1 tsp. dried

2 garlic cloves, peeled

1 bay leaf

Pour water into the slow cooker. Add chicken pieces, carrot, onion, celery, peppercorns, parsley, thyme, garlic, and bay leaf. Cook on Low for 10 to 12 hours or on High for 5 to 6 hours. Strain stock through a sieve into a mixing bowl. Press down on the solids with the back of a spoon to extract as much liquid as possible. Discard the solids.

Chill stock. Remove and discard the fat layer from the top. Ladle stock into containers and either use it refrigerated within 4 days, or freeze it for up to 6 months.

Quick Chicken Stock

Prep time: less than 15 minutes • Minimum cooking time: 3 hours • Makes 1½ quarts

1 (48-oz.) can chicken stock

1 carrot, scrubbed, trimmed, and cut into ½-inch chunks

1 medium onion, peeled and sliced

1 celery stalk, trimmed and sliced

6 black peppercorns

3 sprigs fresh parsley

3 sprigs fresh thyme or 1 tsp. dried

2 garlic cloves, peeled

1 bay leaf

Pour stock into the slow cooker. Add carrot, onion, celery, peppercorns, parsley, thyme, garlic, and bay leaf. Cook on Low for 6 to 8 hours or on High for 3 to 4 hours or until vegetables are soft. Strain stock through a sieve into a mixing bowl. Press down on the solids with the back of a spoon to extract as much liquid as possible. Discard the solids.

Chill stock. Remove and discard the fat layer from the top. Ladle the stock into containers and either use it refrigerated within 4 days, or freeze it for up to 6 months.

Beef Stock

Prep time: less than 15 minutes • Minimum cooking time: 5 hours • Makes 2 quarts

2 lb. beef shank (or 1 lb. beef stew meat or chuck roast)

2 quarts water

1 carrot, scrubbed, trimmed, and cut into ½-inch chunks

1 medium onion, peeled and sliced

1 celery stalk, trimmed and sliced

6 black peppercorns

3 sprigs fresh parsley

3 sprigs fresh thyme or 1 tsp. dried

2 garlic cloves, peeled

1 bay leaf

Preheat the oven broiler, and line a broiler pan with aluminum foil. Broil beef for 3 minutes per side or until browned. Transfer beef to the slow cooker, and add water, carrot, onion, celery, peppercorns, parsley, thyme, garlic, and bay leaf. Cook on Low for 10 to 12 hours or on High for 5 to 6 hours. Strain stock through a sieve into a mixing bowl. Press down on the solids with the back of a spoon to extract as much liquid as possible. Discard the solids.

Chill stock. Remove and discard the fat layer from the top. Ladle stock into containers and either use it refrigerated within 4 days, or freeze it for up to 6 months.

Slow Savvy

Saving meat and poultry scraps in plastic bags in the freezer is the most economical way to make stocks because your base flavor is right there in your freezer. Cut your own stew meat from a chuck roast, then freeze the bones. And keep the tips from chicken wings and the necks and gizzards from whole chickens (but not the livers).

Vegetable Stock

Prep time: less than 15 minutes • Minimum cooking time: 3 hours • Makes 2 quarts

2 quarts water

2 carrots, scrubbed, trimmed, and thinly sliced

2 celery stalks, trimmed and sliced

2 leeks, white part only, trimmed, rinsed, and thinly sliced

1 small onion, peeled and thinly sliced

6 black peppercorns

3 sprigs fresh parsley

3 sprigs fresh thyme or 1 tsp. dried

2 garlic cloves, peeled

1 bay leaf

Pour water into the slow cooker, and add carrots, celery, leeks, onion, peppercorns, parsley, thyme, garlic, and bay leaf. Cook on Low for 6 to 8 hours or on High for 3 to 4 hours or until vegetables are soft. Strain stock through a sieve into a mixing bowl. Press down on the solids with the back of a spoon to extract as much liquid as possible. Discard the solids.

Ladle stock into containers and either use it refrigerated within 4 days, or freeze it for up to 6 months.

 Seafood Stock

Prep time: less than 15 minutes • Minimum cooking time: 4 hours • Makes 3 quarts

3 lobster bodies (whole lobsters from which the tail and claw meat has been removed) or 2 lobster bodies and the shells from 2 lb. raw shrimp

2 quarts water

1 cup dry white wine

1 carrot, scrubbed, trimmed, and cut into 1-inch chunks

1 medium onion, peeled and sliced

1 celery stalk, trimmed and sliced

6 black peppercorns

3 sprigs fresh parsley

3 sprigs fresh thyme or 1 tsp. dried

2 garlic cloves, peeled

1 bay leaf

Pull the top shell off a lobster body. Scrape off and discard the feathery gills, then break the body into small pieces. Place pieces into the slow cooker, and repeat with remaining lobster bodies. Add shrimp, if used.

Pour water and wine into the slow cooker, and add carrots, onion, celery, peppercorns, parsley, thyme, garlic, and bay leaf. Cook on Low for 8 to 10 hours or on High for 4 to 5 hours or until vegetables are soft. Strain stock through a sieve into a mixing bowl. Press down on the solids with the back of a spoon to extract as much liquid as possible. Discard the solids.

Ladle stock into containers and either use it refrigerated within 4 days, or freeze it for up to 6 months.

Slow Savvy _____
Seafood stock is perhaps the hardest to make if you don't live near the coast. A good substitute is bottled clam juice. Use it in place of the water, and simmer it with vegetables and wine, as in the Quick Chicken Stock recipe, to intensify its flavor.

The Least You Need to Know

- Slow cookers are simple electrical devices that cook food for long periods of time at low temperatures by indirect heat.

- A slow cooker's Low setting is 180° to 200°F; the High setting is 280° to 300°F.

- Slow cookers kill any bacteria that might be present in the uncooked food if food safety precautions are followed.

- By keeping a cache of canned goods, spices, and basic dairy products around, it's not time-consuming to shop for food destined for the slow cooker.

- It's easy to make homemade stocks, and they add a depth of flavor to dishes made in the slow cooker.

Chapter 2

Food for Thought

In This Chapter

- Preparing foods for slow cooking
- Converting recipes for slow cookers
- Serving slow cooked food
- Using your slow cooker insert with versatility

Now that you're convinced slow cooking should be part of your routine—if it isn't already—this chapter will give you all sorts of knowledge on how to make the best meals in your slow cooker. Think of this chapter as a quick reference guide to slow cooking. It will help you improvise slow cooked recipes and give you guidance on making substitutions if a particular cut of meat or other ingredient is not available.

"Meating" the Challenge

It's a happy coincidence that the cuts of meat best suited for slow cooking are also the least expensive ones. Even when set on High, a slow cooker is still cool enough to slowly convert the meat's connective tissue from collagen to gelatin. (That's why slow cooked meat is described as "fork-tender.") The well-*marbled* meat with the collagen comes from the parts of the animals that get the most exercise.

Ellen on Edibles

Marbling has nothing to do with stone, but the patterns that swirl through some polished sheets of marble are echoed by the fat patterns in cuts of meat. Although marbling is not wanted in lean cuts of meat like a tenderloin, the fat, which leaches out of the meat during slow cooking, is desirable for cuts destined for the slow cooker. It's this fat that punctuates the strong muscle fibers and makes the food tender after cooking.

Picking Your Parts

Imagine that you're running around in a field. Your leg muscles are getting much more of a workout than your back muscles are. And if you're running around on four legs, you can count your front legs and shoulders amongst those well-used muscles, too.

When shopping in the supermarket for meat destined for your slow cooker, here are the cuts to look for:

Slow Savvy

If you've bought a larger piece of meat than you need for one recipe, cut it all and freeze any you don't use. Freeze the pieces on a plastic-wrapped baking sheet until solid. Then place the frozen pieces in a heavy plastic bag and then pull out just the quantity you need to defrost for your next recipe.

- Shanks
- Shoulder
- Round
- Rump

Even if they are not labeled as such, you'll know you've selected the proper slow cooker cuts when you compare the price of these cuts with cuts such as tenderloin, sirloin, and rib. And there is no need to go for the high-priced Prime grade meats. Choice and Standard quality are just fine.

Stew meat is usually cut from the chuck, and you pay a premium price to buy it already cut up. Save some money and instead, spend a few minutes to cut it yourself. In addition to saving money, there are many advantages to cutting meat yourself:

- You can trim off all visible fat.
- You can make the pieces a uniform size or the size specified in the recipe.
- If cutting up beef or veal, you can save the scraps for grinding into hamburger or making stock.

For slow cooking, make the cubes about 1 inch square, unless instructed otherwise in the recipe. At this size, the meat will finish cooking at the same time as your vegetables.

Benefits of Browning

Whether or not to brown meat before putting it in the slow cooker is a matter of choice. I suggest it for all ground meat, because browning also rids the meat of inherent fat and keeps it from clumping. This has to be done in a skillet on the stove. If you're preparing a stew or roast, the meat can be browned under a preheated oven broiler in a broiler pan lined with aluminum foil. Turn the meat so it browns on all sides. The juices that seep out go into the pot and add flavor to the dish.

All beef and lamb should be browned before slow cooking. Browning adds a rich color to both the meat and the finished sauce. Browning is optional for pork, veal, and chicken. These lighter foods absorb color from the sauce.

Cooker Caveats _____
Although you can prepare many ingredients in a slow cooked dish the night before, meat cannot be browned in advance and then refrigerated. Once it has browned, it should be cooked immediately to ensure that no bacteria are growing.

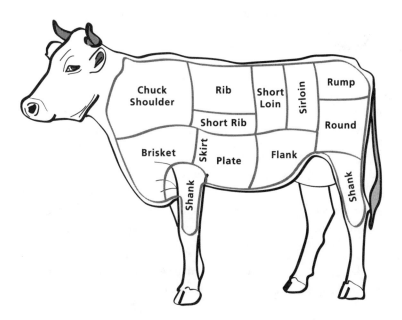

The cuts of meat from the legs, shoulders, and hindquarters are the best cuts for slow cooking.

Here's the Beef

The terminology for the major cuts of meat is similar for beef, lamb, pork, and veal. Beef is usually also broken into more portions. The cuts good for slow cooking are the short ribs (also called flanken), brisket, and chuck (which is part of the shoulder). You'll also find oxtails, which are really from cattle, not from oxen.

Other Grazing Greats

Pork, lamb, and veal have all the same parts as cattle, and once they are butchered, are usually labeled the same way. There are some names unique to each animal to watch for, however.

When you're buying pork, the shoulder is sometimes called the Boston butt, and the upper leg can be called the picnic shoulder. Although some people do slow cook spare ribs, I think they are better served by oven baking or grilling. Country ribs, cut from the blade end of the loin, are best suited for slow cooking.

Lambs don't run around the way cattle do, so there are fewer cuts of meat that are enhanced by long hours of slow cooking. The shanks are my favorite and remind me of the lusty, raucous eating scene from the film *Tom Jones*. They are so large that it looks as if there's a whole roast on the plate, although they are mostly bone. The other good cut for roasts and stews is from the shoulder.

Slow Savvy
Veal cooks in less time than other meats, but beef, lamb, and pork are about even. Feel free to substitute one meat for another in any stew recipe.

Veal are young cattle, so the same cuts apply as for beef.

Poultry with Panache

Chicken is one of the most versatile and popular meats to cook, and in the slow cooker, it's almost impossible for the meat to become dry—yet another advantage of slow cooking!

Chicken and all meats should always be rinsed under cold running water after being taken out of the package. If it's going to be pre-browned in the oven or in a skillet on the stove, pat the pieces dry with paper towels and then wash your hands. Chicken often contains salmonella, a naturally occurring bacteria that is killed by cooking, but you don't want to transfer this bacteria to other foods.

It's a good rule for food safety that all boards and knives that have held raw meats should always be scrubbed well before cooked foods are placed on them. And make sure to wash your hands well, too!

For the sake of food safety, it's best not to cook a whole chicken in the slow cooker except if cooking on High, because the low heat might keep the meat of a whole bird in the bacterial danger zone for more than two hours. But as with beef, you save money and get trimmings for stock if you cut it up yourself.

Ellen on Edibles

White meat or dark? In my book, there's nothing like the texture of succulent dark meat that's been through the slow cooker. Skinless thighs are my favorite cut, and they can be used in place of mixed pieces in any of these recipes. Although dark meat is slightly higher in calories than white meat, the amount is very small, assuming the skin has been removed.

If you do choose to cut the bird yourself, here's how to do it:

♦ Start by breaking back the wings until the joints snap, then use a boning knife to cut through the ball joints to detach the wings.

♦ Cut off the wing tips and save them for stock.

♦ When holding the chicken on its side, you will see a natural curve outlining the boundary between the breast and leg quarters. Cut along this line using sharp kitchen shears. Don't be afraid to feel for the joints with your fingers first. Your cutting will be more accurate if you know exactly where to make the first slice.

♦ Cut the breast in half by cutting down the meat on both sides of the breast bone. Chicken will fit into most slow cookers better if you cut the breast into two or three pieces.

♦ Last, divide the thigh and leg parts by cutting through the joint that joins them. Again, don't be afraid to feel for the joints with your fingers first.

For chicken dishes cooked with the skin on, it's more visually appealing if the chicken is browned before it's placed in the slow cooker. The easy way to do this is to broil it under a preheated oven broiler for 3 to 4 minutes, turning the legs and wings so they brown on both sides.

Fragile Fish

Fish and the slow cooker are not natural buddies, and care must be taken to ensure that fish does not become woefully overcooked. That's why there are so few fish recipes in this book, and most of those recipes have a long cooking time for the other ingredients; then the fish is added last so it doesn't overcook.

When choosing a fish for your slow cooker, select sturdy fish like swordfish, salmon,

Slow Savvy

An easy way to remove pesky little pin bones from fish fillets is with your vegetable peeler. Run the blade of the peeler against the grain of the fish and the bones will stick out. If you can't remove them with your fingers, try using a pair of tweezers. Or if you are a gadget lover, you can buy a special tweezerlike fish-boning tool.

halibut, cod, and tuna. The fish should be cut into 1-inch pieces or larger, and they are added during the last hour of cooking, at the most. To test whether or not the fish is cooked, flake it with a fork. If it's fully cooked, it should flake easily.

Shellfish toughens if it's overcooked, so the same timing principle holds true for shellfish such as shrimp and scallops. Stir them in for the last 15 to 60 minutes of cooking time, depending on the quantity and cooking temperature.

Delicate fish like sole and flounder should not be used in slow cooked recipes. They are too thin for slow cookers and will fall apart.

Versatile Veggies

Sturdy vegetables like carrots, potatoes, and celery are staples for the stew pot and, by extension, the slow cooker. And believe it or not, it takes longer for these vegetables to cook in the slow cooker than it takes most meats or chicken. When prepping hard vegetables, peel and trim them as usual, then cut them into bite-size pieces so they'll cook faster.

More delicate vegetables, like green beans, peas, and snow peas, should be added for the last hour of the cooking time. If you're anxious to serve food as soon as you walk in the door, it's better to cook these tender vegetables in the microwave and then stir them into the slow cooker. If they cook for the whole time, they will be an unappealing gray color and very mushy.

You'll see that in most recipes one of the first steps is to *sauté* the onions and garlic before being adding them to the slow cooker. This preliminary cooking process makes the onions and garlic sweeter and less sharp. (I've skipped the step in recipes where this doesn't matter.)

Ellen on Edibles

Sauté is a common cooking term taken from French. It literally means "to jump." The idea is to keep food moving in the pan by stirring it frequently, if not constantly. Sautéed food is cooked in a little hot fat in a shallow pan, over medium-high or high heat. This causes the food to release its natural sugars and intensify in flavor. Sautéed food should sit lightly in the fat and should not be submerged in it.

Bountiful Beans and Plentiful Pulses

Slow cookers are perfect for cooking beans and pulses. After all, today's slow cookers evolved from a bean pot. There is no end to the list of delicious slow cooked dishes made with healthful, inexpensive dried beans.

The first step for all bean recipes is to rinse the beans in a sieve or colander and look them over carefully to discard any broken beans or the occasional pebble that sneaks into the bag. Also, keep in mind when you're cooking beans to not fill the slow cooker more than one third with beans because they more than double in volume once they're cooked.

Although guidelines are given for how long each bean recipe takes to cook, there are variables that influence this time. If beans are a few years old, they'll take longer to cook. Also, the minerals in your tap water can retard the softening and require a longer cooking time.

The Soaking Step

Most beans benefit from pre-soaking. For many years, it was believed that soaking was beneficial because the enzymes that make beans difficult for some people to digest leach out into the soaking water, which is then discarded. Lately, researchers have questioned whether the amount of enzyme removed in this way is significant. Many cooks agree, however, that soaking does soften the beans and save cooking time. (You can start cooking skinless or thin-skinned legumes such as split peas and lentils without any preliminary soaking.) Soaking also softens the beans, reducing cooking time.

> **Crock Tales**
> Traditional Hawaiian cooks add a few slices of ginger to the water in which dried beans are cooking as a way to alleviate the potential gas problem.

There are two methods you can use to soak beans. The first is to cover them with water and let them sit on the counter overnight. This method is consistent with slow cooking because you might have already decided to cook a recipe the next morning.

The second method is the "quick soak." In a medium saucepan, cover the beans with water and bring to a boil over high heat. Boil the beans for 1 minute, then cover the pan and turn off the heat. Let the beans soak for 1 hour.

Whichever method you use, drain the beans and discard the soaking liquid after soaking. Cooking should then begin as soon as possible. If this isn't possible, drain the beans and refrigerate them.

A Bean by Any Other Name

Bean recipes are also very tolerant to substitutions, so if you can't find or don't have a specific bean on hand, don't despair. Instead, consult the following table for a substitution.

Name of Legume	What to Substitute
Black (also called turtle)	Kidney
Black-eyed peas	Kidney
Cannellini	Small navy
Cranberry	Kidney
Fava (broad beans)	Large lima
Flageolet	Small navy
Kidney (pink and red, pinto)	Small navy
Lentils (red, brown, green)	Split peas
Split peas	Lentils

Although many dried beans can be substituted for one another, don't substitute with canned beans in the slow cooker. Canned beans are already fully cooked, and they'll fall apart before they absorb the flavoring from the slow cooked dish.

Bean Cuisine

It's best to soften the beans before adding other ingredients to the slow cooker because certain foods can actually harden beans while they're cooking—exactly what you don't want! When they're cooking is the time you're hoping the beans will soften.

There are two families of ingredients that can retard bean softening as they cook: sweeteners and acids. Sweeteners include the following:

◆ Honey

◆ Any type of sugar

◆ Molasses

◆ Maple syrup

Acids include the following:

- Tomatoes
- Any sort of vinegar
- Red and white wine
- Lemon juice
- Lime juice

If you use any of these ingredients in your bean dishes, make sure you soften the beans beforehand.

Say Cheese

Dairy products are not treated kindly by the slow cooker. Cheeses, cream, and milk tend to curdle or separate after even a few hours of low heat. One solution is to use processed cheeses, such as American cheese or Velveeta instead of natural cheeses. I don't like the taste of processed cheeses, so they're not listed in many of these recipes. The alternative is to add cheese at the end of the cooking process and cook it just long enough to melt it.

Condensed or evaporated milk hold up a little better than regular milk and cream, if you want to use these in your dishes instead. Stock holds up even better; that's why the cream soup recipes in this book use stock as a medium to cook the ingredients, then the cream is added to smooth out the flavors at the end of the cooking time.

Crock Tales

Velveeta, a processed cheese, was introduced by Kraft in 1928. One of the benefits touted was that it melted smoothly and never curdled. That's why it is used extensively by cooks for dips and cheese sauces still today.

Slowing Down Family Favorites

Once you feel comfortable with your slow cooker, you'll probably want to use it to prepare your favorite recipes you now cook on the stove or in the oven. The best recipes to convert are "wet" ones with a lot of liquid, like stews, soups, chilies, and other braised foods. Make sure the food fills the slow cooker at least half-way to ensure food safety. If it's a smaller quantity, you might want to increase the size of the batch.

The easiest way to convert your recipes is to find a similar one in this book and use its cooking time for guidance. When looking for a similar recipe, take into account the amount of liquid specified as well as the quantity of food. The liquid transfers the heat from the walls of the insert into the food itself, and the liquid heats in direct proportion to its measure.

Cooker Caveats _____
Not all dishes can be easily converted to slow cooked dishes. Even if a dish calls for liquid, if it's supposed to be cooked or baked uncovered, chances are it will not be successfully transformed to a slow cooker recipe, because the food will not brown and the liquid will not evaporate.

You should look for similar recipes as well as keep in mind some general guidelines:

◆ Most any stew or roast takes 8 to 12 hours on Low and 4 to 6 hours on High.

◆ Chicken dishes cook more rapidly. Count on 6 to 8 hours on Low and 3 to 4 hours on High.

◆ Quadruple the time from conventional cooking to cooking on Low, and at least double it for cooking on High.

Retooling the Recipe

The quantity of ingredients and when to add them also change when converting recipes to the slow cooker. Here are some considerations:

◆ Cut back on the amount of liquid used in stews and other braised dishes by about half. Unlike cooking on the stove or in the oven, there is little to no evaporation in the slow cooker.

◆ If the food isn't totally covered with liquid when you start to cook, don't worry. Ingredients like meat, chicken, and many vegetables give off their own juices as they cook.

◆ For soups, cut back on the liquid by one third if the soup is supposed to simmer uncovered, and cut back by one fourth if the soup is simmered covered. Even when covered, a soup that is simmering on the stove has more evaporation than one cooked in the slow cooker.

◆ Put the vegetables in the slow cooker first, at the bottom. They take longer to cook than the meat.

◆ Use leaf versions of herbs such as thyme and rosemary rather than ground versions. Ground herbs tend to lose potency during many hours in the slow cooker.

◆ Season the dishes with pepper at the end of cooking, because it can become harsh.

◆ Remember, this dish is cooking in your slow cooker, so don't peek at or stir it.

Other Adaptations

You might find that even though you cut back on liquid, a dish still doesn't have the intense flavor it did when it was cooked on the stove. Don't fret. After the dish has finished cooking, remove as much liquid as possible from the slow cooker with a bulb baster or strain the liquid from the solids in a colander. *Reduce* the liquid in a saucepan on the stove until it has the right flavor and consistency. Then add it back into the slow cooker before serving.

Ellen on Edibles

To **reduce** is to make something smaller, and when the word is used in cooking, it means to cut down on the volume of liquid by applying heat, which speeds evaporation. Simmering a gravy or sauce evaporates some of the water, which concentrates the flavor of the resulting liquid. Many recipes call for liquid to be reduced by half, but it can be a greater or smaller amount.

If rice or small pasta is part of a recipe, add it only during the last 2 hours of cooking on Low or 1 hour on High. The same rules apply to tender vegetables and dairy products as mentioned earlier in this chapter. Add them at the end of the cooking time.

Glorious Garnishes

One aspect many cooks perceive as a downside of the slow cooker is that most food is soft and has a uniform texture when it finishes cooking. Now that you've mastered the basics of slow cooking and how to prepare foods, here are some ideas to help those delicious dishes garner a "Wow!" when they appear on the table:

- Instead of adding cheese to a dish for the last part of the cooking time, sprinkle it on top of the food right before you serve it. This is especially good with hard cheeses like Parmesan and feta.
- For an unexpected crunch, add toasted croutons to the tops of stews and soups before serving.
- Sprigs of fresh herbs used while cooking the dishes add color.

Slow Savvy

If you have problems separating strips of bacon, pull off the total number of strips you want and place the whole block in the skillet. Within a few minutes, the slices will soften, and they'll be easy to pull apart.

- Toast nuts like slivered almonds and chopped walnuts in a 350°F oven for 5 minutes and sprinkle on stews before serving.
- Crumbled bacon is a good garnish for pork stews and hearty soups.

Versatile Value

The crockery insert in your slow cooker is delicate, but it's not a marshmallow. It can be placed in the microwave, if your microwave is large enough to hold it, and a warmed insert can go right in a preheated oven.

Cooker Caveats

Remember that the crockery insert to your slow cooker is pottery, not metal. Never place it on a cold surface when it's hot, or it can crack. Also, do not scrub it with an abrasive like steel wool because it can scratch the surface.

You can shortcut steps like pre-cooking onions by cooking them in the insert in the microwave rather than cooking them on the stove. (If you go this route, know the onions will not achieve the same caramelized flavor.)

If you want to brown the top of a casserole, preheat the oven broiler or set the oven temperature at 450°F and set the warmed insert containing the finished dish inside for a few minutes. Then use the insert as a serving dish by placing it on a trivet right on the table.

The Least You Need to Know

- Meats chosen for slow cooker dishes should be the less-expensive cuts with connective tissue. (See, slow cooking saves time *and* money!)
- Fish should be chosen carefully and added to the slow cooker at the very end of the cooking time.
- Slow cookers are great for cooking beans.
- Many recipes can be adapted to utilize the slow cooker by making a few liquid and cooking time adjustments.
- Garnishes are a great way to add textural diversity to slow cooked dishes.
- The slow cooker's crockery insert can be placed in the microwave and conventional oven—and right on the table!

Part

Enticing Appetizers

When you're planning a party, you often think you need an extra set of hands—or two—because there are usually many more dishes to prepare than for your average meal.

Enter your kitchen pal, your slow cooker. Now you can go about your party-prepping, confident that the slow cooker's low heat is producing delicious hot dips that aren't burning. And when it's time, you can whisk the slow cooker out to the table and use it as a serving dish that will keep the dips hot.

The slow cooker proves its versatility for hors d'oeuvres beyond just dips, though. It can also make foods to spear right out of the pan or fillings for foods that are served many different ways.

Chapter 3

Dippity Do

In This Chapter

- ◆ Traditional cheese dips from many countries
- ◆ Hearty dips with meats and beans
- ◆ Delicate dips with vegetables and seafood

If you haven't guessed by now, the slow cooker can be used to make every part of your meal—including, as you'll see by the recipes in this chapter, dips to serve as appetizers or that precede the main event.

Of course, there are many advantages to using a slow cooker. Hot dips made in the slow cooker don't burn and stay hot. And if you like to serve hot dips as an hors d'oeuvre, it's worth the small expense of buying a 1-quart slow cooker. Dips can be cooked in a larger cooker in greater quantities, but a small cooker doubles as a serving dish. Plus, you'll have one less dish to clean up!

What to Dip With

All the dips in this chapter are thick dips and would break delicate potato chips you might serve them with. You'll find that sturdy corn chips work best for dipping with all the Mexican and Southwestern dips. Bread cubes

Cooker Caveats _____

If you're making a dip in advance, do not reheat it in the slow cooker once it's been refrigerated. Reheat it in a small saucepan over low heat or in a microwave oven, then keep it hot in the slow cooker set on Low.

on bamboo skewers or slices of bread and crackers are better choices for the subtle flavors of cheese and vegetable dips.

If you want to cut back on calories, celery and carrot sticks also make great dippers. But avoid vegetables like cucumber spears, because they will add liquid to the dips.

The Least You Need to Know

- If you want to make hot dips for parties, it's worth investing in a 1-quart slow cooker.
- Cheese dips are excellent candidates for slow cooking because the cheese melts slowly.
- The foods used for dipping should be consistent with the flavors of the dip. Corn chips are the best choice for Mexican fare, and simple bread cubes can be used for subtle cheese dips. Other good choices are toast points, pita toasts, carrot sticks, and celery sticks.

Cheese Fondue

Prep time: less than 15 minutes   •   Minimum cooking time: 1½ hours   •   Makes 6 to 8 servings

¾ cup dry white wine

½ lb. Gruyère cheese, grated

½ lb. Swiss cheese, grated

2 TB. cornstarch

3 TB. *kirsch*

Cubes or slices of French bread for dipping

Pour wine into a 1-quart slow cooker. Stir in Gruyère and Swiss cheeses. Cook on High for 1 to 2 hours or until cheeses are melted and bubbly. Stir cornstarch into kirsch, then stir mixture into cheese. Cook for an additional 15 to 20 minutes on High until cheese has thickened. Serve with bread for dipping.

Ellen on Edibles _____

Kirsch, also called **kirschwasser,** is a clear, tart cherry-flavored liqueur. There is really no substitute for its taste. It's excellent sprinkled on fresh berries and enhances their fruity taste. It can also be added to sweetened whipped cream to give it a more complex flavor.

Pizza Dip

Prep time: less than 15 minutes • Minimum cooking time: 1 hour • Makes 8 to 12 servings

1 lb. mild or hot bulk Italian sausage	1 tsp. dried oregano
1 cup spaghetti sauce	1 tsp. dried basil
4 cups (1 lb.) grated mozzarella cheese	Slices of Italian bread or pita toasts for dipping

Place a medium skillet over medium-high heat. Add sausage and break up lumps with a fork. Cook sausage for 6 to 10 minutes or until it is no longer pink and is cooked through. Remove sausage from the pan with a slotted spoon, and place it in a 1-quart slow cooker. Add spaghetti sauce, mozzarella cheese, oregano, and basil to the slow cooker. Stir well.

Cook on Low for 2 to 3 hours or on High for 1 to 2 hours or until the mixture is simmering. Serve with bread for dipping.

Slow Savvy

Pita toasts are really easy to make. Separate pita breads into their two natural layers and spread each layer with melted butter. Sprinkle the pieces with salt, pepper, and any herbs you like—anything from oregano to chili powder. Then bake the bread at 375°F for 10 to 15 minutes or until browned and crisp. Then break into dipping-size pieces.

Chili Con Queso

Prep time: less than 15 minutes   •   Minimum cooking time: 2 hours   •   Makes 8 to 10 servings

1 cup refrigerated commercial tomato salsa

1 lb. pasteurized process cheese spread, cut into 1-inch cubes

4 scallions, trimmed and finely chopped

Tortilla chips for dipping

Combine salsa, cheese, and scallions in a 1-quart slow cooker. Cook on Low for 2 to 3 hours or until cheese is melted and bubbly. Serve with tortilla chips for dipping.

Cooker Caveats

Refrigerated salsa is like the good stuff you make yourself—but easier because it's already made for you! It's a real convenience product, with all the chopped tomato, onion, garlic, and chili pepper right there mixed for you. Don't substitute the bottled stuff you can find in the aisle with the Mexican foods. It just won't taste as good.

Refried Bean Dip

Prep time: less than 15 minutes • Minimum cooking time: 1 hour • Makes 8 to 12 servings

1 (15-oz.) can refried beans

1 cup (¼ lb.) shredded Monterey jack or cheddar cheese

4 scallions, trimmed and thinly sliced

2 tomatoes, cored, seeded, and finely diced

2 garlic cloves, peeled and minced

2 to 4 TB. taco sauce

Tortilla chips for dipping

Combine refried beans, cheese, scallions, tomatoes, garlic, and taco sauce in a 1-quart slow cooker. Stir well. Cook on Low for 2 to 3 hours or on High for 1 to 2 hours or until hot and bubbly. Serve with tortilla chips for dipping.

Slow Savvy

If you want to serve this dip as nachos, add only half the cheese to the slow cooker. After the dip is hot, spread it on large tortilla chips, sprinkle the remaining cheese on top, and pop the nachos under a preheated broiler until the cheese is melted and browned.

Welsh Rarebit Dip

Prep time: less than 15 minutes • Minimum cooking time: 1¼ hours • Makes 8 to 12 servings

¾ cup beer

4 cups (1 lb.) grated sharp cheddar cheese

1 TB. prepared mustard

¼ lb. bacon, cooked until crisp and crumbled (optional)

2 tomatoes, cored, seeded, and finely chopped

1 TB. cornstarch

1 TB. cold water

Salt and cayenne to taste

Bread slices or pita toasts for dipping

Combine beer, cheese, mustard, bacon (if used), and tomatoes in a 1-quart slow cooker. Cook on Low for 2 to 3 hours or on High for 1 to 2 hours or until cheese is melted and mixture is bubbly. If cooking on Low, raise the heat to High. Stir cornstarch into cold water, and stir the mixture into the slow cooker. Cook for an additional 10 to 20 minutes or until dip is bubbly and thickened. Season with salt and pepper, and serve with bread for dipping.

Crock Tales

Welsh Rarebit, sometimes called Welsh Rabbit, is a classic dish served for high tea in English pubs. Unlike afternoon tea, which was for the gentry, high tea was the supper of the working class because their main meal of the day was at noontime.

Cheeseburger Dip

Prep time: less than 20 minutes • Minimum cooking time: 1¼ hours • Makes 8 to 12 servings

2 TB. vegetable oil

1 medium onion, peeled and diced

3 garlic cloves, peeled and minced

1 lb. lean ground beef

3 plum tomatoes, cored, seeded, and diced

2 (10¾-oz.) cans condensed cheddar cheese soup

2 cups (½ lb.) grated cheddar cheese

Salt and black pepper to taste

Pita toasts or tortilla chips for dipping

Heat vegetable oil in a medium skillet over medium heat; add onion and garlic. Cook and stir for 3 minutes or until onion is translucent. Scrape mixture into the slow cooker. Add beef to the pan, and break up lumps with a fork. Cook beef over medium-high heat for 5 to 7 minutes or until browned. Remove beef from the pan with a slotted spoon, and add it to the slow cooker.

Stir tomatoes and cheese soup into the slow cooker. Cook on Low for 2 to 3 hours or on High for 1 to 2 hours or until meat is cooked and mixture is bubbly. If cooking on Low, raise the heat to High. Stir in grated cheese, and cook for an additional 15 to 20 minutes or until cheese is bubbly and blended. Season with salt and pepper, and serve with pita toasts for dipping.

Spinach and Artichoke Dip

Prep time: less than 20 minutes   •   Minimum cooking time: 1 hour   •   Makes 8 to 12 servings

1 (10-oz.) box frozen chopped spinach, thawed

1 (10-oz.) box frozen artichoke hearts, thawed

1 (8-oz.) package refrigerated Alfredo sauce

½ lb. Gruyère cheese, grated

½ tsp. dried thyme

Pinch of dried tarragon

Salt and black pepper to taste

Pita toasts or crackers for dipping

Place spinach in a colander, and push on it with the back of a spoon to extract as much liquid as possible. Place spinach in a 1-quart slow cooker. Drain artichoke hearts, and chop finely in a food processor fitted with the steel blade using the on-and-off pulsing action or chop finely by hand. Add artichoke hearts to the slow cooker, and stir in Alfredo sauce, grated cheese, thyme, and tarragon.

Cook on Low for 2 to 3 hours or on High for 1 to 2 hours or until the mixture is bubbly and cheese has melted. Stir once the mixture begins to simmer. Season with salt and pepper, and serve with pita toasts for dipping.

Slow Savvy

Artichokes do not pair well with wine because they contain cynarine, an enzyme that causes food eaten immediately after to take on a sweet taste. If you're serving wine with this dip, try a strong white wine, served very cold.

Crab Dip

Prep time: less than 15 minutes   •   Minimum cooking time: 1½ hours   •   Makes 8 to 12 servings

½ lb. crabmeat, picked over

2 TB. butter

1 small onion, peeled and finely chopped

1 (8-oz.) package cream cheese, softened

¾ cup mayonnaise

½ to 1 tsp. Old Bay Seasoning

Toast points or crackers for dipping

Place crabmeat in a 1-quart slow cooker. Melt butter in a small skillet over medium heat, then add onion. Cook and stir for 3 minutes or until onion is translucent. Scrape onion into the slow cooker, and stir in cream cheese and mayonnaise.

Cook on Low for 1½ to 2 hours or until cheese is bubbly. Stir in Old Bay Seasoning, and serve with toast points for dipping.

Cooker Caveats

It's almost impossible to find fresh or frozen crabmeat that doesn't have some shell fragments hidden in it somewhere. It's really nasty to bite down on a piece when you're eating. The best way to ensure this won't happen is to spread out the crab on a dark plate. Rub your fingers over the meat and you'll be able to find and pick out the shell bits.

Chapter 4

Finger Lickin' Good

In This Chapter

- ◆ Finger foods
- ◆ Hot bits to spear
- ◆ Nuts to nibble

A wide variety of hors d'oeuvres can be made in the slow cooker. In some cases, the foods are cooked and served right out of the slow cooker—making for easy preparation *and* easy cleanup! Have some long bamboo skewers handy because many slow cookers are too deep to make tooth-picks an option.

In other cases, hors d'oeuvre fillings are simmered in the slow cooker. The foods can then be encased in a variety of wrappers to turn a saucy fill-ing into a tasty finger food.

Some slow cooked dishes need time to chill, or at least reach room temperature, so allow for that cooling time when planning your party.

Asian Beef and Barley Lettuce Cups

Prep time: less than 20 minutes • Minimum cooking time: 2¼ hours • Makes 18 lettuce cups

2 TB. sesame oil

4 scallions, trimmed and thinly sliced

2 garlic cloves, peeled and minced

1 TB. grated fresh ginger

½ lb. lean ground beef

¼ cup pearl barley, rinsed

¾ cup water

2 TB. soy sauce

1 TB. cornstarch

1 TB. cold water

⅔ cup fresh bean sprouts, rinsed and cut into 1-inch pieces

Salt and black pepper to taste

18 Boston or iceberg lettuce leaves

Heat sesame oil in a medium skillet over medium heat; add scallions, garlic, and ginger. Cook and stir for 3 minutes or until scallions soften. Scrape mixture into a 1-quart slow cooker. Add ground beef to the skillet, and break up any lumps with a fork. Cook until beef is browned. Remove it from the skillet with a slotted spoon, and place it into the slow cooker. Add barley, water, and soy sauce to the slow cooker.

Slow Savvy

Some cookbooks tell you to pinch the ends off the bean sprouts. This is not necessary and takes a lot of time. Once the bean sprouts are stirred into a dish, no one will ever notice the ends.

Cook on Low for 3 to 4 hours, on High for 2 to 3 hours, or until barley is tender. Then, if cooking on Low, raise the heat to High. Combine cornstarch and cold water in a small cup, and stir the mixture into the slow cooker. Cook for an additional 15 to 20 minutes or until the juices are bubbly and thickened. Turn off the slow cooker, stir in bean sprouts, and season with salt and pepper.

Place 1 tablespoon of the mixture at the stem end of each lettuce leaf. Tuck the sides over the filling, and roll up the cup like an eggroll. Serve immediately.

Steamed Pork Dumplings

Prep time: less than 30 minutes   •   Minimum cooking time: 2 hours   •   Makes 20 dumplings

2 TB. sesame oil

3 scallions, trimmed and thinly sliced

2 garlic cloves, peeled and minced

¾ lb. ground pork

1 TB. rice wine or dry sherry

¼ cup ketchup

¼ cup firmly packed light brown sugar

2 TB. soy sauce

1 TB. rice wine vinegar

Salt and black pepper to taste

2 (7½-oz.) pkg. refrigerated home-style biscuit dough (not buttermilk biscuits)

Heat oil in a medium skillet over medium heat; add scallions and garlic. Cook and stir for 1 minute, then scrape the mixture into a 1-quart slow cooker. Place pork into the skillet, breaking up any lumps with a fork, and cook over medium-high heat for 4 to 5 minutes or until meat is no longer pink. Remove meat from the pan with a slotted spoon, and place in the slow cooker. Combine rice wine, ketchup, brown sugar, soy sauce, and vinegar in a small bowl; stir this mixture into the contents of the slow cooker.

Cook on Low for 4 to 5 hours or on High for 2 to 3 hours or until the mixture is bubbly and thickened. Season with salt and pepper.

Spread the mixture in a shallow pan, and press a sheet of plastic wrap directly into the top. Chill filling until cold; this can be done up to 1 day in advance. Cut a piece of parchment or waxed paper into 20 2-inch squares.

To form dumplings, separate biscuit dough into individual portions about 2 inches in diameter. Place one dough section on a plate, and press out the edge of the dough circle, leaving the center the original thickness, until the circle is 3²/₃ inches in diameter.

Place 1 tablespoon filling in the center of the dough circle. Using your fingers, gather the edges around the filling, and seal dumplings closed by pinching the dough. Place dumpling seam side down on the square of paper, and shape dumpling into a round ball. Repeat with the remaining filling.

Place dumplings in a bamboo steamer. Pour ½ inch water into a stockpot, and when it comes to a boil, place the bamboo steamer in the pot (stack the steamers if you're using more than one). Cover the pot, and steam dumplings for 10 minutes. Serve immediately.

Slow Savvy

If you don't want to go to the trouble of making the dumplings, serve the filling on chips made from fried wonton skins or in small filo cups found in the frozen food section of your supermarket.

Chinese Chicken in Lettuce Cups

Prep time: less than 20 minutes • Minimum cooking time: 2 hours • Makes 18 lettuce cups

2 TB. sesame oil	2 TB. soy sauce
6 scallions, trimmed and thinly sliced	2 TB. *hoisin sauce*
3 garlic cloves, peeled and minced	1 TB. cider vinegar
1 TB. grated fresh ginger	1 TB. cornstarch
1 lb. ground chicken or ground turkey	1 TB. cold water
1 (8-oz.) can water chestnuts, drained and chopped	Salt and black pepper to taste
	18 Boston or iceberg lettuce cups

Heat oil in a medium saucepan over medium heat. Add scallions, garlic, and ginger. Cook and stir for 1 minute or until the mixture is fragrant. Scrape the mixture into a 1-quart slow cooker. Stir in chicken and water chestnuts. Combine soy sauce, hoisin sauce, and vinegar in a small bowl, then stir into the slow cooker.

Ellen on Edibles

Hoisin (pronounced *HOY-zan*) **sauce** is like a great Asian ketchup. It's a mixture of soybeans, garlic, chilies, and Chinese five-spice powder. It's a thick, reddish-brown sauce that's simultaneously sweet and spicy.

Cook on Low for 4 to 5 hours or on High for 2 to 3 hours or until chicken is cooked through. Then, if cooking on Low, raise the heat to High. Mix cornstarch and cold water in a small bowl. Stir cornstarch mixture into the slow cooker, and cook for an additional 5 to 15 minutes or until the mixture is bubbly and thickened. Season with salt and pepper.

Place 1 tablespoon mixture at the stem end of each lettuce cup. Tuck the sides over the filling, and roll up the cup like an egg roll. Serve immediately.

Stuffed Grape Leaves

Prep time: less than 30 minutes   •   Minimum cooking time: 3 hours   •   Makes 3 dozen pieces

2 (8-oz.) jars grape leaves packed in brine

1 lb. lean ground lamb

1 small onion, peeled and grated

2 garlic cloves, peeled and minced

½ cup uncooked white rice

3 TB. chopped fresh parsley

1 TB. chopped fresh oregano or ½ tsp. dried

½ tsp. dried thyme

Salt and black pepper to taste

3 TB. olive oil

3 TB. fresh lemon juice

1 cup chicken stock

Separate grape leaves, and rinse under cold running water. Place in a mixing bowl, and cover with boiling water. Soak for 1 hour, then drain in a sieve, and run under cold water again.

While leaves are soaking in the hot water, combine ground lamb, onion, garlic, rice, parsley, oregano, thyme, salt, and pepper in a mixing bowl. Stir well to combine.

Place a grape leaf vein side up on a plate. Place 1 heaping tablespoon stuffing on the stem end, and pat the mixture into an oval. Fold the sides of the leaf over the filling; then roll the leaf like an eggroll. Place the stuffed leaf in the slow cooker, and continue with the remaining leaves, placing them tightly together in the slow cooker.

Combine olive oil, lemon juice, and chicken stock. Pour the liquid over the stuffed grape leaves. Cook on Low for 6 to 8 hours, on High for 3 to 4 hours, or until the meat is cooked through and the rice is soft. Serve hot, at room temperature, or cold.

Slow Savvy

If you want to make vegetarian Stuffed Grape Leaves, substitute 1 pound zucchini for the lamb. Trim off the zucchini ends and chop it finely by hand or in a food processor fitted with the steel blade.

Spicy Asian Chicken Wings

Prep time: less than 20 minutes • Minimum cooking time: 2 hours • Makes 3 dozen
wings

18 chicken wings (about 3 lb.)	¼ cup soy sauce
2 scallions, trimmed and finely chopped	¼ cup dry sherry
2 garlic cloves, peeled and minced	2 TB. rice wine vinegar
2 TB. grated fresh ginger	¼ cup hoisin sauce
¾ cup chicken stock	¼ to ½ tsp. red pepper flakes

Cut off tips from chicken wings, and save them for making stock. Cut wings into two sections at
the joint, and arrange wings in the slow cooker.

Slow Savvy
You'll sometimes find the
lower part of roaster wings in the
poultry case. They're called
"chicken drumettes." These are
larger than fryer wings, so you'll
need to add about 1 hour to the
cooking time on Low or 30 minutes
on High.

Combine scallions, garlic, ginger, chicken stock, soy
sauce, sherry, vinegar, hoisin sauce, and red pepper
flakes in a mixing bowl. Stir well and pour the mixture
over chicken wings.

Cook on Low for 4 to 6 hours or on High for 2 to 3
hours or until wings are tender.

Preheat the oven broiler, and line a broiler pan with
aluminum foil. Arrange wings in the broiler pan. Broil
wings for 3 to 4 minutes on a side or until they are
lightly browned. Serve hot, at room temperature, or
chilled.

Glazed Chicken Wings

Prep time: less than 15 minutes   •   Minimum cooking time: 2 hours   •   Makes 3 dozen wings

18 chicken wings (about 3 lb.)

½ cup cider vinegar

½ cup cocktail sauce

1 cup orange marmalade

2 garlic cloves, peeled and crushed

1 TB. Old Bay Seasoning

Cut off tips from chicken wings, and save them for making stock. Cut wings into two sections at the joint, and arrange wings in the slow cooker.

Combine the vinegar, cocktail sauce, orange marmalade, garlic, and Old Bay Seasoning in a mixing bowl. Stir well and pour over chicken wings.

Cook on Low for 4 to 6 hours, on High for 2 to 3 hours, or until wings are tender.

Preheat the oven broiler, and line a broiler pan with aluminum foil. Broil the wings for 2 to 3 minutes on a side or until they are lightly browned. Serve hot, at room temperature, or chilled.

Cooker Caveats

Be careful when broiling any food that has been marinated or cooked in a liquid with a high sugar content, such as this marinade. The food will brown much faster than a similar dish cooked without a sweet component.

Kielbasa Nibbles

Prep time: less than 15 minutes • Minimum cooking time: 1½ hours • Makes 6 to 8 servings

1½ lb. kielbasa, or other smoked sausage, cut into ¾-inch slices

½ cup chili sauce

½ cup barbecue sauce

¼ cup cider vinegar

¼ cup firmly packed dark brown sugar

1 TB. prepared mustard

Salt and black pepper to taste

Preheat the oven to 500°F, and line a broiler pan with aluminum foil. Arrange sausage slices in the pan, and bake for 7 to 10 minutes or until sausage is lightly browned. Using a slotted spoon, transfer sausage to a 1-quart slow cooker.

Combine chili sauce, barbecue sauce, vinegar, brown sugar, and mustard in a bowl. Stir well and pour over sausage.

Cook on Low for 3 to 4 hours or on High for 1½ to 2 hours or until sausage is cooked through and sauce is bubbling. Season sauce with salt and pepper. Serve hot with toothpicks.

Italian Sausage Balls

Prep time: less than 15 minutes • Minimum cooking time: 2 hours • Makes 3 dozen

2 lb. mild or hot bulk Italian sausage

1 egg, lightly beaten

½ cup Italian-style bread crumbs

2 TB. chopped fresh parsley

¾ cup spaghetti sauce

¼ cup dry red wine

2 garlic cloves, peeled and minced

2 tsp. dried oregano

1 tsp. dried basil

½ tsp. dried thyme

Salt and black pepper to taste

Preheat the oven to 500°F. Line a broiler pan with aluminum foil, and grease the foil with vegetable oil spray or vegetable oil. Combine sausage, egg, bread crumbs, and parsley in a mixing bowl. Mix well and form into three dozen balls. Place sausage balls on the aluminum foil, and bake for 10 to 12 minutes or until they are lightly browned. Using a slotted spoon, transfer sausage balls to a 1-quart slow cooker.

Combine spaghetti sauce, wine, garlic, oregano, basil, and thyme in a mixing bowl. Stir well and pour the mixture over sausage balls. Cook on Low for 4 to 5 hours or on High for 2 to 3 hours or until sausage balls are cooked through. Season sauce with salt and pepper. Serve sausage balls with toothpicks.

Slow Savvy

I have a great use for the leftover red wine—it's called drinking it. If you don't want to drink it, here's what to do: Boil it down in a saucepan until it's reduced by half, then freeze it in ice cube trays. When you're making a dish in the future that calls for red wine, just pull out a few cubes.

Garlicky Shrimp

Prep time: less than 15 minutes • Minimum cooking time: 1½ hours • Makes 6 to 8 servings

½ cup olive oil	3 TB. chopped fresh parsley
6 garlic cloves, peeled and crushed	Salt to taste
1 TB. paprika	Red pepper flakes to taste
2 lb. medium shrimp, peeled and *deveined*	

Combine olive oil, garlic, paprika, shrimp, and parsley in the slow cooker. Cook on Low for 3 to 4 hours or on High for 1½ to 2 hours or until shrimp are pink and cooked through. Season shrimp with salt and red pepper flakes. Serve shrimp with toothpicks.

Ellen on Edibles

When you buy shrimp that are still in their shells, they need to be peeled. That's step one. Step two is to **devein** them. In one hand, hold the shrimp with its back facing up. With the other hand, cut gently down the back with a small paring knife. If there is a thin black line, scrape it out. That's the "vein"—actually the intestinal tract, which can be bitter and gritty. Many shrimp don't have anything to devein, so don't worry if there's nothing to scrape out.

Barbecued Sparerib Nuggets

Prep time: less than 15 minutes • Minimum cooking time: 3 hours • Makes 8 to 10 servings

3 lb. country spareribs

1 (8-oz.) can tomato sauce

½ cup cider vinegar

½ cup firmly packed dark brown sugar

1 TB. Old Bay Seasoning

Cut ribs into 1-inch sections; remove and discard any bones. Arrange pieces in the slow cooker. Combine tomato sauce, vinegar, brown sugar, and Old Bay Seasoning in a mixing bowl. Stir well and pour the mixture over ribs.

Cook on Low for 5 to 7 hours or on High for 3 to 4 hours or until pork is cooked through and tender. Serve with toothpicks.

Slow Savvy

A variation on this yummy hors d'oeuvre is to use balls of ground pork instead of the spare ribs. If you want to do that, brown the balls under a preheated oven broiler for 3 to 5 minutes before placing them into the slow cooker.

Chinese Chicken Liver Pâté

Prep time: less than 20 minutes • Minimum cooking time: 1 hour • Makes 1 pint

2 TB. sesame oil

6 scallions, trimmed and finely chopped

3 garlic cloves, peeled and minced

1 TB. finely chopped fresh ginger

1 lb. chicken livers, rinsed, trimmed, and cut into ½-inch pieces

2 TB. rice wine or dry sherry

2 TB. Chinese oyster sauce

2 TB. soy sauce

½ cup finely chopped fresh water chestnuts

Salt and black pepper to taste

Heat sesame oil in a small skillet over medium heat; add scallions, garlic, and ginger. Cook and stir for 2 minutes or until the mixture is fragrant. Scrape the mixture into the slow cooker.

Arrange chicken livers on top of vegetables. Combine rice wine, Chinese oyster sauce, and soy sauce in a small bowl, then pour the mixture over livers. Cook on Low for 3 to 4 hours or on High for 1 to 2 hours or until livers are cooked through.

Ellen on Edibles

Sesame oil is an Asian product made from toasted sesame seeds. It's very potent, so a little goes a long way. Look for one that is rich, dark brown, and translucent.

Scrape the mixture into a food processor fitted with a steel blade or a blender, and purée until smooth. Scrape the mixture into a mixing bowl, and stir in water chestnuts. Season with salt and pepper.

Line a decorative mold or small mixing bowl with plastic wrap, and pack pâté into the container. Cover with plastic wrap, and refrigerate until well chilled. To serve, invert the container onto a serving dish, and remove the plastic wrap.

Serve with crackers or crisps made from fried wonton skins.

Fall Chicken Liver Mousse

Prep time: less than 15 minutes • Minimum cooking time: 1½ hours • Makes 2 pints

2 TB. walnut oil

4 TB. (½ stick) butter

2 Golden Delicious apples, peeled, cored, and thinly sliced

2 tsp. granulated sugar

1 lb. chicken livers, rinsed, trimmed, and cut into ½-inch pieces

¼ lb. walnuts, toasted in a 350°F oven for 5 minutes

2 TB. Calvados or apple brandy

Salt and black pepper to taste

Heat walnut oil and butter in a medium skillet over medium heat; add apples and sprinkle them with sugar. Cook, stirring, for 5 minutes or until apples are almost soft. Scrape apples into the slow cooker, and arrange chicken livers on top of them.

Cook on Low for 3 to 4 hours or on High for 1½ to 2 hours or until livers are cooked through. Scrape the mixture into a food processor fitted with a steel blade or a blender, and purée until smooth. Add walnuts and Calvados and chop finely, using the on-and-off pulsing action, or chop by hand. Season the mixture with salt and pepper to taste.

Line a decorative mold or small mixing bowl with plastic wrap, and pack mousse into the container. Cover it with plastic wrap, and refrigerate until well chilled. To serve, invert the container onto a platter, and remove the plastic wrap.

Serve with crackers, pita toasts, or sliced French or Italian bread.

Ellen on Edibles

There's a good reason why you should toast nuts, even if they're going to end up in a wet dish. Toasting releases the oils so the nuts become more aromatic. That translates to a more flavorful food.

Glazed Walnuts

Prep time: less than 15 minutes • Minimum cooking time: 2½ hours • Makes 1 pound

1 lb. walnut halves

2 TB. walnut oil

¼ cup granulated sugar

1 TB. kosher salt

Slow Savvy

These walnuts are great additions to lots of dishes—if you have any left in the bowl after nibbling. Try them as a topping on a tossed salad along with some crumbled blue cheese. Or chop them and stir them into a chicken salad.

Bring a large pot of water to a boil over high heat. Stir in walnuts, and remove the pan from the stove. Let nuts soak for 1 hour, then drain and pat dry with paper towels. While nuts are soaking, preheat the oven to 350°F. Spread walnuts on a large baking sheet, and bake them in the preheated oven for 45 minutes or until they are dry.

Place walnuts into the slow cooker, and drizzle with walnut oil. Stir to coat nuts evenly, then sprinkle with sugar and kosher salt. Cook on Low for 2 to 3 hours or until nuts are glazed. Raise the heat to High, and cook an additional 30 minutes uncovered. Once nuts have cooled, store them in an airtight container.

Slow Savvy

The universal benefit of slow cookers' low heat extends to spiced and glazed nuts. Nuts toast best, and absorb the best flavor, at low heat. And the low heat means the sugar won't burn.

Chili Pecans

Prep time: less than 15 minutes   •   Minimum cooking time: 2½ hours   •   Makes 1 pound

2 TB. vegetable oil

1 lb. pecan halves

¼ cup granulated sugar

2 TB. chili powder

1 TB. herbes de Provence

1 TB. *kosher salt*

Place oil and pecans into the slow cooker, and stir to coat. Combine sugar, chili powder, herbes de Provence, and kosher salt in a small bowl. Sprinkle the mixture over nuts and stir well.

Cook on Low for 2 to 3 hours or until sugar is melted. Uncover the pan, and cook on High for an additional 30 minutes or until nuts are crisp. Serve warm or cold.

Ellen on Edibles _____

Kosher salt is a coarse-grained salt that is made without any additives or iodine. Religious Jews use it in the rituals of preparing meats, and many cooks like using it because it doesn't have any chemical flavor. It's used for dishes such as this nut dish because it is granular. If using table salt instead, use one-third the amount.

The Least You Need to Know

- Chicken wings should be browned under the broiler after they are cooked in the slow cooker.
- The slow cooker can be used to make hot hors d'oeuvres like meatballs that can be speared with toothpicks or bamboo skewers.
- Use your slow cooker to make the fillings for finger foods that can be served both hot and cold.
- Slow cooked fillings can be presented in everything from lettuce leaves to steamed biscuit dough.
- Slow cookers are excellent for making flavored nuts because you don't have to worry that the sugar will burn.

Part 3

Satisfying Soups

Soups are the quintessential comfort food. Lewis Carroll of *Alice in Wonderland* fame wrote "Beautiful soup! Who cares for fish, game, or any other dish? Who would not give all else for two pennyworth only of beautiful soup?"

In Part 3, you'll find a range of recipes for satisfying soups. Some are vegetarian soups intended as first courses, and then there are the nutritious bean soups, flocks of chicken soups, and hearty, meat-based soups.

Vegetarian Soups as a Starter

In This Chapter

- ◆ Creamy soups made with a variety of vegetables
- ◆ Hearty vegetable and grain soups
- ◆ Vegetable soups from the world over

There's nothing as warming at the start of a meal as a bowl of soup, and this chapter contains a number of easy and delicious soups that can be served before an entrée or augmented with other ingredients to serve as supper itself. Some are puréed so they become thick and creamy, while others remain chunky. Whatever your preference, you're sure to find something to your liking.

Making It a Meal

Although these soups are intended to serve as small starters, there's no reason why they can't become the main event. For a vegetarian meal, simply serve extra-large portions—perhaps with the addition of cubes of tofu—along with some good, crusty bread and a salad. For the

meat-eaters at your table, you can add leftover poultry or meat—as long as these were roasted and not prepared in a sauce so there will not be conflicting flavors. Dice the leftovers and add them to the soup at the end of the cooking process. Add a few minutes to the cooking time to ensure the new additions get warmed.

Fresh from the Freezer

In most of the recipes in this chapter, I've assumed fresh vegetables will be used as the base for the soups, but frozen vegetables can be substituted with a few exceptions. Frozen carrot slices, cauliflower, broccoli, butternut squash, and chopped green pepper can be used successfully, but don't use frozen onions if they are going to be sautéed. They won't hold up.

Vegetarian Versatility

All the soups in this chapter are fine vegetarian fare if you make them using vegetable stock. (Refer to the recipe for Vegetable Stock in Chapter 1, or just add some additional carrots, celery, and herbs to the soup to boost the flavor.) If you desire, chicken stock can be used in place of vegetable stock.

The stock is the medium that actually cooks the vegetables in these creamed soups. The cream itself is added at the end of the cooking cycle. This is because cream and other dairy products tend to curdle and separate if cooked for long hours, even at low heat.

The Least You Need to Know

◆ Cream should be added to soups at the end of the cooking cycle so it doesn't curdle from long hours of simmering.

◆ Frozen vegetables can be substituted for fresh vegetables in most soups.

◆ First-course soups can be turned into entrées by adding cubes of tofu, or diced poultry or meat that was roasted without a strong sauce—a great way to use leftovers.

◆ Using vegetable stock instead of chicken stock makes any of these recipes truly vegetarian.

Potato Leek Soup

Prep time: less than 20 minutes   •   Minimum cooking time: 3¼ hours   •   Makes 4 to 6 servings

6 leeks, white part only	4 cups vegetable or chicken stock
2 TB. butter	½ cup heavy cream
2 large boiling potatoes (about 1½ lb.), peeled and cut into ½-inch dice	Salt and white pepper to taste

Trim ends of leeks, and split them lengthwise. Rinse them well under cold running water to get rid of all dirt. Slice leeks into thin arcs. Melt butter in a medium saucepan over medium heat. Add leeks and toss with butter. Cover the pan, reduce the heat to low, and cook for 10 minutes. Then scrape leeks into the slow cooker.

Add potatoes and stock to the slow cooker. Cook on Low for 6 to 8 hours or on High for 3 to 4 hours or until potatoes are tender. Then, if cooking on Low, raise the heat to High. Add cream to the soup, and season it with salt and pepper. Cook the soup for an additional 15 to 20 minutes or until it is simmering.

For a chunky soup, use a potato masher to crush some of the potatoes right in the slow cooker. For a smooth soup, drain the solids into a colander set over a mixing bowl. Purée leeks and potatoes in a food processor fitted with a steel blade or in a blender. Stir the purée back into the soup.

Slow Savvy

This is a really versatile soup. It can also be puréed and served chilled, at which time it's called Vichyssoise. You'll probably want to add a bit more salt to the soup if you serve it chilled.

Butternut Squash Bisque

Prep time: less than 20 minutes   •   Minimum cooking time: 3½ hours   •   Makes 4 to 6 servings

3½ lb. butternut or acorn squash, peeled and cut into 1-inch chunks

2½ cups vegetable or chicken stock

⅓ cup molasses

⅓ cup bourbon

2 TB. chopped fresh parsley

½ tsp. ground cinnamon

Pinch of ground nutmeg

1 cup half-and-half

Salt and white pepper to taste

Slow Savvy

Many supermarkets now have pre-peeled butternut squash—at least during the winter months—a huge time-saver when making a soup such as this one. Cut back to 3 pounds squash to compensate for the peels.

Place squash, stock, molasses, bourbon, parsley, cinnamon, and nutmeg in the slow cooker. Cook on Low for 6 to 8 hours or on High for 3 to 4 hours or until squash is tender.

Then, if cooking on Low, raise the heat to High. Add half-and-half, and cook for an additional 20 to 30 minutes or until bubbly. Drain soup into a colander placed over a mixing bowl, and purée squash in a food processor fitted with a steel blade or in a blender. Stir the purée back into the soup, and season it with salt and pepper.

Curried Carrot Soup

Prep time: less than 20 minutes   •   Minimum cooking time: 3½ hours   •   Makes 6 to 8 servings

2 TB. butter

1 medium onion, peeled and diced

2 TB. all-purpose flour

1½ to 2 tsp. curry powder or to taste

6 carrots, peeled and sliced

1 apple, peeled, cored, and diced

5 cups vegetable or chicken stock

½ cup heavy cream

Salt and black pepper to taste

Melt butter in a medium saucepan over medium heat; add onion. Cook and stir for 3 minutes or until onion is translucent. Reduce the heat to low, and stir in flour and curry powder. Cook for 2 minutes, stirring constantly. Scrape the mixture into the slow cooker.

Add carrots, apple, and stock to the slow cooker. Cook on Low for 6 to 8 hours or on High for 3 to 4 hours or until carrots are tender.

Then, if cooking on Low, raise the heat to High. Add cream and cook for an additional 20 to 30 minutes or until bubbly. Drain the soup into a colander placed over a mixing bowl, and purée the solids in a food processor fitted with a steel blade or in a blender. Stir the purée back into the soup, and season it with salt and pepper.

Cooker Caveats

One small step that will make a big difference in your final results is properly stirring and cooking the flour used as a thickener for a good 2 minutes, until the flour is thoroughly incorporated into the liquid and fully cooked. These few minutes of stirring will ensure that your soup will not have the underlying flavor of library paste.

Beet and Cabbage Borscht

Prep time: less than 20 minutes • Minimum cooking time: 4 hours • Makes 4 to 6 servings

2 large boiling potatoes (about ½ lb.), peeled and cut into 1-inch cubes

1½ lb. beets, peeled and cut into 1-inch cubes

1 large onion, peeled and cut into 1-inch cubes

4 cups vegetable or chicken stock

2 cups shredded green cabbage (about ¼ small head)

2 TB. granulated sugar

1 TB. lemon juice

Salt and black pepper to taste

Sour cream

Crock Tales

Borscht, always made with beets and sometimes made with meat, is of Russian and Polish origin. It was popular with the Jews who emigrated from those countries, and during the 1930s, resorts in New York's Catskill Mountains that featured Jewish entertainers became known as the "Borscht Belt."

Place potatoes, beets, and onion in the work bowl of a food processor fitted with a steel blade. Chop finely using the on-and-off pulsing action or chop by hand. Scrape the mixture into the slow cooker. Stir stock, cabbage, sugar, and lemon juice into the slow cooker.

Cook on Low for 8 to 10 hours or on High for 4 to 5 hours or until cabbage is tender. Remove half the vegetables from the soup using a slotted spoon. Purée vegetables in a food processor fitted with a steel blade or in a blender until smooth. Return the purée to the soup and stir well. Season with salt and pepper. Serve the soup garnished with a dollop of sour cream.

Mushroom Barley Soup

Prep time: less than 20 minutes   •   Minimum cooking time: 3 hours   •   Makes 6 to 8 servings

½ oz. dried *porcini* mushrooms

1 cup hot water

1 large onion, peeled and cut into 1-inch pieces

1 stalk celery, cut into 1-inch pieces

1 carrot, peeled and cut into 1-inch pieces

4 TB. (½ stick) butter

½ lb. white mushrooms, rinsed, stemmed, and sliced

5 cups vegetable or chicken stock

1 cup pearl barley, rinsed

4 TB. chopped fresh parsley

2 tsp. fresh thyme or ½ tsp. dried

1 bay leaf

Salt and black pepper to taste

Soak porcinis in hot water for 30 minutes. Strain liquid through a sieve lined with a coffee filter into the slow cooker. Finely chop porcinis in a food processor fitted with a steel blade or by hand. Add porcinis to the slow cooker.

Place onion, celery, and carrot in the work bowl of a food processor fitted with a steel blade. Chop finely using the on-and-off pulsing action or by hand. Heat butter in a large skillet over medium heat; add chopped onion, celery, and carrot. Cook, stirring, for 3 minutes or until onion is translucent. Raise the heat to medium-high, and add sliced white mushrooms. Cook for an additional 3 minutes or until mushrooms begin to soften. Scrap the mixture into the slow cooker, and stir in stock, barley, parsley, thyme, and bay leaf.

Cook on Low for 6 to 7 hours or on High for 3 to 4 hours or until barley is soft. Discard bay leaf, and season with salt and pepper.

Ellen on Edibles

Although the name actually means "little pigs" in Italian, **porcini** mushrooms are extremely flavorful and aromatic when dried. If you can't find porcini mushrooms, dried Polish mushrooms are a good substitute. Dried shiitake mushrooms do not have the same flavor, but they can be used in a pinch.

Cream of Onion Soup

Prep time: less than 30 minutes   •   Minimum cooking time: 3¼ hours   •   Makes 6 to 8 servings

3 TB. butter

2½ lb. onions, peeled and thinly sliced

½ tsp. salt

1 tsp. sugar

4 cups vegetable or chicken stock

1 cup dark beer

3 TB. chopped fresh parsley

2 bay leaves

1 TB. fresh thyme or 1 tsp. dried

1 TB. chopped fresh rosemary or 1 tsp. dried

1 cup heavy cream

Salt and black pepper to taste

Cooker Caveats

Don't leave your onions alone while they're browning. They need some attention, especially as they reach the chestnut brown stage. If the onions stick to the pan, stir to incorporate the browned juices into the onions and then continue stirring often.

Heat butter in a large saucepan over low heat. Add onions, toss to coat, and cover the pan. Cook over low heat for 10 minutes, stirring occasionally. Uncover the pan, raise the heat to medium, and stir in salt and sugar. Cook for 20 to 30 minutes, stirring frequently, until onions are browned. Scrape onions into the slow cooker.

Add stock, beer, parsley, bay leaves, thyme, and rosemary to the slow cooker. Stir well. Cook on Low for 6 to 8 hours or on High for 3 to 4 hours. Then, if cooking on Low, raise the heat to High. Stir in cream, and season the soup with salt and pepper. Cook for an additional 15 to 20 minutes or until the soup is simmering.

Portuguese Kale Soup

Prep time: less than 20 minutes • Minimum cooking time: 5 hours • Makes 6 servings

2 TB. olive oil

1 large onion, peeled and diced

2 garlic cloves, peeled and minced

1 lb. Portuguese *linguiça* sausage, cut into ½-inch dice

1½ pounds boiling potatoes, peeled and diced

5 cups vegetable or chicken stock

¾ lb. kale

Salt and black pepper to taste

Heat olive oil in a medium skillet over medium heat; add onion and garlic. Cook and stir for 3 minutes or until onion is translucent. Scrape the mixture into the slow cooker. Add sausage to the pan, and cook over medium heat for 5 to 7 minutes, stirring frequently. Turn off the heat, transfer sausage to a covered storage container, and refrigerate until ready to use.

Add potatoes and stock to the slow cooker. Cook on Low for 8 to 10 hours or on High for 4 to 5 hours or until potatoes are tender.

While the soup is cooking, prepare kale. Rinse kale and discard the stems and center of the ribs. Cut the leaves crosswise into thin slices.

Drain the soup through a sieve over a mixing bowl. Purée the solids in a food processor fitted with a steel blade or in a blender. Return the soup to the slow cooker, and stir in purée, sausage, and kale. Cook on High for 1 to 2 hours or until kale is cooked and tender. Season with salt and pepper.

Ellen on Edibles

Many sausages got their start on the Iberian Peninsula, and most of them are characterized by a moderate spice level. **Linguiça** sausage is Portuguese, often spiced with garlic, cumin, and cinnamon. The best substitute for it is Spanish or Mexican chorizo.

Southwest Corn Soup

Prep time: less than 15 minutes • Minimum cooking time: 4½ hours • Makes 6 to 8 servings

8 ears fresh corn, shucked, or 2 (10-oz.) boxes frozen corn, thawed

2 garlic cloves, peeled and minced

¼ cup yellow cornmeal

1 (4-oz.) can chopped mild green chilies, drained

2 cups vegetable or chicken stock

2 cups half-and-half

Salt and black pepper to taste

Cut off kernels from the ears of corn. Combine corn, garlic, cornmeal, chilies, and stock in the slow cooker and stir well. Cook on Low for 7 to 9 hours or on High for 4 to 5 hours or until corn is tender and broth has thickened.

Remove half the corn from the slow cooker with a slotted spoon. Purée corn in a food processor fitted with a steel blade or in a blender. If cooking on Low, raise the heat to High. Stir the purée back into the soup, and stir in half-and-half. Season with salt and pepper. Cook on High for 20 to 30 minutes or until the soup is simmering.

Slow Savvy

Try making this soup with grilled corn. Grilling adds a fantastic, smoky flavor. To grill corn, pull off all but one layer of husks, and reach in to pull out as much corn silk as possible. Soak the ears in cold water for 10 minutes, then place them on the grill and close the lid. Cook the corn for 10 to 15 minutes, turning it with tongs from time to time.

Cream of Cauliflower Soup

Prep time: less than 15 minutes • Minimum cooking time: 3½ hours • Makes 6 to 8 servings

6 cups finely chopped cauliflower (1 medium head)

1 small onion, peeled and chopped

1½ cups vegetable or chicken stock

1 (10¾-oz.) can condensed cheddar cheese soup

1 cup half-and-half

¼ lb. (1 cup) grated sharp cheddar cheese

Salt and black pepper to taste

Combine cauliflower, onion, stock, and cheddar cheese soup in the slow cooker and stir well. Cook on Low for 7 to 9 hours or on High for 3 to 4 hours or until cauliflower is tender. Remove half the cauliflower from the slow cooker with a slotted spoon, and purée it in a food processor fitted with a steel blade or in a blender. Return the purée to the soup, and stir in half-and-half and cheddar cheese.

If cooking on Low, raise the heat to High. Cook the soup for 30 to 45 minutes or until the soup is simmering. Stir well and season with salt and pepper.

Slow Savvy

Broccoli can be substituted for all or some of the cauliflower in this soup; the rest of the ingredients and directions remain the same. This is a good way to use up the broccoli stalks that are not as pretty to serve on the vegetable plate as the florets are.

Chapter 6

Those Luscious Legumes

In This Chapter

- ◆ Bean soups of many colors
- ◆ Bean soups with aromatic herbs and spices
- ◆ Bean soups with and without meat

Beans are an essential in the slow cooker's pantry. Healthful and hearty, bean soups are easy to make in a slow cooker—that's justification enough for owning one. The great advantage to simmering bean soups in the slow cooker is the low heat. You'll never find burned beans stuck to the bottom of the pot.

Famous for Fiber

You might already know that beans are a good source of both protein and dietary fiber, but did you know they also add B vitamins to your diet, contain little or no fat depending on the variety, and contain no cholesterol?

In today's Food Pyramid, beans are part of the complex carbohydrates group at the base of the pyramid, and they should be eaten a few times a day—which is easy to do if you have a slow cooker.

The Soaking Standard

Although pre-soaking beans is not totally essential, it's suggested for almost all the recipes in this chapter, as it cuts down cooking time. Keep in mind that other members of the legume family, such as lentils and split peas, don't require soaking. They will soften easily during a relatively short cooking time.

There are two ways to soak beans. The first is to cover them with water for at least six hours. This is called the "overnight method," but you can cover them with water early in the morning and then begin cooking them in the early afternoon.

The second method is the "quick soak." *Quick* means a total time of about an hour and a half. Cover the beans with hot tap water and bring them to a boil on top of the stove. After boiling for 1 minute, turn off the heat, cover the pan, and let the beans soak for 1 hour.

Whichever method you use, discard the soaking water and start cooking with fresh.

The Least You Need to Know

- ◆ Dried bean soups are excellent in the slow cooker because the beans at the bottom do not scorch and stick to the pan.
- ◆ Beans are high in protein, fiber, and B vitamins, are also low in fat, and contain no cholesterol.
- ◆ Soaking beans before cooking them speeds the cooking time and can be done in two ways, either at room temperature covered with water overnight or brought to a boil and allowed to sit covered for 1 hour.

Cuban Black Bean Soup

Prep time: less than 15 minutes   •   Minimum cooking time: 4 hours   •   Makes 6 to 8 servings

1 lb. dried black beans	1 TB. ground cumin
¼ cup olive oil	2 tsp. ground coriander
1 large onion, peeled and diced	6 cups vegetable or stock
1 green bell pepper, seeds and ribs removed, and finely chopped	Salt to taste
6 garlic cloves, peeled and minced	¼ cup chopped cilantro
1 or 2 jalapeño peppers, seeds removed, and finely diced	Black pepper to taste
	Sour cream (optional)
	Lime wedges

Rinse beans in a colander, place them in a mixing bowl, and cover with cold water. Allow beans to soak overnight. Or place beans in a saucepan, and bring to a boil over high heat. Boil 1 minute. Turn off the heat, cover the pan, soak beans for 1 hour. Drain and discard the soaking water.

Heat oil in a medium skillet over medium heat; add onion, green bell pepper, garlic, and jalapeño pepper. Cook and stir for 3 minutes or until onion is translucent. Reduce the heat to low; add cumin and coriander. Stir for 1 minute. Scrape the mixture into the slow cooker.

Place beans in the slow cooker, and stir in stock. Cook the mixture on Low for 8 to 10 hours or High for 4 to 5 hours or until beans are soft. Add salt during the last hour of cooking.

Purée the soup in a food processor fitted with a steel blade or in a blender. Stir in cilantro, and season with pepper. Top with a dollop of sour cream, if desired, and serve with lime wedges.

 **Cooker Caveats**

Some cookbooks tell you to wear rubber gloves when handling hot chilies. That's not really necessary (unless you have sensitive skin), but you do need to take care. I cut the chilies on a glass plate rather than on my cutting board so the volatile oils do not penetrate the wood. What's most important is that you wash your hands thoroughly after handling chilies.

White Bean Soup with Prosciutto

Prep time: less than 15 minutes • Minimum cooking time: 4 hours • Makes 6 to 8 servings

2 cups dried navy beans or other small dried white beans

3 TB. olive oil

1 large onion, peeled and diced

6 garlic cloves, peeled and minced

1 (14½-oz.) can diced tomatoes, drained

½ cup finely chopped carrots

½ cup finely chopped celery

¼ lb. prosciutto, finely chopped

6 cups chicken or ham stock

1 TB. fresh thyme or 1 tsp. dried

1 TB. fresh rosemary, chopped, or 1 tsp. dried

Salt and black pepper to taste

Rinse beans in a colander, place them in a mixing bowl, and cover with cold water. Allow beans to soak overnight. Or place beans in a saucepan, and bring to a boil over high heat. Boil 1 minute. Turn off the heat, cover the pan, and soak beans for 1 hour. Drain and discard the soaking water, and place beans into the slow cooker.

Heat olive oil in a medium skillet over medium heat; add onion and garlic. Cook and stir for 3 minutes or until onion is translucent. Add the mixture to the slow cooker, and stir in tomatoes, carrots, celery, prosciutto, stock, thyme, and rosemary. Cook on Low for 8 to 10 hours or on High for 4 to 5 hours or until beans are tender.

Using a slotted spoon, transfer half the solids to a food processor fitted with a metal blade or a blender, and purée until smooth. Return the purée to the soup, and season with salt and pepper. Reheat soup, if necessary, by cooking on High for 15 to 20 minutes.

> ### Crock Tales
> Prosciutto has been made for more than 2,000 years in the region of Italy near Parma and must come from Parma, San Daniele, or the Veneto to be authentic. If you've wondered why prosciutto seems to go so well with Parmesan cheese, it might be because the whey from Parmigiano Reggiano is one of the foods fed to the pigs prosciutto comes from.

Seven-Bean Soup

Prep time: less than 20 minutes   •   Minimum cooking time: 5 hours   •   Makes 6 to 8 servings

¼ cup each dried baby lima beans, kidney beans, black-eyed peas, navy beans, chickpeas, pinto beans, and red beans (or some combination of beans to equal 1¾ cups)

¼ cup olive oil

1 large onion, peeled and chopped

1 carrot, peeled and chopped

1 celery stalk, peeled and chopped

1 green or red bell pepper, seeds and ribs removed, and chopped

1 Anaheim green chili pepper, seeds and ribs removed, and chopped

3 garlic cloves, peeled and minced

3 cups vegetable or chicken stock

1 (14½-oz.) can crushed tomatoes

2 TB. tomato paste

2 TB. granulated sugar

2 TB. balsamic vinegar

1 TB. dried oregano

1 tsp. dried thyme

1 bay leaf

Salt to taste

Red pepper flakes to taste

Rinse beans in a colander, place them in a mixing bowl, and cover with cold water. Allow beans to soak overnight. Or place beans in a saucepan, and bring to a boil over high heat. Boil 1 minute. Turn off the heat, cover the pan, and soak beans for 1 hour. Drain and discard the soaking liquid, then place beans into the slow cooker.

Heat oil in a large skillet over medium heat; add onion, carrot, celery, green bell pepper, chili pepper, and garlic. Cook and stir for 3 to 5 minutes or until onion is translucent and peppers have begun to soften. Scrape the mixture into the slow cooker. Stir in stock, tomatoes, tomato paste, sugar, vinegar, oregano, thyme, and bay leaf. Cook on Low for 10 to 12 hours or on High for 5 to 6 hours or until beans are soft. Discard bay leaf, and season with salt and red pepper flakes.

Crock Tales

There is a veritable rainbow of colored peppers at the market today. The two peppers most closely related are green and red bell peppers. Green peppers are immature red peppers, which is why you'll see some with orange stripes that were beginning to mature when they were harvested. If you have trouble digesting green peppers, using red peppers might solve the problem because they are not as bitter.

Split Pea Soup

Prep time: less than 15 minutes • Minimum cooking time: 3 hours • Makes 8 to 10 servings

1 lb. green split peas, rinsed

6 cups chicken or vegetable stock

1 ham bone or smoked pork hock (optional)

1 onion, peeled and finely chopped

1 carrot, peeled and finely chopped

2 garlic cloves, peeled and minced

2 TB. chopped fresh parsley

1 TB. fresh thyme or 1 tsp. dried

1 bay leaf

Salt and black pepper to taste

Slow Savvy

Unless you want a vegetarian soup, adding a ham bone is a wonderful flavor addition to any soup. It adds a smoky flavor as well as salt to the broth. If you're using a bone, don't salt the soup until the very end.

Place split peas into the slow cooker. Add stock, ham bone or pork hock (if used), onion, carrot, garlic, parsley, thyme, and bay leaf. Cook on Low for 6 to 8 hours or on High for 3 to 4 hours or until split peas have disintegrated. Discard bay leaf, and season with salt and pepper.

Remove ham bone (if used), and cut meat from the bone. Return meat to the soup.

Lentil and Carrot Soup

Prep time: less than 15 minutes　•　Minimum cooking time: 3 hours　•　Makes 6 to 8 servings

3 TB. olive oil

2 carrots, peeled and finely chopped

2 garlic cloves, peeled and minced

1 large onion, peeled and finely chopped

1 tsp. ground cumin

1 tsp. ground coriander

1 tsp. turmeric

2 cups red lentils, rinsed

6 cups vegetable or chicken stock

1 TB. grated orange *zest*

Salt and black pepper to taste

Heat olive oil in a medium skillet over medium heat; add carrots, garlic, and onion. Cook and stir for 3 to 5 minutes or until onion is translucent. Stir in cumin, coriander, and turmeric. Stir for 1 minute, then scrape the mixture into a slow cooker.

Add lentils and stir in stock and orange zest. Cook on Low for 7 to 9 hours or on High for 3 to 5 hours or until lentils are very soft. Remove 2 cups of the solids from the soup with a slotted spoon. Purée until smooth in a food processor fitted with a steel blade or in a blender. Return the purée to the soup, and season with salt and pepper.

Ellen on Edibles

The **zest** is the very thin, colored coating on citrus fruits that contains the aromatic oils. You can buy a gizmo called a zester that strips off the zest in neat little strips, or you can use the fine side of a box grater to remove it. Don't try to do it by hand with a paring knife, though, because there's a good chance you'll also get some of the bitter white pith beneath the zest.

Chapter 7

Soup as Supper

In This Chapter

- ◆ Filling soups that are complete meals
- ◆ Hearty Italian vegetable soups
- ◆ Chicken soups from around the world

When soups are served as supper, they should be thick enough that the spoon can stand up by itself. Those are the kinds of soups you'll find in this chapter. The only real difference between these soups and stews is that the soups have a bit more liquid—but just a bit.

Soups have traditionally been a way to stretch a small amount of protein so it can fill a large number of stomachs, so these soups are not haute cuisine. They are the definition of comfort food, and almost every culture and climate has its own versions.

Personalize with Pleasure

Soup recipes are always open to improvisation. If you like one vegetable more than another or if you have a lot of one vegetable around, changing the proportion will not change the delicious outcome. When making soups in the slow cooker, the important thing is to have the correct amount of food in the pot. Ideally, it should be at least half full and not more than three-quarters full. Feel free to change around the ingredients and proportions, but try to keep the quantity the same.

Extras for Insurance

I don't think of making more food than you need for one night as creating *leftovers*. That word has a negative connotation. I think of it instead as *dinner insurance*—and everyone should have a few of these policies in his or her freezer!

Strategy for Success

If you've decided in advance that part of a batch of soup is destined for the freezer, two things are important to consider: the ingredients used (some hold up better than others when frozen) and timing.

Soups that freeze the best are the ones made without potatoes. Potatoes tend to break down and become mushy when thawed and reheated and are not good candidates for a second supper. The same fate awaits pasta and noodles. Many of the recipes in this chapter call for adding the noodles at the end of the cooking process. So if you plan on freezing all or part of the soup, take out the amount you want to freeze *before* adding the pasta to the pot.

Freeze in a Flash

Heavy quart plastic bags are the freezer's best friend. Remember that liquid expands when it freezes, so don't fill a bag more than three-quarters full. Lay the filled bag on its side until it's frozen solid, and it will be easy to defrost in the microwave on a future night.

Vibrant and Vegetarian

Even devoted meat eaters are becoming occasional vegetarians today. The soups in this chapter are so hearty and filling that no meat-eater who eats them will say "Where's the beef?"

Chicken Soups for the Soul

It's not just your grandmother who says to eat chicken soup when you're sick. Some medical studies have also touted the virtues of chicken soup, and here are some from a number of different cultures that are sure to make you healthy if you're not already.

Because chicken has an innately mild flavor, most of these soups rely on herbs, spices, and other flavors to perk the palate. If you want to create a soup with leftover roast or grilled chicken, go ahead. Just add the chicken at the end of the cooking process.

The Least You Need to Know

- Recipes for hearty soups are found in all the world's cuisines.
- It's possible to make a large batch of soup and freeze a portion for a future meal. Select recipes to freeze that do not contain potatoes, and do not add pasta to a soup before freezing it.
- Personalize a recipe by substituting a food you don't like for more of one you do like.

Minestrone
(Italian Mixed Vegetable and Pasta Soup)

Prep time: less than 30 minutes • Minimum cooking time: 4 hours • Makes 6 to 8 servings

2 TB. olive oil

1 large onion, peeled and diced

3 garlic cloves, peeled and minced

1½ cups shredded green cabbage

1 (28-oz.) can diced tomatoes

3 cups vegetable or chicken stock

1 carrot, peeled and thinly sliced

1 celery stalk, trimmed and sliced

1 tsp. dried thyme

1 tsp. dried oregano

1 bay leaf

2 small zucchini, cut into ½-inch cubes

1 (10-oz.) box frozen Italian green beans, thawed

1 (15-oz.) can white cannellini beans, drained and rinsed

½ cup small elbow macaroni or small pasta shells

Salt and black pepper to taste

Freshly grated Parmesan cheese

 Crock Tales

If you think this hearty Italian soup changes from pot to pot, you're right. *Minestrone* is the Italian word for "big soup"; it comes from the Latin *ministro*, which means "to serve." As a big soup, it always contains a number of different vegetables, depending on what the chef has on hand or what's in season.

Heat olive oil in a medium skillet over medium heat; add onion and garlic. Cook and stir for 3 minutes or until onion is translucent. Scrape the mixture into the slow cooker, and add cabbage, tomatoes, stock, carrot, celery, thyme, oregano, and bay leaf.

Cook on Low for 6 to 8 hours or on High for 3 to 4 hours or until vegetables are tender. Then, if cooking on Low, raise the heat to High. Stir in zucchini, green beans, cannellini beans, and pasta. Cook for 1 to 1½ hours or until pasta is cooked. Season with salt and pepper, and serve with grated Parmesan cheese.

Zuppa al Quattro Formaggi (Italian Vegetable Soup with Four Cheeses)

Prep time: less than 20 minutes • Minimum cooking time: 4¼ hours • Makes 4 to 6 servings

3 TB. butter

1 onion, peeled and diced

3 garlic cloves, peeled and minced

2 carrots, peeled and thinly sliced

2 small zucchini (about ½ lb.), trimmed and thinly sliced

1 large potato, peeled and cut into ½-inch dice

1 quart vegetable or chicken stock

1 (14½-oz.) can diced tomatoes

½ cup grated Swiss cheese

½ cup grated Gruyère cheese

¼ cup grated Parmesan cheese

¼ cup finely chopped Bel Paese or Brie cheese

Salt and black pepper to taste

Thick slices of toast from French or Italian bread

Heat butter in a medium skillet over medium heat; add onion and garlic. Cook and stir for 3 minutes or until onion is translucent. Scrape the mixture into the slow cooker.

Add carrots, zucchini, potato, stock, and tomatoes to the slow cooker. Cook on Low for 8 to 10 hours or on High for 4 to 5 hours or until vegetables are tender. Then, if cooking on Low, raise the heat to High. Stir in Swiss, Gruyère, Parmesan, and Bel Paese cheeses. Cook for 15 to 20 minutes or until cheeses are melted and the soup is bubbly. Season with salt and pepper, and ladle the soup over toast slices.

Slow Savvy
While the soup is chunky like this, you can serve it as a main course dish. If you'd prefer a smooth, first-course soup, purée it in a food processor fitted with a steel blade or in a blender. It will make 6 to 8 servings.

Mediterranean Chicken and Vegetable Soup

Prep time: less than 15 minutes   •   Minimum cooking time: 4 hours   •   Makes 6 to 8 servings

3 TB. olive oil

1 large onion, peeled and diced

3 garlic cloves, peeled and diced

5 cups chicken stock

1 (14½-oz.) can diced tomatoes

1 TB. tomato paste

2 boneless, skinless chicken breast halves, cut into 1-inch dice

1 carrot, peeled and sliced

2 celery stalks, trimmed and sliced

1 TB. dried oregano

1 (10-oz.) box frozen lima beans, thawed

1 (10-oz.) box frozen Italian-style green beans, thawed

2 cups cooked small pasta, such as macaroni or small shells

Salt and black pepper to taste

Heat olive oil in a medium skillet over medium heat; add onion and garlic. Cook and stir for 3 minutes or until onion is translucent. Scrape the mixture into the slow cooker. Stir in stock, tomatoes, tomato paste, chicken, carrot, celery, and oregano. Stir well.

Cook on Low for 7 to 9 hours or on High for 4 to 5 hours. Add lima beans and green beans during the last hour of cooking. Stir in cooked pasta, and continue to cook until pasta is hot. Season with salt and pepper.

Cooker Caveats _____

Don't add green vegetables to slow cooked dishes until the last hour of cooking. These tender foods will take on a dull gray-green color and mushy texture if added sooner. Also, frozen vegetables, once thawed, have already been partially cooked, so a brief time in the slow cooker is all that is needed.

Mexican Tortilla Soup

Prep time: less than 30 minutes • Minimum cooking time: 3 hours • Makes 4 to 6 servings

Soup:

2 TB. olive oil

2 medium onions, peeled and sliced

4 garlic cloves, peeled and minced

1 TB. dried oregano

1 TB. dried basil

2 tsp. ground cumin

1 (14½-oz.) can diced tomatoes

5 cups chicken stock

2 TB. tomato paste

3 boneless, skinless chicken breast halves, or 6 boneless, skinless chicken thighs cut into ½-inch pieces

1 celery stalk, trimmed and sliced

1 small zucchini, trimmed and cut into ¾-inch dice

1 carrot, peeled and sliced

1 medium potato, peeled and cut into ½-inch dice

Salt and black pepper to taste

Garnish:

½ cup vegetable oil

4 corn tortillas, cut into ½-inch strips

1 ripe avocado, peeled and diced

Grated Monterey Jack cheese

Heat olive oil in a large skillet over medium heat; add onions and garlic. Cook and stir for 3 minutes or until onion is translucent. Add oregano, basil, and cumin to the pan. Cook for 1 minute, stirring constantly. Add tomatoes and stir well. Purée the mixture in a food processor fitted with a steel blade or a blender. Scrape the purée into the slow cooker, and add stock and tomato paste. Stir well.

Add diced chicken, celery, zucchini, carrot, and potato to the slow cooker. Cook on Low for 6 to 8 hours or on High for 3 to 4 hours or until chicken is cooked through and no longer pink and potatoes are tender. Season with salt and pepper.

About 30 minutes before the soup will be finished, heat vegetable oil in a medium skillet over high heat. Add tortilla strips, and fry until crisp. Remove strips from the pan with a slotted spoon, and drain on paper towels.

To serve, ladle the soup into bowls, and garnish each serving with fried tortilla strips, avocado, and cheese.

Cooker Caveats

Fried food that is crisp and not greasy is the result of properly heated oil cooking the right amount of food. Heat your oil over high heat until you see a thin haze or ripple, then fry only as much food as will fit in one layer. Filling a pan too full results in food that steams instead of fries.

Slow Savvy

Like potatoes and apples, avocados turn brown when exposed to air. It's best to peel and dice this delicate fruit just before eating it. If you're only using half, keep the pit in the unused half and coat the cut surface with lemon juice to keep it green.

Old-Fashioned Chicken Noodle Soup

Prep time: less than 15 minutes • Minimum cooking time: 3 hours • Makes 4 to 6 servings

3 TB. butter

2 medium onions, peeled and diced

2 garlic cloves, peeled and minced

5 cups chicken stock

2 boneless, skinless chicken breast halves or 4 boneless, skinless chicken thighs, cut into 1-inch pieces

1 carrot, peeled and sliced

1 parsnip, peeled and sliced (or 1 additional carrot)

1 celery stalk, trimmed and sliced

2 ripe tomatoes, cored, seeded, and diced

2 TB. chopped fresh parsley

1 TB. fresh thyme or 1 tsp. dried

1 bay leaf

Salt and black pepper to taste

1 cup frozen peas, thawed

2 cups cooked egg noodles

Slow Savvy

There's a reason why bay leaves should always be discarded. Although they add a pungent and woodsy flavor and aroma to dishes, they can be quite a bitter mouthful if you accidentally eat one. That's also why bay leaves are always added whole. If they were broken into pieces, it would be a real scavenger hunt to retrieve them.

Heat butter in a medium skillet over medium heat; add onions and garlic. Cook and stir for 3 minutes or until onion is translucent. Scrape the mixture into the slow cooker.

Add stock, chicken, carrot, parsnip, celery, tomatoes, parsley, thyme, and bay leaf to the slow cooker and stir well. Cook on Low for 6 to 8 hours or on High for 3 to 4 hours or until chicken is cooked through and no longer pink and vegetables are tender. Discard bay leaf, and season with salt and pepper.

Then, if cooking on Low, raise the heat to High. Add peas and egg noodles. Cook an additional 15 to 20 minutes or until the soup is bubbling.

Cream of Chicken and Wild Rice Soup

Prep time: less than 15 minutes • Minimum cooking time: 4¼ hours • Makes 6 to 8 servings

6 cups chicken stock

2 boneless, skinless chicken breast halves, cut into ½-inch cubes

1 large onion, peeled and diced

2 carrots, peeled and sliced

2 celery stalks, trimmed and sliced

½ cup *wild rice*, rinsed

1 TB. fresh thyme or ½ tsp. dried

1 (10¾-oz.) can condensed cream of celery or cream of chicken soup

½ cup heavy cream

Salt and black pepper to taste

Combine chicken stock, chicken cubes, onion, carrots, celery, wild rice, and thyme in the slow cooker. Cook on Low for 8 to 10 hours or on High for 4 to 5 hours or until wild rice is puffed and vegetables are tender.

Then, if cooking on Low, raise the heat to High. Stir in condensed soup and heavy cream. Cook for an additional 15 to 20 minutes or until the soup is simmering. Season with salt and pepper.

Ellen on Edibles

Wild rice is not a grain; it's actually a grass that is native only to North America. Called *Zizania aquatica* in Latin, the grass is harvested from lakes in the northern states and Canada in the fall. The best rice is still harvested by hand. Select grains that are long and unbroken—signs of a gentle harvest.

Mulligatawny (Indian Curried Chicken Soup)

Prep time: less than 30 minutes • Minimum cooking time: 3½ hours • Makes 6 to 8 servings

2 TB. vegetable oil

1 large onion, peeled and diced

3 garlic cloves, peeled and minced

2 TB. all-purpose flour

2 TB. curry powder or to taste

½ tsp. ground cumin

4 cups chicken stock

4 boneless, skinless chicken breast halves

1 carrot, peeled and diced

2 large boiling potatoes (about 1 lb.), peeled and diced

1 cup blanched almonds

1 cup canned unsweetened coconut milk

2 TB. lime juice

3 TB. chopped fresh cilantro

Salt and black pepper to taste

3 cups cooked basmati or white rice

Heat vegetable oil in a medium skillet over medium heat; stir in onions and garlic. Cook and stir for 3 minutes or until onion is translucent. Reduce the heat to low and stir in flour, curry powder, and cumin. Cook and stir over low heat for 2 minutes. Stir in 1 cup chicken stock, and bring to a boil over medium heat. Stir well and pour the mixture into the slow cooker. Stir in remaining 3 cups stock, along with chicken breast halves, carrot, potatoes, and almonds.

Crock Tales

The British popularized this curry-flavored soup when they brought it home with them from India during the Raj era of the nineteenth century. It was originally called *Milakutanni*, which means "pepper water." Recipes vary widely, with chicken and curry as the only two constants.

Cook on Low for 7 to 9 hours or on High for 3 to 4 hours or until chicken is cooked through and no longer pink and vegetables are soft. Remove chicken from the slow cooker with tongs and set aside. Strain the soup over a mixing bowl, and purée the solids in a food processor fitted with a steel blade or in a blender. Return the soup to the slow cooker, and stir in vegetable purée, coconut milk, lime juice, and cilantro. Dice chicken meat, and add it to the soup.

Then, if cooking on Low, raise the heat to High. Cook the soup for an additional 30 to 45 minutes or until it is simmering. Season with salt and pepper, and serve the soup over rice.

Chapter 8

Soups for Carnivore Cravings

In This Chapter

◆ Thick soups starring beef, lamb, and pork
◆ Main course soups made with ever-popular meatballs
◆ Hearty soups from many countries

Few things duplicate the feeling of warmth that eating a bowl of steaming soup can bring on a cold winter night. This group of meat-based soups are tailor-made for such occasions.

Although these soups are clearly on the hearty side, they are simultaneously healthful. The meat is always balanced by a large number of vegetables, so the actual amount of cholesterol and saturated fat in each serving of soup is relatively low.

Degrees of Degreasing

The meat in these soups is always meltingly tender; however, one problem with using the inexpensive cuts of meat suited for soups is that they frequently contain a high degree of hidden fat that cannot be trimmed off prior to cooking.

In an ideal world, you'd chill the cooked soup overnight, then discard the hard layer of fat that forms when the soup is chilled. But chances are, you make the soup the night you plan to serve it.

In that case, turn off the slow cooker and don't stir the soup. Let it sit for 5 to 10 minutes and much of the fat will float to the top. Use a soup ladle to skim it off, then discard it.

The Least You Need to Know

- ◆ Soups made with beef, lamb, and pork remain relatively healthful because the meats are balanced by many vegetables and carbohydrates.
- ◆ You can remove much of the saturated fat from meat soups either at the end of the cooking time or by chilling them.
- ◆ Soups can be served over a variety of carbohydrates to balance the meal.
- ◆ Soups made with meat take from 3 to 8 hours to cook.

Eastern European Sweet and Sour Cabbage Soup with Brisket

Prep time: less than 30 minutes • Minimum cooking time: 4 hours • Makes 4 to 6 servings

1½ lb. beef brisket

¼ cup vegetable oil

1 large onion, peeled and diced

3 garlic cloves, peeled and diced

1 small head green cabbage, about 1½ lb., cored and shredded

6 cups beef stock

1 (14½-oz.) can diced tomatoes

¼ cup cider vinegar

¼ cup firmly packed dark brown sugar

¼ cup golden raisins

¼ cup dried currants

1 tsp. dried thyme

1 bay leaf

Salt and black pepper to taste

2 to 3 cups cooked egg noodles

Preheat the oven broiler, and line a broiler pan with aluminum foil. Trim fat from brisket, and cut brisket into 1-inch cubes. Broil cubes for 3 minutes per side or until browned. Spoon meat into the slow cooker along with any juices that have collected in the pan.

Heat oil in a medium skillet over medium heat; add onion and garlic. Cook and stir for 3 minutes or until onion is translucent. Scrape the mixture into the slow cooker. Add cabbage, stock, tomatoes, vinegar, brown sugar, raisins, currants, thyme, and bay leaf. Stir well.

Cook on Low for 8 to 10 hours or on High for 4 to 5 hours or until meat is tender. Discard bay leaf, and season with salt and pepper. Ladle the soup over hot egg noodles.

Slow Savvy _____

If brisket is hard to find, you can always substitute well-trimmed chuck roast for this soup. And if you want to transform it into a vegetarian dish, omit the beef, use vegetable stock, and add some additional cabbage and perhaps a can of small white beans.

Beefy Tomato Soup with Barley

Prep time: less than 15 minutes • Minimum cooking time: 4 hours • Makes 6 to 8 servings

2 lb. beef stew meat, cut into 1-inch pieces	1 celery stalk, diced
1 envelope dehydrated onion soup mix	⅔ cup pearl barley, rinsed
6 cups water	1 tsp. dried thyme
1 (28-oz.) can crushed tomatoes in tomato purée	1 bay leaf
1 large onion, peeled and diced	1 (10-oz.) box frozen mixed vegetables, thawed
1 carrot, peeled and diced	Salt and black pepper to taste

Preheat the oven broiler, and line a broiler pan with aluminum foil. Broil beef cubes for 3 to 4 minutes per side or until browned. Spoon beef into the slow cooker, and pour in any juices from the pan.

Add onion soup mix, water, tomatoes, onion, carrot, celery, barley, thyme, and bay leaf to the slow cooker; stir well. Cook the soup on Low for 8 to 10 hours or on High for 4 to 5 hours or until beef is tender and barley is cooked. Add mixed vegetables for the last hour of cooking. Discard bay leaf, and season with salt and pepper.

Cooker Caveats

Always thaw vegetables or any ingredients before placing them in the slow cooker. Especially when cooking on Low, the addition of ice-cold items can drastically increase the cooking time. In a pinch, place the whole box of frozen vegetables into the microwave to defrost, or completely cook the vegetables separately and stir them into the slow cooker just before serving.

Moroccan Lamb and Chickpea Soup

Prep time: less than 20 minutes   •   Minimum cooking time: 4 hours   •   Makes 4 to 6 servings

1 cup dried chickpeas	1 carrot, peeled and sliced
1½ lb. lamb stew meat, cut into 1-inch cubes	3 cups beef or chicken stock
2 TB. olive oil	1 (14½-oz.) can diced tomatoes
2 large onions, peeled and diced	¼ cup chopped fresh cilantro
3 garlic cloves, peeled and minced	Salt and cayenne to taste
½ tsp. ground cumin	2 cups hot *couscous*
½ tsp. ground coriander	

Rinse chickpeas in a colander, and place them into a mixing bowl covered with cold water. Allow chickpeas to soak overnight. Or place chickpeas into a saucepan, and bring to a boil over high heat. Boil 1 minute. Turn off the heat, cover the pan, and soak chickpeas for 1 hour. Drain, discard the soaking water, and place chickpeas into the slow cooker.

Preheat the oven broiler, and line a broiler pan with aluminum foil. Broil lamb cubes for 3 minutes per side or until browned. Spoon lamb into the slow cooker, and add any juices that have collected in the pan.

Heat olive oil in a medium skillet over medium heat; add onion and garlic. Cook and stir for 3 minutes or until onion is translucent. Reduce the heat to low, and stir in cumin and coriander. Cook for 1 minute, stirring constantly. Scrape the mixture into the slow cooker.

Add carrot, stock, and tomatoes to the slow cooker. Cook on Low for 9 to 11 hours or on High for 4 to 5 hours or until chickpeas and lamb are tender. Transfer half the chickpeas to a food processor fitted with a steel blade or a blender. Purée until smooth, and stir the mixture back into the soup. Stir in cilantro, and season with salt and cayenne. Ladle the soup over hot couscous.

Ellen on Edibles

Contrary to popular belief, **couscous** is not a grain even though it is cooked like one. It's a fine pasta made from semolina. There are many instant couscous mixes that miraculously fluff up in tap water, but you'll have a much fluffier product if you buy regular couscous and steam it for 15 to 20 minutes. In a pinch, pour 1½ cups boiling water over each 1 cup couscous and cover the pan until the water is absorbed. Always end by fluffing the couscous with a fork.

Albondigas (Mexican Meatball Soup)

Prep time: less than 20 minutes • Minimum cooking time: 4 hours • Makes 6 to 8 servings

Meatballs:

1½ lb. lean ground beef

¼ cup yellow cornmeal

¼ cup milk

1 egg, lightly beaten

1 TB. chili powder

Salt and black pepper to taste

Soup:

2 TB. olive oil

1 large onion, peeled and diced

4 garlic cloves, peeled and minced

1 TB. chili powder

1 tsp. ground cumin

½ tsp. dried oregano

1 (28-oz.) can diced tomatoes

3 cups beef stock

½ cup refrigerated commercial tomato salsa

2 TB. chopped fresh cilantro

⅓ cup uncooked converted long-grain rice

Salt and black pepper to taste

Preheat the oven to 500°F. Line a broiler pan with aluminum foil, and grease the foil with vegetable oil spray or vegetable oil. Combine ground beef, cornmeal, milk, egg, chili powder, salt, and pepper in a mixing bowl, and mix well. Form the mixture into 1-inch balls, and place them on the greased foil. Brown meatballs in the preheated oven for 10 minutes or until lightly browned.

Crock Tales

Maize, the grain we know as corn from which cornmeal is ground, has been cultivated in North America for more than 2,000 years. Because it served as the staple of the Native American diet, most tribes honored deities who were responsible for ensuring successful corn crops.

While meatballs are browning, heat olive oil in a medium skillet over medium heat; add onion and garlic. Cook and stir for 3 minutes or until onion is translucent. Reduce the heat to low and stir in chili powder, cumin, and oregano. Cook for 1 minute; then scrape the mixture into the slow cooker. Stir in tomatoes, stock, salsa, and cilantro. Stir well. Transfer meatballs to the slow cooker with a slotted spoon.

Cook on Low for 8 to 10 hours or on High for 4 to 5 hours or until meatballs are cooked through. Add rice for the last hour of cooking. Season with salt and pepper.

Italian Wedding Soup

Prep time: less than 30 minutes   •   Minimum cooking time: 4 hours   •   Makes 4 to 6 servings

Meatballs:

2 eggs, lightly beaten

⅓ cup Italian-flavored breadcrumbs

¼ cup milk

¼ cup grated mozzarella cheese

2 garlic cloves, peeled and crushed

1½ lb. lean ground beef

Salt and black pepper to taste

Soup:

6 cups chicken or beef stock

1 fennel bulb, trimmed and thinly sliced

4 garlic cloves, peeled and minced

1 (10-oz.) box frozen whole-leaf spinach, thawed

¾ cup uncooked orzo or other small pasta

Salt and black pepper to taste

Preheat the oven to 500°F. Line a broiler pan with aluminum foil, and grease the foil with vegetable oil spray or vegetable oil. Place eggs, breadcrumbs, milk, cheese, and garlic into a mixing bowl and stir well. Add beef, mix well, and season with salt and pepper. Form the mixture into 1-inch balls, and place them on the greased foil. Brown meatballs in the preheated oven for 10 minutes or until lightly browned. Transfer meatballs to the slow cooker with a slotted spoon.

Add stock to the slow cooker along with fennel and garlic. Cook on Low for 7 to 9 hours or on High for 3½ to 4½ hours or until meatballs are cooked through and fennel is soft.

Then, if cooking on Low, raise the heat to High. Place spinach into a strainer, and press it with the back of a spoon to extract as much liquid as possible. Add spinach and orzo to the slow cooker. Cook on High for 20 to 30 minutes or until orzo is cooked *al dente*. Season with salt and pepper.

Ellen on Edibles

Al dente literally means "to the tooth" in Italian. In cooking, it means that pasta or rice is cooked to the point that it's still chewy. It's that magical point between hard and mushy.

Chinese Hot and Sour Soup with Pork

Prep time: less than 20 minutes   •   Minimum cooking time: 3½ hours   •   Makes 4 to 6 servings

1 oz. dried *black tree fungus mushrooms*	¼ cup rice wine vinegar
½ oz. dried *lily buds*	2 TB. soy sauce
6 large dried shiitake mushrooms	1 TB. sesame oil
1 lb. pork tenderloin	½ tsp. chili oil
5 cups chicken stock	3 TB. cornstarch
½ lb. firm tofu, well drained and cut into ½-inch dice	2 TB. cold water
	2 eggs, lightly beaten
1 (8-oz.) can sliced water chestnuts, drained and rinsed	2 cups hot cooked white rice
	2 scallions, trimmed and thinly sliced

Soak black tree fungus mushrooms, lily buds, and shiitake mushrooms in 1 cup hot tap water. Trim off the *silverskin* from pork tenderloin, and cut tenderloin into ¹/₂-inch slices. Cut the slices into thin shreds. Place pork into the slow cooker.

Remove mushrooms from the cup, and strain the liquid through a coffee filter into the slow cooker. Rinse mushrooms well to remove any grit. Discard the stems from the shiitake mushrooms, and slice shiitake and black tree fungus mushrooms into thin slices; leave lily buds whole. Add mushrooms and lily buds to the slow cooker along with stock, tofu, water chestnuts, vinegar, soy sauce, sesame oil, and chili oil. Cook on Low for 6 to 8 hours or on High for 3 to 4 hours or until pork is cooked through.

Then, if cooking on Low, raise the heat to High. Combine cornstarch and water in a small cup. Stir cornstarch mixture into soup. Cook on High for 10 to 20 minutes or until the liquid has thickened and is bubbly. Stir eggs into the soup, and continue to stir so eggs form thin strands. Cover the pan, and bring soup back to a simmer. Serve over rice, garnished with scallion slices.

Ellen on Edibles

Black tree fungus and **lily buds** are dried mushrooms traditionally used in hot and sour soup. They can be found in the Asian food aisle of some supermarkets or in Asian markets. If you can't find them, use dried shiitake mushrooms. **Silverskin** is the almost iridescent membrane that covers a pork or beef tenderloin. It is extremely tough and causes meat to curl as it cooks. With a boning knife, scrape away at the end of the silverskin while pulling with your fingers down the length of the meat. Repeat, turning the meat as necessary, until the membrane is pulled away.

Hungarian Pork Goulash and Noodle Soup

Prep time: less than 20 minutes   •   Minimum cooking time: 3¼ hours   •   Makes 4 to 6 servings

3 TB. olive oil

1 large onion, peeled and diced

3 garlic cloves

1½ lb. pork loin, cut into 1-inch dice

2 TB. Hungarian paprika

1 tsp. caraway seeds, crushed

2 TB. tomato paste

4 cups beef or chicken stock

½ cup dry white wine

1 carrot, peeled and sliced

2 celery stalks, sliced

3 cups cooked egg noodles

Salt and black pepper to taste

Sour cream

Heat olive oil in a large skillet over medium heat; add onion, garlic, and pork. Cook and stir for 3 minutes or until onion is translucent. Reduce the heat to low, and stir in paprika and caraway seeds. Cook for 1 minute, stirring constantly. Scrape the mixture into the slow cooker.

Stir tomato paste, stock, and wine into the slow cooker. Add carrot and celery. Cook on Low for 6 to 8 hours or on High for 3 to 4 hours or until pork is tender. Then, if cooking on Low, raise the heat to High. Add egg noodles, and season with salt and pepper. Cook for an additional 15 minutes to heat noodles. Ladle the soup into bowls, and garnish with sour cream.

Slow Savvy

It's best to crush large seeds like caraway and fennel before adding them to a dish. The seeds release more flavor crushed, and they can be bitter if eaten whole. The easiest way to crush the seeds is with a mortar and pestle. If you don't have a mortar and pestle, place the seeds into a small, heavy plastic bag and pound them with the back of a small skillet or saucepan. This does the trick.

Part 4

Stews to Savor

The first food almost everyone makes in a slow cooker is some sort of stew. Stews are meals in a bowl. Most of the time every component you need for a balanced meal is right in the pot, or it's just minutes to cook a dish that completes the meal.

Part 4 features poultry and meat stews from many cuisines, from the American Southwest to the southwest of France.

There are also a number of variations of ever-popular chili. Some are made with meat, but there is also a vegetarian version. There are also dishes close to chili that true "chili heads" will embrace.

Chapter 9

Best of the Barnyard

In This Chapter

- ◆ Old-fashioned American chicken stews
- ◆ Chicken and turkey stews from Mexico to Morocco and China
- ◆ Stews topped with dumplings

Lean skinless, boneless chicken and turkey breasts are becoming the mainstays of diets today. The inherently mild flavor of chicken and turkey makes them ideal candidates for a wide range of seasonings. There are endless ways to prepare them, and they cook in less time than beef, lamb, or pork.

You can substitute chicken for turkey or turkey for chicken in any of these recipes. They cook at the same rate.

Jump-Start Dinner

Are you stressed just getting out the door on time in the morning, let alone preparing tonight's meal before you leave for work? There's no reason you can't have everything ready to roll the night before—but be careful.

Cooker Caveats

Bacteria have a better chance of growing if food has been partially cooked and then re-refrigerated That's why it's okay to cook onions but not brown meat.

It's fine to cut all the vegetables and measure all the ingredients beforehand, but don't layer them in the slow cooker until just before you turn it on. It's fine to do steps like sautéing the onions and garlic, but don't brown the meat. And keep the meat or poultry separate from the vegetables for food safety until you put them into the slow cooker.

Serve-Alongs

The main part of dinner is set as soon as you turn on the slow cooker in the morning. But it's nice to have a few crunchy things as a textural contrast to the silky soft stew your slow cooker will cook.

Slow Savvy

You can easily make salad dressings at home in any jar with a tight-fitting lid. The general ratio is one part acid (any vinegar, lemon juice, or lime juice) to three parts oil. Always add your seasoning to the vinegar first and shake it well, because seasoning doesn't dissolve in oil. Add the oil last and shake it again.

A tossed green salad is a great start to any stew dinner. Pick a dressing that's in the same flavor family as the stew. For example, if you're serving a French or Italian stew, a vinaigrette dressing is always a good choice. If the stew is Mexican, add a bit of cumin to the dressing. And if it's Asian, use soy sauce instead of salt.

Along with a tossed salad, bread is always welcome. Once again, tie it to the theme of the meal. If it's a Mexican dish, serve heated flour or corn tortillas instead of bread.

The Least You Need to Know

- All most stews need for a complete meal is a tossed salad and perhaps some bread.
- Boneless, skinless chicken and turkey breast meat can be substituted for each other in any recipe.
- The preparatory dicing and cutting for stews can be done the night before, but to avoid any bacterial growth, the ingredients should not be placed in the slow cooker until it's time to cook.

Chicken Stew with Wild Mushrooms

Prep time: less than 15 minutes • Minimum cooking time: 3¼ hours • Makes 4 to 6 servings

2 TB. butter

2 TB. vegetable oil

1 onion, peeled and chopped

3 garlic cloves, peeled and minced

¾ lb. fresh shiitake or other wild mushrooms, stems discarded and halved if large

4 boneless, skinless chicken breast halves, cut into 1-inch cubes

2 carrots, peeled and sliced

1 celery stalk, trimmed and sliced

1 cup chicken stock

½ cup dry white wine

2 TB. chopped fresh parsley

1 TB. fresh thyme, or 1 tsp. dried

1 TB. cornstarch

½ cup heavy cream

Salt and black pepper to taste

Cooked white or brown rice

Heat butter and oil in a medium skillet over medium heat; add onion and garlic. Cook and stir for 2 minutes. Add mushrooms; cook and stir for 3 to 4 minutes or until mushrooms begin to soften. Scrape the mixture into the slow cooker. Add chicken, carrots, celery, stock, wine, parsley, and thyme to the slow cooker. Stir well.

Cook for 6 to 8 hours on Low or 3 to 4 hours on High or until chicken is cooked through and no longer pink and vegetables are tender. Then, if cooking on Low, raise the heat to High. Stir cornstarch into cream, and stir cornstarch-cream mixture into the slow cooker. Cook for an additional 15 to 30 minutes or until the juices are bubbly. Season with salt and pepper, and serve over rice.

Cooker Caveats
Dairy products like cream and cheese tend to curdle if cooked in a slow cooker for the entire cooking time. Add them at the end and let them cook for no more than 1 hour, unless otherwise directed in the recipe.

Mexican Chicken Stew

Prep time: less than 15 minutes • Minimum cooking time: 4 hours • Makes 4 servings

3 TB. vegetable oil

1 large onion, peeled and diced

3 garlic cloves, peeled and minced

½ green bell pepper, seeds and ribs removed, and finely chopped

1 TB. chili powder

1 tsp. ground cumin

4 boneless, skinless chicken breast halves, cut into 1-inch cubes

1 cup refrigerated commercial tomato salsa

1 (8-oz.) can tomato sauce

1 (15-oz.) can kidney beans, drained and rinsed

Salt and black pepper to taste

Cooked white or brown rice

Heat oil in a medium skillet over medium heat; add onion, garlic, and green bell pepper. Cook and stir for 3 minutes or until onion is translucent. Stir in chili powder and cumin. Cook 1 minute, stirring constantly.

Scrape the mixture into the slow cooker. Add chicken, salsa, tomato sauce, and kidney beans. Cook on Low for 4 to 6 hours or on High for 2 to 3 hours. Season with salt and pepper, and serve it over rice.

Slow Savvy

Here's an easy way to remove the seeds and ribs from bell peppers: Cut a slice off the bottom so the pepper stands up straight. You'll see that there are natural curves to the sections. Holding the pepper by its stem, cut down those curves, and you'll be left with a skeleton of ribs and seeds. Throw it out, and you're ready to chop the pepper.

Chicken and Dumplings

Prep time: less than 20 minutes • Minimum cooking time: 3½ hours • Makes 4 to 6 servings

Stew:

3 TB. butter

1 large onion, peeled and diced

2 garlic cloves, peeled and minced

3 TB. all-purpose flour

2 lb. boneless, skinless chicken breast halves, cut into 1-inch cubes

3 medium red-skinned potatoes, scrubbed and cut into ½-inch cubes

2 carrots, peeled and thinly sliced

1 celery stalk, thinly sliced

2 cups chicken stock

3 sprigs fresh thyme or 1 tsp. dried

2 TB. chopped fresh parsley

1 bay leaf

1 (10-oz.) box frozen baby peas, thawed

½ cup heavy cream

Salt and black pepper to taste

Dumplings:

1½ cups dry biscuit mix, such as Bisquick

1 tsp. *fines herbs* or Italian herbs

½ cup milk

Heat butter in a medium skillet over medium heat; add onion and garlic. Cook and stir for 3 minutes or until onion is translucent. Reduce the heat to low, and stir in flour. Cook for 1 minute, stirring constantly. Scrape the mixture into the slow cooker.

Add chicken, potatoes, carrots, celery, stock, thyme, parsley, and bay leaf to the slow cooker. Stir well. Cook on Low for 6 to 8 hours or on High for 3 to 4 hours or until chicken is cooked and no longer pink and potatoes are tender. Then, if cooking on Low, raise the heat to High. Stir peas and cream into chicken mixture, discard bay leaf, and season with salt and pepper.

To make the dumplings, combine biscuit mix and fines herbs in a small bowl. Add milk and stir until a dough forms. Shape the dough with your hands to make walnut-size dumplings, and place them on top of the stew. Cook on High for 20 to 25 minutes or until dumplings are cooked through and a toothpick inserted into the center of a dumpling comes out clean.

Ellen on Edibles

Fines herbs (pronounced *feen erb*) is a simple blend of equal parts of parsley, tarragon, chervil, and chives. Although it's already mixed in the spice section of supermarkets, it's easy to make it yourself, and it's lovely if you use fresh herbs.

Moroccan Chicken Stew with Dried Apricots

Prep time: less than 15 minutes • Minimum cooking time: 3¼ hours • Makes 4 to 6 servings

4 boneless, skinless chicken breast halves, or 6 boneless, skinless chicken thighs, cut into 1-inch cubes

4 garlic cloves, peeled and minced

¾ cup dry white wine

¾ cup chicken stock

⅓ cup white wine vinegar

2 TB. olive oil

¼ lb. dried apricots, finely chopped

½ cup sliced pimento-stuffed green olives

¼ cup firmly packed dark brown sugar

3 TB. dried oregano

2 tsp. ground cumin

Salt and black pepper to taste

2 TB. cornstarch

2 TB. cold water

2 cups hot couscous or rice

Slow Savvy

An easy way to chop dried apricots is in a food processor fitted with a steel blade, using the on-and-off pulsing action. The dried apricots will not stick to the blade if you chop them with the brown sugar. In recipes that call for flour, you can chop the apricots with that as well.

Arrange chicken in the slow cooker. Combine garlic, wine, stock, vinegar, oil, apricots, olives, brown sugar, oregano, and cumin in a bowl. Pour over chicken.

Cook on Low for 6 to 8 hours or on High for 3 to 4 hours or until chicken is cooked through and no longer pink. Then, if cooking on Low, raise the heat to High. Season with salt and pepper. Mix cornstarch and cold water in a small cup; then stir the mixture into chicken. Cook for an additional 15 to 20 minutes or until the sauce is bubbly and thickened. Serve the stew over couscous or rice.

Chinese Curried Chicken

Prep time: less than 20 minutes • Minimum cooking time: 3¼ hours • Makes 4 to 6 servings

3 boneless, skinless chicken breast halves, cut into 1-inch cubes

1 carrot, peeled and sliced

½ red bell pepper, seeds and ribs removed, and cut into 1-inch squares

1 cup sliced Napa or *bok choy* cabbage

1 TB. grated fresh ginger

3 scallions, trimmed and chopped

3 garlic cloves, peeled and minced

1 cup chicken stock

1 cup canned unsweetened coconut milk

2 TB. rice wine vinegar

2 TB. firmly packed dark brown sugar

1 TB. soy sauce

1½ tsp. curry powder or to taste

2 TB. cornstarch

2 TB. cold water

Cooked white rice

Condiments:

Chutney

Raisins

Thinly sliced scallions

Sweetened coconut

Slivered almonds, toasted in a 350°F oven for 5 minutes or until browned

Place chicken, carrot, red bell pepper, and cabbage into the slow cooker. Combine ginger, scallions, garlic, stock, coconut milk, vinegar, brown sugar, soy sauce, and curry powder in a mixing bowl and stir well. Pour the mixture over chicken and vegetables.

Cook on Low for 6 to 8 hours or on High for 3 to 4 hours or until chicken is cooked through and no longer pink. Then, if cooking on Low, raise the heat to High. Mix cornstarch with cold water, and stir cornstarch mixture into the slow cooker. Cook for an additional 15 to 20 minutes or until the sauce is bubbly and thickened. Serve over cooked rice, and pass condiments separately.

Ellen on Edibles

Bok choy is part of the family of Asian cabbages and is the one with the most delicate flavor. Select small heads with snowy white stalks, and use just the stalks when cooking. Save the leaves for a salad or toss them into a soup.

Brunswick Stew

Prep time: less than 20 minutes   •   Minimum cooking time: 4 hours   •   Makes 6 to 8 servings

1 lb. boneless, skinless chicken breast halves, cut into 1-inch cubes

1 lb. smoked pork butt or smoked ham, cut into 1-inch cubes

8 bacon slices, cooked and crumbled

3 medium red-skinned potatoes, scrubbed and cut into 1-inch cubes

2 celery stalks, sliced

2 garlic cloves, peeled and minced

1 large onion, peeled and diced

½ green bell pepper, seeds and ribs removed, and finely chopped

1 (14½-oz.) can diced tomatoes

2 cups chicken stock

2 TB. tomato paste

2 TB. Worcestershire sauce

2 bay leaves

1 tsp. dried oregano

1 (10-oz.) box frozen succotash, thawed

Salt to taste

Red pepper sauce to taste

2 cups hot cooked white or brown rice or squares of cornbread

Crock Tales

Brunswick Stew hails from Brunswick County, but from which state? Both North Carolina and Virginia contain a Brunswick County, and both of them claim the stew. What we do know is that it dates from Colonial times and used to be made with squirrel.

Combine chicken, smoked pork, bacon, potatoes, celery, garlic, onion, and green bell pepper in the slow cooker. Stir in tomatoes, stock, tomato paste, Worcestershire sauce, bay leaves, and oregano. Cook on Low for 8 to 10 hours or on High for 4 to 5 hours or until chicken is cooked through and no longer pink and potatoes are tender. Add succotash for the last hour of cooking. Discard bay leaf, and season with salt and red pepper sauce. Serve with rice or cornbread.

Turkey Molé

Prep time: less than 20 minutes   •   Minimum cooking time: 3¼ hours   •   Makes 4 to 6 servings

3 TB. vegetable oil

2 large onions, peeled and diced

3 garlic cloves, peeled and minced

3 TB. chili powder

2 TB. unsweetened cocoa powder

2 TB. peanut butter

1 tsp. *Chinese five-spice powder*

½ tsp. ground coriander

1½ lb. turkey breast, cut into 1-inch cubes

1 (14½-oz.) can diced tomatoes

1¼ cups chicken stock

1 TB. cornstarch

2 TB. cold water

Salt and cayenne to taste

2 cups cooked white or brown rice

Heat oil in a medium skillet over medium heat; add onion and garlic. Cook and stir for 3 minutes or until onion is translucent. Reduce the heat to low, and stir in chili powder, cocoa powder, peanut butter, Chinese five-spice powder, and coriander. Stir for 1 minute; then scrape the mixture into the slow cooker. Stir in turkey, tomatoes, and stock.

Cook on Low for 6 to 8 hours or on High for 3 to 4 hours or until turkey is cooked through and tender. Then, if cooking on Low, raise the heat to High. Mix cornstarch and water in a small cup, and stir it into the slow cooker. Cook for 15 to 20 minutes or until the juices are bubbly and thickened. Season with salt and cayenne, and serve it over rice.

Ellen on Edibles

Chinese five-spice powder is a spice mixture I use in place of cinnamon in dishes from many cultures. Cinnamon is one of the ingredients, along with anise, ginger, fennel, and pepper. It has a complex flavor and aroma that I love in this dish, with apologies to Mexicans and Mexican food lovers who might take issue with its authenticity.

Turkey Stew with Cornmeal Dumplings

Prep time: less than 20 minutes • Minimum cooking time: 5 hours • Makes 4 to 6 servings

Stew:

2 TB. vegetable oil

1 onion, peeled and diced

2 garlic cloves, peeled and minced

2 lb. turkey breast or boneless turkey thigh, cut into 1-inch cubes

1 carrot, peeled and sliced

2 Granny Smith apples, peeled, cored, and thinly sliced

¼ cup chopped dried apricots

¼ cup raisins

1½ cups chicken stock

½ cup apple cider

2 TB. chopped fresh parsley

1 TB. chopped fresh sage or 1 tsp. dried

2 tsp. fresh thyme or ½ tsp. dried

½ tsp. ground cinnamon

1 (10-oz.) box frozen mixed vegetables, thawed

Salt and black pepper to taste

Dumplings:

½ cup all-purpose flour

½ cup yellow cornmeal

1 tsp. baking powder

½ tsp. salt

1 egg, lightly beaten

¼ cup milk

3 TB. melted butter

Heat oil in a medium skillet over medium heat; add onion and garlic. Cook and stir for 3 minutes or until onion is translucent. Scrape the mixture into the slow cooker. Add turkey, carrot, apples, apricots, raisins, stock, cider, parsley, sage, thyme, and cinnamon to the slow cooker. Stir well.

Slow Savvy _____

When you're making a pretty apple tart, how the apples look matters. But in a stew like this one, who cares? They fall apart anyway. Here's an easy way to slice them: Peel the apples, then, turning the apple, slice off the sides. Soon all you'll be left with is the core to throw away.

Cook the stew on Low for 7 to 9 hours or on High for 4 to 5 hours or until turkey and vegetables are tender. Then, if cooking on Low, raise the heat to High. Stir in mixed vegetables, and cook for 30 minutes. Season with salt and pepper.

To make the dumplings, combine flour, cornmeal, baking powder, and salt in a mixing bowl. Stir in egg, milk, and melted butter and mix well. Drop the batter by 1 tablespoon measures onto the stew. Cover the slow cooker, and cook on High for 35 to 45 minutes or until a toothpick inserted into the center of a dumpling comes out clean.

10

The Meat of the Matter

In This Chapter

- ◆ Beef stews from plain to fancy
- ◆ Pork and ham as stars of hearty stews
- ◆ European lamb stews
- ◆ Mediterranean veal stews

The term *stew* is almost synonymous with hearty meats. The stew pot has always been the repository of meat odds and ends that were left over from sectioning larger cuts. It's only in the past few decades that stew meat has found its way into the meat case in its own name.

In this chapter, you'll find a wide variety of ways to season and sauce stews. Many of these are historic dishes that have been enjoyed for centuries.

The key to the success of these stews is patience. You can't rush the cooking time. Although pork and veal become tender before beef or lamb, all these dishes need many hours to reach their goal of tenderness.

Party Pleasers

A great advantage of serving stews at buffet parties is that your guests don't have to grow extra arms to eat their meals. The pieces of meat in stews are bite-size, so a fork is all that's needed. I suggest serving stews in shallow bowls because gravy dripping down their legs is not a memory you want your guests to take away from the evening.

A Cache from the Cow

The beef stews in this chapter are both cosmopolitan and cozy. Some are perfect for parties, and others are favorites families in countries around the world have loved for generations.

One key to the success of beef stews is browning the meat. The browning adds a distinctive flavor to the finished dishes and makes the beef more visually appealing.

Porking Out

One little piggy might have gone to market, but lots of little and big piggies end up in my slow cooker as stews each year, especially now that "the other white meat" has shed its bad rap as being fatty.

One time-saver of pork stews is that it's not really necessary to brown the meat. Browning really doesn't add the same depth of flavor to pork as it does to beef or lamb, and the pork will absorb the color of the sauce so it's visually pleasing.

Versatile Veal

Veal, a young calf, is one of the most tender and delicate of all meats. More veal is eaten per capita in Italy than any other country, which is why you see so many dishes with *vitello* on Italian menus. But veal is "segmenting," to use marketing jargon; you either love it or hate it. The recipes in this chapter can all be done with chicken or pork, too.

Luscious Lamb

It's only been in the past few decades that great lamb has been widely available in our supermarkets, and I think the best comes from Australia and New Zealand. There's a richness to lamb that infuses every bite of lamb stews. But for some people, lamb is an acquired taste they have yet to acquire. If you're one of them, don't fret. Beef can be substituted for lamb in any of the recipes in this chapter.

Boeuf Bourguignon (Beef in Red Wine)

Prep time: less than 30 minutes • Minimum cooking time: 4 hours • Makes 6 to 8 servings

2 lb. stewing beef, fat trimmed and cut into 1-inch cubes

2 TB. olive oil

1 large onion, peeled and diced

3 garlic cloves, peeled and minced

½ lb. white mushrooms, rinsed, stemmed, and sliced

2 cups dry red wine

½ cup beef stock

1 TB. tomato paste

1 TB. chopped fresh parsley

1 tsp. *herbes de Provence*, or 1 tsp. dried thyme

1 bay leaf

2 TB. cornstarch

2 TB. cold water

Salt and black pepper to taste

1½ lb. steamed new potatoes or 2 cups cooked buttered egg noodles

Preheat the oven broiler, and line a broiler pan with aluminum foil. Broil beef for 3 minutes per side or until browned. Transfer beef to the slow cooker, and pour in any juices that have collected in the pan.

Heat olive oil in a medium skillet over medium heat. Add onion, garlic, and mushrooms; cook and stir for 4 to 5 minutes or until onion is translucent and mushrooms are soft. Scrape the mixture into the slow cooker.

Stir in wine, stock, tomato paste, parsley, herbes de Provence, and bay leaf. Cook on Low for 8 to 10 hours or on High for 4 to 5 hours or until beef is tender. Then, if cooking on Low, raise the heat to High. Mix cornstarch and cold water in a small cup; then stir cornstarch mixture into beef. Cook for an additional 15 to 20 minutes or until bubbly and the sauce has thickened. Discard bay leaf, and season with salt and pepper. Serve the stew with steamed new potatoes or buttered egg noodles.

Ellen on Edibles
Herbes de Provence is one of my favorite blended seasonings, and it's now found in many supermarkets and specialty food stores. If you can't find it, blend equal parts of dried thyme, tarragon, chervil, rosemary, basil, and lavender.

Beef Stroganoff

Prep time: less than 15 minutes • Minimum cooking time: 4¼ hours • Makes 4 to 6 servings

2 lb. stewing beef, fat trimmed and cut into 1-inch cubes

3 TB. butter

3 TB. vegetable oil

2 large onions, peeled and diced

3 garlic cloves, peeled and minced

¾ lb. white mushrooms, rinsed, trimmed, and sliced

2 TB. paprika

1 (8-oz.) can tomato sauce

¾ cup beef stock

1 TB. prepared mustard

1 (1.2-oz.) pkg. dehydrated mushroom gravy mix

¾ cup sour cream

Salt and black pepper to taste

2 cups cooked buttered egg noodles

Preheat the oven broiler, and line a broiler pan with aluminum foil. Arrange beef on the foil, and broil for 3 to 4 minutes per side or until beef is lightly browned. Transfer beef to the slow cooker, and pour in any juices that have collected in the pan.

Crock Tales

Beef Stroganoff was named for a nineteenth-century Russian diplomat, Count Paul Stroganoff. It was one of the dishes that became a hallmark of what Americans called "continental cuisine" many years ago.

Heat butter and oil in a large skillet over medium heat; add onions, garlic, and mushrooms. Cook and stir for 4 to 5 minutes or until onion is translucent and mushrooms are soft. Reduce the heat to low, and stir in paprika. Cook for 1 minute, and scrape the mixture into the slow cooker. Stir in tomato sauce, stock, mustard, and gravy mix. Cook on Low for 8 to 10 hours or on High for 4 to 5 hours or until beef is tender. Then, if cooking on High, reduce the heat to Low. Stir in sour cream, and season with salt and pepper. Cook for 15 to 20 minutes or until the mixture is hot. Do not let it boil. Serve over buttered egg noodles.

Carbonnades à la Flamande (Belgian Beef Stew Cooked in Beer)

Prep time: less than 20 minutes • Minimum cooking time: 4 hours • Makes 6 to 8 servings

2 lb. stewing beef, fat trimmed and cut into 1-inch cubes

2 TB. vegetable oil

4 large onions, peeled and thinly sliced

2 garlic cloves, peeled and minced

1 (12-oz.) can beer

1 cup beef stock

2 TB. firmly packed dark brown sugar

2 TB. chopped fresh parsley

1 TB. fresh thyme or 1 tsp. dried

1 bay leaf

2 TB. cornstarch

2 TB. cold water

Salt and black pepper to taste

2 cups cooked buttered egg noodles

Preheat the oven broiler, and line a broiler pan with aluminum foil. Place beef in a single layer in the pan, and broil for 3 minutes per side or until beef is lightly browned. Place beef into the slow cooker along with any juices that have collected in the pan.

Heat oil in a medium skillet over medium heat; add onion and garlic. Cook and stir for 3 minutes or until onion is translucent. Scrape the mixture into the slow cooker. Add beer, stock, brown sugar, parsley, thyme, and bay leaf. Stir well.

Cook the stew on Low for 8 to 10 hours or on High for 4 to 5 hours or until beef is very tender. Then, if cooking the stew on Low, raise the heat to High. Mix cornstarch with cold water in a small cup. Add cornstarch mixture to the slow cooker, cover, and cook for an additional 10 to 15 minutes or until the juices are bubbling and slightly thickened. Discard bay leaf, and season with salt and pepper. Serve the stew with buttered egg noodles.

Slow Savvy

The general ratio of fresh herbs vs. dried herbs is about three to one. So if a recipe doesn't give you an equivalent and calls for 1 tablespoon fresh herb, you'll be fine using 1 teaspoon dried herb.

Old-Fashioned Beef Stew

Prep time: less than 20 minutes • Minimum cooking time: 4 hours • Makes 6 servings

2 lb. stewing beef, fat trimmed and cut into 1-inch cubes

2 TB. vegetable oil

1 onion, peeled and chopped

2 garlic cloves, peeled and minced

½ lb. white mushrooms, rinsed, trimmed, and halved, if large

3 carrots, peeled, and cut into ½-inch slices

2 celery stalks, trimmed and sliced

4 large red-skinned potatoes, scrubbed and cut into 1-inch dice

1 large turnip, peeled and cut into 1-inch dice

1 (10-oz.) box frozen pearl onions, thawed

3 cups beef stock

2 TB. Worcestershire sauce

2 TB. tomato paste

1 TB. fresh thyme or 1 tsp. dried

1 bay leaf

1 cup frozen peas, thawed

2 TB. butter, softened

3 TB. all-purpose flour

Salt and black pepper to taste

Preheat the oven broiler, and line a broiler pan with aluminum foil. Place beef into the pan in a single layer, and broil for 3 minutes per side or until beef is lightly browned. Place beef into the slow cooker along with any juices that have collected in the pan.

Heat oil in a medium skillet over medium heat; add onion, garlic, and mushrooms. Cook and stir for 3 to 5 minutes or until onion is translucent and mushrooms are soft. Scrape the mixture into the slow cooker, and add carrots, celery, potatoes, turnip, pearl onions, stock, Worcestershire sauce, tomato paste, thyme, and bay leaf.

> **Slow Savvy**
> When you're thickening a sauce or stew with a mixture of butter and flour, you'll sound very sophisticated if you refer to it by the French term, *beurre manié.* Mixing the butter and flour together coats the proteins in the flour so they don't give the gravy a pasty taste.

Cook the stew on Low for 8 to 10 hours or on High for 4 to 5 hours or until beef is very tender. Add peas for the last hour of cooking. Then, if cooking on Low, raise the heat to High. Mix softened butter with flour in a small cup to make a thick paste. Stir butter-flour mixture in small bits into the slow cooker, cover, and cook for an additional 10 to 15 minutes or until the juices are bubbling and slightly thickened. Discard bay leaf, and season with salt and pepper.

Chinese Beef Stew

Prep time: less than 30 minutes   •   Minimum cooking time: 4½ hours   •   Makes 4 to 6 servings

2 lb. stewing beef, fat trimmed and cut into 1-inch cubes

2 TB. sesame oil

3 scallions, trimmed and thinly sliced

2 TB. grated fresh ginger

4 garlic cloves, peeled and minced

1 small red onion, peeled and thinly sliced

½ lb. white mushrooms, rinsed, trimmed, and sliced

10 baby carrots, peeled and halved lengthwise

1½ cups beef stock

3 TB. soy sauce

2 TB. Chinese *oyster sauce*

1 TB. firmly packed dark brown sugar

1 TB. Chinese chili oil or ¼ tsp. red pepper flakes

½ lb. asparagus, trimmed and cut into ½-inch slices

2 TB. cornstarch

2 TB. cold water

Salt and black pepper to taste

2 cups cooked white rice or Chinese noodles

Preheat the oven broiler, and line a broiler pan with aluminum foil. Place beef into the pan in a single layer, and broil for 3 minutes per side or until beef is lightly browned. Place beef into the slow cooker along with any juices that have collected in the pan.

Heat sesame oil in a medium skillet over medium heat; add scallions, ginger, garlic, red onion, and mushrooms. Cook and stir for 3 to 5 minutes or until mushrooms begin to soften. Scrape the mixture into the slow cooker, and stir in carrots, stock, soy sauce, oyster sauce, brown sugar, and Chinese chili oil.

Cook stew on Low for 8 to 10 hours or on High for 4 to 5 hours or until beef is very tender. Add asparagus for the last hour of cooking. Then, if cooking stew on Low, raise the heat to High. Mix cornstarch with cold water in a small cup. Add cornstarch mixture to the slow cooker, cover, and cook for an additional 10 to 15 minutes or until the juices are bubbling and slightly thickened. Season with salt and pepper, and serve stew over rice or Chinese noodles.

Ellen on Edibles

Oyster sauce is another seasoning staple of the Chinese pantry. It's made from oysters, brine, and soy sauce, and it's cooked until it's deep brown, thick, and concentrated. It gives dishes a rich flavor, and it's not as salty as soy sauce.

New Mexican Pork Pozole

Prep time: less than 20 minutes   •   Minimum cooking time: 3¼ hours   •   Makes 4 to 6 servings

2 TB. olive oil

2 onions, peeled and finely chopped

1 carrot, peeled and finely chopped

4 garlic cloves, peeled and finely chopped

1 jalapeño or serrano chili, seeds and ribs removed, and finely chopped

2 TB. chili powder

1 TB. ground cumin

1 TB. dried oregano

2 lb. pork shoulder or loin, cut into 1-inch cubes

2½ cups chicken or beef stock

2 (15-oz.) cans hominy, drained and rinsed

Salt and black pepper to taste

Garnishes:

Grated radishes

Chopped cilantro

Sliced black or green olives

Grated Monterey Jack cheese

Crock Tales

Pozole is a traditional dish made on both sides of the Mexican border, and its key ingredient is hominy. Hominy is dried corn from which the hull and germ have been removed. The dish originated in Jalisco, on Mexico's Pacific Coast. It's traditionally served for Christmas, but it's enjoyed all year.

Heat oil in a medium skillet over medium heat; add onion, carrot, garlic, and japaleño pepper. Cook and stir for 3 minutes or until onion is translucent. Reduce the heat to low, and stir in chili powder, cumin, and oregano. Cook for 1 minute. Scrape the mixture into the slow cooker.

Add pork cubes. Stir in stock, and cook on Low for 6 to 8 hours or on High for 3 to 4 hours or until pork is tender. Stir in hominy, and season the stew with salt and pepper. Cook for 15 to 20 minutes or until hominy is hot. Serve the stew in shallow bowls, and pass small dishes with radishes, cilantro, olives, and cheese separately.

Pork Stew with Dried Fruit

Prep time: less than 15 minutes   •   Minimum cooking time: 3¼ hours   •   Makes 4 to 6 servings

2 lb. pork shoulder, cut into 1-inch cubes

1 bunch scallions, trimmed and cut into 1-inch pieces

2 carrots, peeled and sliced

2 parsnips, peeled and sliced

½ cup chopped dried apricots

½ cup raisins

2 cups chicken stock

2 TB. *Dijon mustard*

1 TB. cornstarch

2 TB. cold water

Salt and black pepper to taste

2 cups cooked buttered egg noodles or rice

Arrange pork, scallions, carrots, parsnips, apricots, and raisins in the slow cooker. Stir together stock and mustard, and add the mixture to the slow cooker. Cook on Low for 6 to 8 hours or on High for 3 to 4 hours or until meat is tender.

Then, if cooking on Low, raise the heat to High. Mix cornstarch with water in a small cup. Stir in cornstarch mixture, and cook for 15 to 20 minutes or until the sauce is bubbly and thickened. Season with salt and black pepper. Serve stew over buttered egg noodles or rice.

Ellen on Edibles

Dijon mustard originated in Dijon, France, and is known for its clean, sharp flavor. Although it's made just about everywhere today, the only "must" is making it with unfermented grape juice. Other than that, the mustard seeds can be brown or black, and it can have a taste from mild to hair-curling hot.

Cajun Stewed Red Beans and Ham

Prep time: less than 15 minutes • Minimum cooking time: 4 hours • Makes 6 to 8 servings

1 lb. dried red kidney beans, rinsed

2 lb. boneless ham steak, cut into 1-inch pieces

2 medium onions, finely chopped

2 celery stalks, finely chopped

1 green bell pepper, seeds and ribs removed, and finely chopped

2 bay leaves

2 tsp. dried thyme

4 cups water

Salt and cayenne to taste

2 to 3 cups cooked white rice

Crock Tales

Jazz great Louis Armstrong, whose name is synonymous with New Orleans jazz, used to sign his letters "Red beans and ricely yours."

Rinse beans in a colander and place them into a mixing bowl covered with cold water. Allow beans to soak overnight. Or place beans into a saucepan, and bring to a boil over high heat. Boil 1 minute. Turn off the heat, cover the pan, and soak beans for 1 hour. Drain beans, discard the soaking water, and place them into the slow cooker. Add ham, onions, celery, green bell pepper, bay leaves, thyme, and water.

Cook on Low for 8 to 10 hours or on High for 4 to 5 hours or until beans are very tender. Season with salt and cayenne, and discard bay leaves. Serve over rice.

Greek Lamb Stew

Prep time: less than 20 minutes • Minimum cooking time: 4 hours • Makes 4 to 6 servings

2 lb. lamb stew meat, fat trimmed, and cut into 1-inch cubes

2 TB. olive oil

2 onions, peeled and diced

3 garlic cloves, peeled and minced

1 TB. dried oregano

½ tsp. ground cinnamon

½ tsp. ground coriander

1 (14½-oz.) can diced tomatoes

1 cup beef stock

½ cup dry red wine

¼ cup orange juice

2 TB. lemon juice

3 TB. firmly packed dark brown sugar

1 TB. grated orange zest

1 lb. frozen pearl onions, thawed

¼ cup dried currants

2 TB. cornstarch

1 TB. cold water

2 cups boiled *orzo* or brown rice

Preheat the oven broiler, and line a broiler pan with aluminum foil. Place lamb cubes into the pan in a single layer, and broil for 3 minutes per side or until lamb is lightly browned. Place lamb into the slow cooker along with any juices that have collected in the pan.

Heat oil in a medium skillet over medium heat; add onions and garlic. Cook and stir for 3 minutes or until onion is translucent. Reduce the heat to low and stir in oregano, cinnamon, and coriander. Stir for 1 minute; then scrape the mixture into the slow cooker. Add tomatoes, stock, wine, orange juice, lemon juice, brown sugar, orange zest, pearl onions, and currants.

Cook the stew on Low for 8 to 10 hours or on High for 4 to 5 hours or until lamb is very tender. Then, if cooking the stew on Low, raise the heat to High. Mix cornstarch with cold water in a small cup. Add cornstarch mixture to the slow cooker, cover, and cook for an additional 10 to 15 minutes or until the juices are bubbling and slightly thickened. Serve stew over orzo or brown rice.

Ellen on Edibles

Orzo is a rice-shape pasta that's used a lot in Greek cooking, and it's now gaining fans on this side of the Atlantic. The best orzo is imported and has very long grains. Unlike most pastas, it absorbs the flavors of sauces beautifully.

Navarin d'Agneau (Classic French Lamb Stew)

Prep time: less than 30 minutes • Minimum cooking time: 4 hours • Makes 6 to 8 servings

2 lb. lamb stew meat, fat trimmed, and cut into 1-inch cubes

2 TB. olive oil

2 onions, peeled and diced

4 garlic cloves, peeled and minced

½ lb. mushrooms, rinsed, stemmed, and halved, if large

3 large carrots, peeled and cut into ½-inch pieces

2 cups beef stock

1 cup dry white wine

3 TB. tomato paste

2 TB. fresh thyme or 2 tsp. dried

2 TB. chopped fresh rosemary or 2 tsp. dried

2 bay leaves

3 TB. chopped fresh parsley

1 (10-oz.) box frozen pearl onions, thawed

1 (10-oz.) box frozen peas, thawed

2 TB. cornstarch

2 TB. cold water

Salt and black pepper to taste

1½ lb. boiled baby potatoes

Preheat the oven broiler, and line a broiler pan with aluminum foil. Place lamb cubes into the pan in a single layer, and broil for 3 minutes per side or until lamb is lightly browned. Place lamb into the slow cooker along with any juices in the pan.

Heat oil in a medium skillet over medium heat; add onion, garlic, and mushrooms. Cook and stir for 3 minutes or until onion is translucent and mushrooms are soft. Scrape the mixture into the slow cooker, and add carrots, stock, wine, tomato paste, thyme, rosemary, bay leaves, parsley, and pearl onions.

Slow Savvy

I've been faithful to the classic French recipe for this stew, but if you want to put the potatoes right into the slow cooker and not cook them separately, go ahead. It will save you cleaning another pot at the end of the night.

Cook stew on Low for 8 to 10 hours or on High for 4 to 5 hours or until lamb is very tender. Add peas for the last hour of cooking. Then, if cooking the stew on Low, raise the heat to High. Mix cornstarch with cold water in a small cup. Add cornstarch mixture to the slow cooker, cover, and cook for an additional 10 to 15 minutes or until the juices are bubbling and slightly thickened. Discard bay leaves, season with salt and pepper, and serve with boiled baby potatoes.

Irish Stew

Prep time: less than 15 minutes   •   Minimum cooking time: 4½ hours   •   Makes 4 to 6 servings

2 lb. lamb stew meat, fat trimmed and cut into 1-inch cubes

2 TB. vegetable oil

1 large onion, peeled and diced

2 garlic cloves, peeled and minced

2 carrots, peeled and diced

1 celery stalk, trimmed and sliced

1 lb. red-skinned potatoes, scrubbed and cut into 1-inch cubes

2 cups beef stock

2 TB. chopped fresh parsley

1 TB. fresh thyme or ½ tsp. dried

1 bay leaf

1 (10-oz.) box frozen mixed vegetables, thawed

Salt and black pepper to taste

Preheat the oven broiler, and line a broiler pan with aluminum foil. Place lamb into the pan in a single layer, and broil for 3 to 4 minutes per side or until lightly browned. Transfer lamb to the slow cooker along with any juices that have collected in the pan.

Heat oil in a small skillet over medium heat; add onion and garlic. Cook and stir for 3 minutes or until onion is translucent. Scrape the mixture into the slow cooker, and add carrots, celery, potatoes, stock, parsley, thyme, and bay leaf.

Cook on Low for 8 to 10 hours or on High for 4 to 5 hours or until potatoes and lamb are tender. Then, if cooking on Low, raise the heat to High. Add mixed vegetables, and cook for an additional 30 to 45 minutes or until vegetables are tender. Discard bay leaf. Remove 1 cup vegetables and purée in a food processor fitted with a steel blade or in a blender. Return the purée to the stew, and season with salt and pepper.

Cooker Caveats

As long as they're scrubbed well, there is no need to peel thin-skinned red potatoes before using. However, if you substitute other potatoes, be sure to peel them first. The skin on russet potatoes will peel off the cubes as they cook, and floating potato skins are not very attractive in the pot.

Veal Marengo

Prep time: less than 20 minutes • Minimum cooking time: 3 hours • Makes 4 to 6 servings

2 lb. veal stew meat, fat trimmed, and cut into 1-inch cubes

All-purpose flour for dredging

¼ cup olive oil

1 large onion, peeled and diced

3 garlic cloves, peeled and minced

1 orange, washed

1 (14½-oz.) can diced tomatoes

½ cup dry white wine

½ cup chicken or beef stock

½ lb. white mushrooms, rinsed, stemmed, and sliced

1 tsp. dried thyme

1 bay leaf

Salt and black pepper to taste

2 cups cooked buttered egg noodles or rice

Crock Tales

This dish was invented to celebrate a victory. When Napoleon's troops won the Battle of Marengo on June 14, 1800, his cook, Dunand, produced this in the camp kitchen. It was originally made with chicken but soon became a veal classic.

Coat veal with flour, shaking off any excess. Heat oil in a large skillet over medium heat. Add veal cubes, and brown them on all sides. Remove veal from the pan, and place it into the slow cooker. Add onion and garlic to the skillet. Cook and stir for 3 minutes or until onion is translucent. Scrape the mixture into the slow cooker.

Grate zest from orange; then squeeze the juice out of orange. Add zest and orange juice to the slow cooker along with tomatoes, wine, stock, mushrooms, thyme, and bay leaf. Cook on Low for 6 to 8 hours or on High for 3 to 4 hours or until meat is tender. Discard bay leaf, and season with salt and pepper. Serve on top of buttered egg noodles or rice.

Veal Marsala

Prep time: less than 15 minutes • Minimum cooking time: 3 hours • Makes 4 to 6 servings

2 lb. veal stew meat, fat trimmed, and cut into 1-inch cubes

All-purpose flour for dredging

¼ cup olive oil

6 garlic cloves, peeled and minced

⅓ cup chopped fresh parsley

¾ cup dry Marsala wine

¼ cup chicken stock

Salt and black pepper to taste

2 cups cooked orzo, pasta, or rice

Coat veal with flour, shaking off any excess. Heat oil in a large skillet over medium heat. Add veal cubes, and brown them on all sides. Remove veal from the pan, and place it into the slow cooker. Add garlic to the skillet. Cook and stir for 2 minutes; then scrape garlic into the slow cooker.

Add parsley, wine, and stock to the slow cooker. Cook on Low for 6 to 8 hours or on High for 3 to 4 hours or until veal is tender. Season with salt and pepper to taste. Serve the stew over orzo, pasta, or rice.

Cooker Caveats

When you're browning meat coated with flour, browning the flour is even more important than browning the meat. This step creates a sauce that thickens slightly but does not taste pasty. If you don't want to brown the veal, thicken the juices with cornstarch instead.

Blanquette de Veau
(French Veal Stew with Mushrooms and Onions)

Prep time: less than 20 minutes • Minimum cooking time: 3 hours • Makes 4 to 6 servings

3 TB. butter

1 large onion, peeled and diced

2 garlic cloves, peeled and minced

½ lb. white mushrooms, rinsed, stemmed, and sliced

3 TB. all-purpose flour

2 cups beef stock

2 lb. veal stew meat, fat trimmed and cut into 1-inch cubes

1 large carrot, peeled and sliced

1 (16-oz.) bag frozen pearl onions, thawed

3 TB. chopped fresh parsley

1 TB. fresh thyme or 1 tsp. dried

1 bay leaf

½ cup heavy cream

Salt and white pepper to taste

2 cups cooked white or brown rice or buttered egg noodles

Heat butter in a medium skillet over medium heat; add onion, garlic, and mushrooms. Cook and stir for 3 minutes or until onion is translucent and mushrooms are soft. Reduce the heat to low, and stir in flour. Cook for 2 minutes, stirring constantly. Stir stock into the skillet, and bring to a boil over high heat. Cook for 2 minutes or until the liquid is slightly thickened. Scrape the contents of the skillet into the slow cooker.

> **Slow Savvy**
> The classic French dish calls for regular white mushrooms, but I've made this dish with fresh shiitake mushrooms and it is equally delicious. The wild mushrooms give a slightly woodsy flavor to the sauce.

Arrange veal, carrot, and pearl onions in the slow cooker. Add parsley, thyme, and bay leaf. Cook on Low for 6 to 8 hours or on High for 3 to 4 hours or until veal is tender. Then, if cooking on Low, raise the heat to High. Stir in cream, discard bay leaf, and season with salt and pepper. Cook for an additional 20 to 30 minutes on High or until the sauce is bubbly. Serve the stew over rice or buttered egg noodles.

The Least You Need to Know

- Stews are good to serve at parties, especially buffet parties, because they don't require the use of a knife.
- Lamb stews are very popular in European countries, and veal stews are a large part of Italian cuisine.
- Meats should be trimmed of all visible fat before cooking.
- Although browning is not essential for veal or pork, beef and lamb should be browned as the first cooking step.

Chapter 11

Chilies to Warm You

In This Chapter

- ◆ Meaty chilies
- ◆ Turkey chilies
- ◆ Vegetarian chilies
- ◆ Chili-related dishes

Chilies and their relations are hardly fussy foods. They're what you serve as you cheer a football game on TV or what simmers on the stove—or in the show cooker—so the family can eat whenever they wish. If you're a "chili head," give some of the recipes in this chapter a try.

In addition to condiments such as grated cheese and chopped onions that are traditionally served with chili, some rice to soak up the sauce is a good idea, too, unless you're piling the dish into tortillas as a wrap.

Chili Con Carne

Prep time: less than 20 minutes • Minimum cooking time: 3 hours • Makes 4 to 6 servings

3 TB. vegetable oil

1 large onion, peeled and diced

4 garlic cloves, peeled and minced

1 jalapeño chili pepper, seeds removed, and finely chopped

½ green bell pepper, seeds and ribs removed, and finely chopped

3 TB. *chili powder*

1 TB. ground cumin

1½ lb. lean ground beef

1 (8-oz.) can tomato sauce

2 (14½-oz.) cans diced tomatoes, drained

1 (15-oz.) can red kidney beans, drained and rinsed

Salt and cayenne to taste

Condiments:

Sour cream

Chopped onion

Grated Monterey Jack cheese

Ellen on Edibles

Chili powder is really a blend of herbs and spices, and if you make it yourself, you can personalize the taste to suit your own. The base should be ground red chilies and ground cumin. Then add as much paprika, ground coriander, cayenne, and oregano as you like. Some brands also include garlic powder and onion powder.

Heat oil in a medium skillet over medium heat; add onion, garlic, jalapeño pepper, and green bell pepper. Cook and stir for 3 minutes or until onion is translucent. Stir in chili powder and ground cumin. Cook for 1 minute, stirring constantly. Spoon the mixture into the slow cooker.

Place ground beef into the skillet, and break up lumps with a fork. Cook beef for 3 to 5 minutes or until it is browned. Remove beef from the pan with a slotted spoon, and place it into the slow cooker. Stir in tomato sauce, tomatoes, and kidney beans. Cook on Low for 6 to 8 hours or on High for 3 to 4 hours. Season with salt and cayenne. When serving, pass sour cream, onion, and cheese separately.

Turkey Chili

Prep time: less than 15 minutes • Minimum cooking time: 3¼ hours • Makes 6 to 8 servings

1½ lb. ground turkey

1 onion, peeled and chopped

1 red bell pepper, seeds and ribs removed, and chopped

3 garlic cloves, peeled and minced

3 TB. chili powder

2 TB. ground cumin

2 (14½-oz.) cans diced tomatoes

1 (15-oz.) can red kidney beans, drained and rinsed

Salt and cayenne to taste

2 cups cooked white or brown rice

Combine turkey, onion, red bell pepper, garlic, chili powder, cumin, and tomatoes in the slow cooker. Stir well. Cook on Low for 6 to 8 hours or on High for 3 to 4 hours.

Then, if cooking on Low, raise the heat to High. Add beans and cook for an additional 20 minutes. Season with salt and cayenne, and serve over rice.

Slow Savvy

Any chili can become a finger food by turning it into nachos. Pile the chili on large nacho corn chips, top with some grated Monterey Jack cheese, and pop under the broiler until the cheese is melted.

Vegetarian Chili

Prep time: less than 20 minutes • Minimum cooking time: 3 hours • Makes 4 to 6 servings

2 TB. vegetable oil

1 large onion, peeled and diced

½ green or red bell pepper, seeds and ribs removed, and chopped

3 garlic cloves, peeled and minced

4 TB. chili powder

1 TB. ground cumin

2 tsp. dried oregano

3 small zucchini (about 1 lb.), trimmed, cut into quarters lengthwise then into ½-inch slices

1 (15-oz.) can red kidney beans, drained and rinsed

1 (28-oz.) can crushed tomatoes in tomato purée

1 (4-oz.) can diced mild green chilies

2 TB. tomato paste

1 TB. granulated sugar

Salt and cayenne to taste

2 cups hot cooked white or brown rice

Condiments:

Chopped scallions

Sour cream or plain yogurt

Grated Monterey Jack cheese

Slow Savvy _____
There are many fresh vegetables you can use in this recipe in place of or along with the zucchini. Try some yellow squash, green beans cut into 1-inch sections, or sliced carrots. The cooking time will be the same.

Heat oil in a medium skillet over medium heat; add onion, green bell pepper, and garlic. Cook and stir for 3 minutes or until onion is translucent. Reduce the heat to low, and stir in chili powder, cumin, and oregano. Cook for 1 minute, stirring constantly. Scrape the mixture into the slow cooker.

Add zucchini, kidney beans, tomatoes, green chilies, tomato paste, and sugar. Stir well. Cook on Low for 6 to 8 hours or on High for 3 to 4 hours or until zucchini is tender. Season with salt and cayenne. Serve it over rice, and pass scallions, sour cream, and cheese separately.

Cincinnati Chili

Prep time: less than 15 minutes • Minimum cooking time: 3 hours • Serves 4 to 6

3 TB. vegetable oil	1 TB. granulated sugar
2 medium onions, peeled and diced	1 tsp. cinnamon
4 garlic cloves, peeled and minced	1 bay leaf
1½ lb. ground beef	Salt and cayenne to taste
1 (8-oz.) can tomato sauce	2 cups hot cooked spaghetti
¾ cup beef stock	**Condiments:**
2 TB. tomato paste	Grated cheddar cheese
2 TB. cider vinegar	Finely chopped onion
1 TB. Worcestershire sauce	Canned red kidney beans, drained and rinsed
1 TB. unsweetened cocoa powder	

Heat the oil in a medium skillet over medium heat; add onion and garlic. Cook and stir for 3 minutes or until onion is translucent. Scrape the mixture into the slow cooker.

Place ground beef into the skillet, and break up lumps with a fork. Cook beef for 3 to 5 minutes or until it is browned. Remove beef from the pan with a slotted spoon, and place it into the slow cooker.

Add tomato sauce, stock, tomato paste, vinegar, Worcestershire sauce, cocoa powder, sugar, cinnamon, and bay leaf to the slow cooker. Stir well.

Cook on Low for 6 to 8 hours or on High for 3 to 4 hours or until the mixture is bubbly and beef is thoroughly cooked. Discard bay leaf, and season with salt and cayenne. Serve it on top of spaghetti, and pass cheese, onion, and kidney beans separately.

Crock Tales

Cincinnati chili was invented by a Macedonian immigrant, Athanas Kiradjieff, in 1922. He served it on hot dogs and called his business the Empress because it was in the same building as the Empress Burlesque Theater. He then opened the Empress Chili restaurant and devised different ways to serve his creation. Cinnamon and a rather watery consistency are the hallmarks of a true Cincinnati chili.

Sloppy Joes

Prep time: less than 15 minutes • Minimum cooking time: 3 hours • Makes 6 to 8 servings

2 TB. vegetable oil

1 large onion, peeled and diced

2 garlic cloves, peeled and minced

1 TB. chili powder

2 lb. ground beef

¾ cup ketchup

½ cup beer

1 (8-oz.) can tomato sauce

1 TB. Worcestershire sauce

Salt and black pepper to taste

6 to 8 toasted hamburger buns

Cooker Caveats

The reason why I specify a slotted spoon in any recipe with ground beef is that it's a shortcut instead of draining the meat in a strainer. The slots let the fat drip back into the pan. If you don't own a slotted spoon, it's a good investment for many dishes.

Heat oil in a medium skillet over medium heat; add onion and garlic. Cook and stir for 3 minutes or until onion is translucent. Reduce the heat to low, and stir in chili powder. Cook for 1 minute, and scrape the mixture into the slow cooker.

Place ground beef into the skillet, and break up lumps with a fork. Cook beef for 3 to 5 minutes or until it is browned. Remove beef from the pan with a slotted spoon, and place it into the slow cooker.

Stir ketchup, beer, tomato sauce, and Worcestershire sauce into the slow cooker. Cook on Low for 6 to 8 hours or on High for 3 to 4 hours. Season with salt and pepper, and serve on toasted hamburger buns.

Picadillo

Prep time: less than 15 minutes   •   Minimum cooking time: 3 hours   •   Makes 4 to 6 servings

2 TB. vegetable oil	1 (14½-oz.) can diced tomatoes
1 large onion, peeled and diced	½ cup beef stock
3 garlic cloves, peeled and minced	1 (4-oz.) can diced mild green chilies
2 TB. chili powder	2 TB. cider vinegar
½ tsp. ground cinnamon	½ cup raisins
1½ lb. ground beef	Salt and black pepper to taste
	2 cups hot cooked white or yellow rice

Heat oil in a medium skillet over medium heat; add onion and garlic. Cook and stir for 3 minutes or until onion is translucent. Reduce the heat to low, and stir chili powder and cinnamon into the mixture. Cook for 1 minute, and scrape the mixture into the slow cooker.

Place ground beef into the skillet, and break up lumps with a fork. Cook beef for 3 to 5 minutes or until it is browned. Remove beef from the pan with a slotted spoon, and place it into the slow cooker.

Add tomatoes, stock, green chilies, vinegar, and raisins to the slow cooker. Cook on Low for 6 to 8 hours or on High for 3 to 4 hours or until beef is thoroughly cooked. Season with salt and pepper, and serve it over rice.

Slow Savvy

Picadillo, or any recipes in this chili section, can be used as the stuffing for bell peppers or the base for a "tamale pie." Steam or microwave the peppers until tender; then fill them. For the pie, make a batch of cornbread batter. Place the hot Picadillo in a 9×13-inch pan, spread the batter over the top, and bake it according to the cornbread directions.

The Least You Need to Know

- Traditionally seasoned chili can be made with turkey and vegetables instead of beef.
- There are many variations on chili dishes that contain different flavors but keep the chili seasoning.
- Chili con carne, a chili relative, means "beans with meat," but you can omit the beans or serve them separately and still keep the essential form of the chili.

Part  Crock Around the Clock: Main Courses for All Times of Day

Up until now, the pieces of food we've been cooking have been small. They've been in appetizers, soups, and stews. Now it's time to get larger. In Part 5, you'll find recipes for whole pieces of chicken still on the bone, as well as shanks and chops of meat. There's also a whole section of pot roasts and a chapter devoted to the ever-popular genre of one-dish dinners.

And because your slow cooker can't tell time, there's a whole chapter of recipes to serve for breakfast and brunch.

Our Feathered Friends

In This Chapter

- ◆ An international collection of chicken recipes
- ◆ Delicious ways to eat turkey when it's not Thanksgiving
- ◆ Recipes that can also be made with other "white meats"

There's no question that chicken in all forms is becoming the mainstay of our diets. And why not? It's a relatively inexpensive source of protein that can be treated myriad ways. And the slow cooker is the perfect pot for cooking chicken because by the way the slow cooker cooks, there is almost no way the chicken can become dry.

Some of the recipes are annotated with nonpoultry alternatives. If you've made a recipe once and liked the results, you're more likely to make it again, so in addition to chicken, this chapter includes a few turkey and duck dishes. If you want further variety, you can also try veal or pork.

Picking Your Parts

When you're cooking conventionally, it's important to remember that white meat cooks a bit faster than dark meat. When you're using a slow cooker, the difference between the parts is so negligible that they are not differentiated.

One thing to keep in mind is that bones make a difference, and boneless pieces, be they breasts or thighs, will cook faster than those with bones.

Crock Tales

Although we credit President Herbert Hoover with the quote about "a chicken in every pot," it was first said by King Henry IV of France at his coronation, when he said he hoped that every peasant could afford a "chicken every Sunday."

Size Matters

You might wonder why you're instructed to use chicken pieces in the recipes in this chapter rather than plunking the whole bird into the slow cooker. The reason is because food in the slow cooker cooks from all sides, and the smaller the pieces, the faster they will cook through. A whole bird should only be cooked on High because its sheer mass keeps it in the bacterial danger zone too long. That's also the reason frozen chicken pieces should never be placed into the slow cooker until they are thawed.

Merrily We Roll Along

One way to serve chicken that is always visually appealing is to pound the breasts thin between two sheets of plastic wrap, layer them with a filling, and roll them tightly. You can keep them closed with toothpicks or kitchen twine. When the chicken is cooked, these rolls get sliced into medallions. Anything from a few leaves of fresh spinach to slices of ham will work well as filling, and the rolls cook in the same time as chicken pieces with bones.

The Least You Need to Know

- All the world's cuisines have delicious ways to prepare chicken.
- Chicken pieces can be substituted for one another, and boneless pieces can be used in place of those with bones. The boneless pieces cook faster.
- Dark and white meat cook at the same rate in the slow cooker.
- Boneless turkey and chicken pieces cook at the same rate.
- For some recipes, other "white meats" such as pork and veal can be substituted for poultry.

Coq au Vin (Chicken in Red Wine)

Prep time: less than 20 minutes   •   Minimum cooking time: 3½ hours   •   Makes 4 to 6 servings

1 (3- to 4-lb.) chicken, cut into serving pieces, or 6 chicken pieces of your choice (breasts, thighs, legs), rinsed and patted dry with paper towels

2 cups dry red wine

½ cup chicken stock

3 garlic cloves, peeled and minced

1 tsp. dried thyme

1 bay leaf

1 (1-lb.) bag frozen pearl onions, thawed

½ lb. white mushrooms, rinsed, stemmed, and halved

1 TB. cornstarch

2 TB. cold water

Salt and black pepper to taste

1½ lb. oven-roasted or steamed potatoes

Preheat the oven broiler, and line a broiler pan with aluminum foil. Place chicken pieces into the pan skin side up in a single layer, and broil for 3 to 5 minutes or until lightly browned. Set aside.

Combine wine, stock, garlic, thyme, bay leaf, pearl onions, and mushrooms in the slow cooker. Arrange chicken pieces in the cooker, skin side down.

Cook on Low for 6 to 8 hours or on High for 3 to 4 hours or until chicken is tender and no longer pink. Remove chicken and vegetables from the cooker with a slotted spoon, and cover with aluminum foil to keep them warm.

Pour cooking liquid from the slow cooker into a saucepan, and bring it to a boil over high heat. Boil until liquid is reduced in volume by half. Mix cornstarch and water in a small cup, and add cornstarch mixture to the boiling liquid. Reduce the heat to low, and simmer the sauce for 2 minutes or until bubbling and thick. Discard bay leaf, season with salt and pepper, and pour the sauce over chicken. Serve chicken with oven-roasted or steamed potatoes.

Cooker Caveats

When cooking with wine or any other acid such as lemon juice, it's important to use a stainless-steel or coated steel pan rather than aluminum. When mixed with the wine or acid, an aluminum pan can impart a metallic taste to the dish.

Chicken Fricassee with Wild Mushrooms

Prep time: less than 15 minutes • Minimum cooking time: 3½ hours • Makes 4 to 6 servings

¼ lb. (1 stick) butter

1 (3- to 4-lb.) chicken, cut into serving pieces, or 6 chicken pieces of your choice (breasts, thighs, legs) with bones, rinsed and patted dry with paper towels

3 shallots, peeled and diced

2 garlic cloves, peeled and minced

3 TB. all-purpose flour

1½ cups chicken stock

3 TB. chopped fresh parsley

1 TB. fresh thyme or 1 tsp. dried

1 TB. fresh rosemary or 1 tsp. dried

¾ lb. wild mushrooms, rinsed, stemmed, and sliced

½ cup heavy cream

Salt and black pepper to taste

2 cups cooked white or brown rice

Heat 3 tablespoons butter in a large skillet over medium heat. Add chicken pieces, brown them on both sides, and cover the pan. Cook for 5 minutes, and transfer the pieces to the slow cooker. Add shallots and garlic to the skillet. Cook and stir for 3 minutes or until shallots are translucent. Reduce the heat to low, and stir in flour. Cook for 1 minute, stirring constantly. Raise the heat to medium-high, and stir in stock. Bring to a boil, and simmer for 2 minutes. Stir in parsley, thyme, and rosemary to the stock. Pour the mixture over chicken.

Ellen on Edibles

Fricassee (pronounced *frick-a-SEE*) is an old method for creating a tender chicken dish. The chicken is lightly cooked in butter before being stewed with liquid and vegetables.

Cook for 6 to 8 hours on Low or 3 to 4 hours on High or until chicken is cooked through, tender, and no longer pink. While chicken is cooking, heat the remaining 5 tablespoons butter in a medium skillet over medium-high heat; add mushrooms. Cook and stir for 5 minutes or until mushrooms are soft.

Then, if cooking on Low, raise the heat to High. Stir mushrooms and cream into the slow cooker, and season with salt and pepper. Cook for an additional 20 to 30 minutes or until the sauce is bubbly. Serve chicken over rice.

Country Captain

Prep time: less than 20 minutes • Minimum cooking time: 3 hours • Makes 4 to 6 servings

1 (3- to 4-lb.) chicken, cut into serving pieces, or 6 chicken pieces of your choice (breasts, thighs, legs) with bones, rinsed and patted dry with paper towels

3 TB. butter

1 large onion, peeled and diced

3 garlic cloves, peeled and minced

1 red bell pepper, seeds and ribs removed, and diced

1 TB. curry powder

½ tsp. ground ginger

½ tsp. ground allspice

½ tsp. dried thyme

⅔ cup dried currants

1 (14½-oz.) can diced tomatoes

⅓ cup chicken stock

⅓ cup dry sherry

2 TB. cornstarch

2 TB. cold water

Salt and black pepper to taste

2 cups cooked white or brown rice

Preheat the oven broiler, and line a broiler pan with aluminum foil. Broil chicken pieces for 3 to 5 minutes or until browned. Turn the pieces, and brown the other side. Arrange chicken in the slow cooker.

Melt butter in a medium skillet over medium heat; add onion, garlic, and red bell pepper. Cook and stir for 3 to 5 minutes or until onion is translucent and pepper begins to soften. Add curry powder, ginger, allspice, and thyme to the pan. Cook for 1 minute, stirring constantly. Scrape the mixture into the slow cooker. Add currants, tomatoes, stock, and sherry. Stir well.

Cook chicken on Low for 6 to 8 hours or on High for 3 to 4 hours or until chicken is cooked through, tender, and no longer pink. Then, if cooking on Low, raise the heat to High. Mix cornstarch and cold water in a small cup. Stir the mixture into the slow cooker, and cook for an additional 10 to 20 minutes or until the liquid is bubbly and has thickened. Season with salt and pepper. Serve chicken with hot rice.

Crock Tales

Country Captain is a chicken dish that dates back to Colonial times. Some food historians say it originated in Savannah, Georgia, a major port for the spice trade. Other sources say a British captain brought the curry-flavored dish back from India.

Chicken Paprikash

Prep time: less than 15 minutes • Minimum cooking time: 3 hours • Makes 6 servings

2 TB. vegetable oil

1 TB. butter

1 large onion, peeled and thinly sliced

3 garlic cloves, peeled and minced

4 TB. paprika

6 skinless chicken thighs

1 (14½-oz.) can diced tomatoes

½ cup chicken stock

½ cup dry white wine

1 TB. fresh thyme or 1 tsp. dried

2 TB. cornstarch

2 TB. cold water

⅓ cup sour cream

Salt and black pepper to taste

2 cups buttered egg noodles

Heat vegetable oil and butter in a large skillet over medium heat; add onion and garlic. Cook and stir for 3 minutes or until onion is translucent. Reduce the heat to low, and stir in paprika. Cook for 1 minute, stirring constantly. Scrape the mixture into the slow cooker.

Cooker Caveats

Because sour cream can curdle if it's allowed to boil, always add it at the end of cooking a dish. Stir in the sour cream, and allow the mixture to cook on Low until the juices are once again hot. Then turn off the heat.

Place chicken into the slow cooker. Stir in tomatoes, stock, wine, and thyme.

Cook on Low for 6 to 8 hours or on High for 3 to 4 hours or until chicken is cooked through, tender, and no longer pink. Mix cornstarch with water, and stir cornstarch mixture into the slow cooker. Cook for an additional 20 to 30 minutes or until the juices are thickened and bubbly. Then, if cooking on High, reduce the heat to Low. Stir in sour cream, and cook for 5 to 10 minutes or until sour cream is heated. *Do not let the mixture come to a boil.* Season with salt and pepper, and serve with buttered egg noodles.

Chicken Cacciatore

Prep time: less than 15 minutes • Minimum cooking time: 2 hours • Makes 4 servings

3 TB. olive oil

1 large onion, peeled and diced

3 garlic cloves, peeled and minced

½ green bell pepper, seeds and ribs removed, and finely chopped

4 boneless, skinless chicken breast halves

1 (8-oz.) can tomato sauce

½ cup dry white wine

½ cup chicken stock

2 TB. fresh oregano or 2 tsp. dried

1 TB. fresh thyme or 1 tsp. dried

1 TB. fresh rosemary or 1 tsp. dried

1 bay leaf

Salt and black pepper to taste

2 cups cooked orzo or rice

Heat oil in a medium skillet over medium heat; add onion, garlic, and green bell pepper. Cook and stir for 3 minutes or until onion is translucent. Scrape the mixture into the slow cooker.

Arrange chicken on top of vegetables. Combine tomato sauce, wine, stock, oregano, thyme, rosemary, and bay leaf in a small bowl. Pour the mixture over chicken. Cook on Low for 4 to 6 hours or on High for 2 to 3 hours or until chicken cooked through, tender, and no longer pink. Discard bay leaf, and season with salt and pepper. Serve chicken with orzo or rice.

Crock Tales

Cacciatore is Italian for "hunter's style." A number of dishes from chicken to beef to veal use cacciatore as a handle, but all it means is that the dish is cooked with tomatoes. The rest of the ingredients are up to the cook.

Chinese Red-Cooked Chicken

Prep time: less than 15 minutes • Minimum cooking time: 3 hours • Makes 4 to 6 servings

1 (3- to 4-lb.) chicken, cut into serving pieces	¾ cup chicken stock
2 TB. sesame oil	¼ cup dry sherry
4 scallions, trimmed and sliced	¼ cup firmly packed dark brown sugar
6 garlic cloves, peeled and minced	1 tsp. Chinese five-spice powder
2 TB. grated fresh ginger	2 cups cooked white rice or fried rice
¾ cup soy sauce	

Slow Savvy

This dish is delicious cold as well as hot. If you're going to serve it cold, one suggestion would be to use boneless, skinless chicken breasts instead of the whole pieces. Reduce the cooking time to 4 to 6 hours on Low or 2 to 3 hours on High if you make that substitution.

Preheat the oven broiler, and line a broiler pan with aluminum foil. Brown chicken for 3 to 5 minutes or until the skin is brown. Turn the pieces, and brown the other side. Transfer chicken to the slow cooker.

Heat oil in a small skillet over medium heat; add scallions, garlic, and ginger. Cook and stir for 2 minutes or until fragrant. Scrape the mixture into a mixing bowl. Add soy sauce, stock, sherry, brown sugar, and Chinese five-spice powder to the bowl. Stir well to dissolve sugar, and pour the mixture over chicken.

Cook on Low for 6 to 8 hours or on High for 3 to 4 hours or until chicken is cooked through, tender, and no longer pink. Serve with white rice or fried rice.

Braised Rock Cornish Hens with Spring Vegetables

Prep time: less than 20 minutes • Minimum cooking time: 3 hours • Makes 4 servings

2 *Rock Cornish hens*, cut into halves or quarters (depending on the shape of your slow cooker)

2 cups chicken stock

1 TB. fresh thyme or 1 tsp. dried

1 TB. fresh chopped rosemary or 1 tsp. dried

1 TB. fresh chervil or 1 tsp. dried

1 bay leaf

2 garlic cloves, peeled and crushed

1 (10-oz.) box frozen pearl onions, thawed

1 (10-oz.) box frozen peas, thawed

2 heads bibb lettuce, rinsed, trimmed, and cut into quarters

Salt and black pepper to taste

1 lb. steamed baby potatoes

Preheat the oven broiler, and line a broiler pan with aluminum foil. Broil hens skin side up for 3 to 5 minutes or until lightly browned. Arrange hens in the slow cooker. Add stock, thyme, rosemary, chervil, bay leaf, garlic, and pearl onions to the slow cooker.

Cook on Low for 6 to 8 hours or on High for 3 to 4 hours or until hens are cooked through and no longer pink. Then, if cooking on Low, raise the heat to High. Add peas and lettuce, and cook for 45 minutes or until lettuce is wilted and the mixture is bubbling. Discard bay leaf, and season with salt and pepper. Serve hens in low soup bowls with vegetables and steamed baby potatoes.

Ellen on Edibles

Although **Rock Cornish hens** are sometimes called Rock Cornish game hens, they are not game at all. These small chickens, which usually weigh about 2 pounds, are a hybrid of Cornish and White Rock chickens that are between 4 and 6 weeks old.

Cranberry-Glazed Turkey Meatloaf

Prep time: less than 15 minutes • Minimum cooking time: 3 hours • Makes 4 to 6 servings

4 TB. (½ stick) butter

2 onions, peeled and diced

2 garlic cloves, peeled and minced

1 celery stalk, trimmed and chopped

1½ lb. ground turkey

2 eggs, lightly beaten

½ cup fresh breadcrumbs

1 TB. chopped fresh sage or 1 tsp. dried

1 TB. fresh thyme or 1 tsp. dried

Salt and black pepper to taste

½ cup Cranberry Chutney (recipe in Chapter 21) or canned whole berry cranberry sauce

3 cups stuffing or mashed potatoes

Melt butter in a medium saucepan over medium heat; add onion, garlic, and celery. Cook and stir for 3 minutes or until onion is translucent. Scrape the mixture into a mixing bowl. Add turkey, eggs, breadcrumbs, sage, thyme, salt, and pepper. Mix well to combine.

Fold a sheet of aluminum foil in half, and place it in the bottom of the slow cooker with the sides of the foil extending up the sides of the slow cooker. Form meat mixture into an oval or round, depending on the shape of your cooker, and place it into the cooker on top of the foil. Spread Cranberry Chutney on top of meat.

Cook meatloaf on Low for 6 to 8 hours or on High for 3 to 4 hours or until a thermometer inserted into the center of meat reads 165°F. Remove meat from the cooker by pulling up the sides of the foil. Drain off any grease from the foil, and slide meatloaf onto a serving platter. Serve meatloaf with stuffing or mashed potatoes.

> **Slow Savvy**
>
> This dish works equally well with ground pork or a combination of pork and veal. The cooking time does not change with the substitution.

Turkey Tonnato

Prep time: less than 20 minutes   •   Minimum cooking time: 3 hours   •   Makes 4 to 6 servings

Turkey:

2 lb. boneless, skinless turkey breast

3 garlic cloves, peeled and cut into quarters

1½ cups chicken stock

½ cup dry white wine

1 onion, peeled and sliced

1 carrot, peeled and sliced

4 sprigs fresh parsley

2 sprigs fresh thyme or 1 tsp. dried

1 bay leaf

Salt and black pepper to taste

Sauce:

1 (6½-oz.) can imported tuna packed in olive oil

¼ cup lemon juice

2 TB. anchovy paste

¼ cup mayonnaise

2 TB. capers, drained and rinsed

Black pepper to taste

1½ lb. cold pasta salad or potato salad

Place turkey breast between two sheets of plastic wrap. Pound it with the flat side of a meat mallet or bottom of a small saucepan until it is a uniform thickness. Roll turkey breast into a shape that will fit into your slow cooker, and tie it with kitchen string. Make 12 slits around turkey breast, and insert a garlic sliver in each one. Place turkey breast into the slow cooker, and add stock, wine, onion, carrot, parsley, thyme, bay leaf, salt, and pepper. Cook turkey on Low for 6 to 8 hours or on High for 3 to 4 hours or until a thermometer inserted in the center of turkey reads 165°F. Remove turkey from the slow cooker and chill well.

For the sauce, combine tuna, lemon juice, and anchovy paste in a food processor fitted with a steel blade or in a blender. Purée until smooth, and scrape the mixture into a mixing bowl. Stir in mayonnaise and capers, and season the sauce with pepper.

To serve, remove and discard the string, and thinly slice turkey. Spoon some sauce on turkey slices, and pass the rest separately. Serve turkey with cold pasta salad or potato salad.

Slow Savvy

Although there is no use for the braising liquid in this recipe, it's a richly flavored stock and it's a shame to throw it away. Freeze it and use it in place of chicken stock when cooking another recipe.

Duck Confit

Prep time: less than 15 minutes,   •   Minimum cooking time: 7 hours   •   Makes 4 servings
plus 1 day for marinating

4 duck legs or 1 duck cut into quarters, rinsed and patted dry with paper towels

6 garlic cloves, peeled and minced

2 bay leaves, broken into pieces

1 TB. dried thyme

2 TB. kosher salt

1 tsp. coarsely ground black pepper

2 cups duck fat, chicken fat, or vegetable oil

1 lb. oven-roasted potatoes

Rinse duck legs, and pat dry with paper towels. Combine garlic, bay leaves, thyme, kosher salt, and pepper in a small bowl. Rub both sides of duck legs with the mixture, and place them in a heavy plastic bag. Marinate duck legs in the refrigerator for 24 hours.

If using duck or chicken fat, heat it in the slow cooker on High for 30 minutes or until it is melted. If using vegetable oil, pour it into the slow cooker. Remove duck legs from the refrigerator, and rinse them under cold running water. Arrange duck legs in the slow cooker skin side down. They should be almost submerged in fat. Cook on Low for 7 to 9 hours or until duck is incredibly tender.

> **Crock Tales**
>
> Confit is a gastronomic specialty of the Gascony region of France. It can be either duck or goose that is gently cooked in fat and then stored submerged in fat. This was one of the earliest methods of preserving meats, and it still produces a dish that is melt-in-your-mouth tender.

Remove duck from fat. If using duck in other dishes, remove meat from the bones when cool enough to handle, and discard the bones. Store duck meat refrigerated, covered with fat from the slow cooker. If serving duck legs as an entrée, place them under a preheated broiler for 4 to 5 minutes or until the skin is brown and crisp. Serve duck with oven-roasted potatoes.

Chapter 13

Beefing Up Dinner

In This Chapter

- ◆ Delicious ways to cook inexpensive cuts of beef
- ◆ The many ways family-pleasing pot roast is made around the world
- ◆ A new look at an old friend—meatloaf

After women started working outside the house in large numbers, dishes like pot roast were reserved for weekends. Very few cooks felt comfortable leaving a pot unattended on a burner or in the oven all day while the house was empty.

Today there's an alternative—the slow cooker. Pot roast can once again become a dish for any evening. In this chapter, you'll find a number of ways to cook large pieces of beef as well as ground beef.

Slowly cooked beef dishes use less-expensive cuts of meat than those reserved for roasting. These succulent cuts, like short ribs and chuck, become meltingly tender after many hours of the slow cooker's gentle heat.

Cheaper Is Better

Even if you know nothing about beef and what the various parts are called, you can pick the right ones. Just look at the price tags. There are many more cuts on a cow that require long, slow cooking than there are parts that are meant to be grilled, broiled, or roasted. Look at the cost of a tenderloin roast, then look at the cost of a brisket. Buy the brisket for the slow cooker.

Choosing Your Cuts

Price is a good guideline, but there are others. Anything that says "chuck," "rump," or "shank" is a good slow cooker choice. One of the best cuts of beef for the slow cooker is the short ribs, also called flanken in some parts of the country.

The shape of your slow cooker is one guide to what to buy. If your slow cooker is round, a rump roast is your best bet. If it's oval, go with a chuck roast or a brisket.

Crock Tales

Our English word *beef* comes from the Latin *bos,* which means "ox." By the Middle Ages, it had become *beef* or *boef* in English. There were cattle at the Jamestown settlement in Virginia in the early seventeenth century, but the Texas longhorns that we use for beef today were brought to that state by the Spanish almost a century after the Jamestown settlement.

Basics of Boning

Some cuts that look like the best buys frequently contain some bones. It's a good idea to cut these away, because they slow down the cooking process. Save the bones for making stock (see the recipe in Chapter 1).

The first step of boning is to cut away the bones. The second step is to decide how the remaining boneless meat should be cut. The rule is to cut across the grain rather than with the grain. If you're not sure which way the grain runs, make a test slice. You should see the ends of fibers if you cut across the grain.

Long Leads to Luscious

You can't rush a great pot roast. It takes hours of low heat for the fibers to tenderize in a large piece of beef. If you don't have the 5 or 6 hours necessary, cut the meat into pieces and make a stew which will cook faster. Plan on about 10 to 12 hours on Low or 5 to 6 hours on High for most of these pot roast variations.

Sunday Pot Roast

Prep time: less than 20 minutes   •   Minimum cooking time: 5½ hours   •   Makes 4 to 6 servings

1 (2- to 2½-lb.) beef rump or chuck roast

3 TB. vegetable oil

1 onion, peeled and diced

3 garlic cloves, peeled and minced

½ lb. white mushrooms, rinsed, stemmed, and sliced

4 medium red-skinned potatoes, scrubbed and cut into 1-inch cubes

2 carrots, peeled and cut into ½-inch pieces

1 celery stalk, trimmed and cut into ½-inch slices

1 (14½-oz.) can diced tomatoes

2 cups beef stock

1 TB. fresh thyme or 1 tsp. dried

1 bay leaf

1 TB. cornstarch

2 TB. cold water

Salt and black pepper to taste

Preheat the oven broiler, and line a broiler pan with aluminum foil. Broil beef for 3 to 5 minutes per side or until browned. Set aside.

Heat oil in a large skillet over medium heat; add onion, garlic, and mushrooms. Cook and stir for 3 to 5 minutes or until onion is translucent and mushrooms are soft. Scrape the mixture into the slow cooker. Add potatoes, carrots, celery, tomatoes, stock, thyme, and bay leaf. Mix well, then place beef into the slow cooker, pushing it down into the liquid. Cook for 10 to 12 hours on Low or 5 to 6 hours on High or until beef and vegetables are very tender.

Then, if cooking on Low, raise the heat to High. Mix cornstarch with water, and stir cornstarch mixture into the slow cooker. Cook for an additional 15 to 20 minutes or until the liquid has thickened and is bubbly. Discard bay leaf, and season pot roast with salt and pepper.

Slow Savvy

You can vary the vegetables in this dish to suit your taste. Turnips, parsnips, fennel, and celery root (celeriac) are all great additions or substitutions.

Pot-au-Feu (French Mixed Braised Meats)

Prep time: less than 20 minutes • Minimum cooking time: 5 hours • Makes 4 to 6 servings

3 short ribs of beef (about 1½ lb.)

2 slices beef shank (about 1½ lb.)

2 carrots, peeled and cut into ½-inch slices

2 onions, peeled and cut into quarters through the root end

1 small celery root (celeriac), peeled and cut into ½-inch cubes

3 cups beef stock

2 TB. chopped fresh parsley

1 TB. fresh thyme or 1 tsp. dried

1 bay leaf

½ small head of cabbage, cored and cut into 6 wedges

Salt and black pepper to taste

1½ lb. steamed baby potatoes

Condiments:

Dijon mustard

Coarse sea salt

Cornichons or other sweet small pickles

Preheat the oven broiler, and line a broiler pan with aluminum foil. Broil short ribs and beef shank slices for 3 to 5 minutes per side or until browned.

Arrange carrots, onions, and celery root in the bottom of the slow cooker. Arrange beef on top of vegetables. Pour stock over meats, and add parsley, thyme, and bay leaf. Arrange cabbage wedges over beef.

Crock Tales

Pot-au-feu literally means "pot of fire," and this classic French dish began centuries ago as one of the original "potluck dinners." Everyone would bring what they had in their larder, and they'd cook it all together.

Cook on Low for 10 to 12 hours or on High for 5 to 6 hours or until beef is very tender. Remove beef from the slow cooker, and slice it into serving pieces. Arrange vegetables around the pieces. Remove as much grease as possible from the top of stock with a ladle, discard bay leaf, and season broth with salt and pepper. Serve broth as a first course and then serve beef and vegetables as the entrée accompanied by steamed baby potatoes. Pass mustard, sea salt, and cornichons separately.

Short Ribs of Beef with Rosemary

Prep time: less than 15 minutes   •   Minimum cooking time: 4 hours   •   Makes 4 to 6 servings

5 lb. meaty short ribs with bones, or 2½ lb. boneless short ribs	2 celery stalks, sliced
¼ cup vegetable oil	3 TB. chopped fresh rosemary or 1 TB. dried
1 large onion, peeled and diced	2 TB. cornstarch
4 garlic cloves, peeled and minced	2 TB. cold water
1 cup beef stock	Salt and black pepper to taste
	2 cups buttered egg noodles

Preheat the oven broiler, and line a broiler pan with aluminum foil. Broil short ribs for 3 to 4 minutes per side or until browned. Arrange short ribs in the slow cooker, and pour in any juices that have collected in the pan.

Heat oil in a medium skillet over medium heat; add onions and garlic. Cook and stir for 3 minutes or until onion is translucent. Scrape the mixture into the slow cooker.

Add stock, celery, and rosemary to the slow cooker and stir well. Cook on Low for 8 to 10 hours or on High for 4 to 5 hours or until short ribs are very tender. Remove as much grease as possible from the slow cooker with a soup ladle. Then, if cooking on Low, raise the heat to High. Mix cornstarch with water in a small cup. Stir cornstarch mixture into the cooker, and cook on High for 15 to 20 minutes or until the juices are bubbly and thickened. Season with salt and pepper, and serve with buttered egg noodles.

Slow Savvy

If you have leftovers from this dish, turn them into barbecue sandwiches the next night. Chop up the meat, heat it in some of the juices; then mound it on buns with barbecue sauce.

Deviled Short Ribs

Prep time: less than 20 minutes • Minimum cooking time: 4 hours • Makes 4 to 6 servings

4 to 6 meaty short ribs of beef on the bone or 2 lb. chuck, cut into 4-inch cubes

2 TB. vegetable oil

2 large onions, peeled and diced

4 garlic cloves, peeled and minced

2 TB. chili powder

½ tsp. ground allspice

1½ cups beef stock

¼ cup Dijon mustard

⅓ cup firmly packed dark brown sugar

2 TB. cider vinegar

Salt and black pepper to taste

3 cups cooked mashed potatoes

Preheat the oven broiler, and line a broiler pan with aluminum foil. Broil short ribs for 3 to 5 minutes per side or until browned. Arrange short ribs in the slow cooker, and pour in any juices that have collected in the pan.

Crock Tales

Deviled is an American term for any sort of dish that's highly seasoned with flavors like cayenne or mustard. The association is with demons in the heat of hell. The word appears in the late eighteenth century, and Washington Irving described some deviled dishes in a few of his books.

Heat oil in a medium skillet over medium heat; add onion and garlic. Cook, stirring, for 3 minutes or until onion is translucent. Add chili powder and allspice to the skillet. Cook for 1 minute, stirring constantly. Scrape the mixture into the slow cooker.

Combine stock, mustard, brown sugar, and vinegar in a mixing bowl. Stir well to dissolve sugar, and pour the mixture into the slow cooker. Cook on Low for 8 to 10 hours or on High for 4 to 5 hours or until short ribs are very tender. Remove as much grease as possible from the slow cooker with a soup ladle. Season short ribs with salt and pepper, and serve with mashed potatoes.

Indonesian Pot Roast

Prep time: less than 20 minutes • Minimum cooking time: 5 hours • Makes 4 to 6 servings

2 lb. chuck roast, trimmed of all visible fat

3 TB. vegetable oil

4 large onions, peeled and *diced*

6 garlic cloves, peeled and minced

3 TB. grated fresh ginger

1 small jalapeño or serrano chili pepper, seeds and ribs removed, and finely chopped

2 TB. ground coriander

1 TB. turmeric

1½ cups canned unsweetened coconut milk

1 cup beef stock

1 bay leaf

1 tsp. grated lemon zest

Salt and black pepper to taste

2 cups cooked white or jasmine rice

½ cup sweetened coconut, toasted at 350°F for 10 minutes

Preheat the oven broiler, and line a broiler pan with aluminum foil. Broil roast for 3 to 5 minutes per side or until lightly browned. Transfer roast to the slow cooker along with any juices that have collected in the pan.

Heat oil in a medium skillet over medium heat; add onion, garlic, ginger, and jalapeño pepper. Cook and stir for 3 minutes or until onion is translucent. Stir in coriander and turmeric. Cook for 1 minute, stirring constantly. Scrape the mixture into the slow cooker, and stir in coconut milk, stock, bay leaf, and lemon zest.

Cook on Low for 10 to 12 hours or on High for 5 to 6 hours or until beef is tender. Discard bay leaf, and season pot roast with salt and pepper. Slice roast and serve it with rice. Spoon some juices over the slices, and garnish with toasted coconut.

Ellen on Edibles

Dice means to cut food into squares of the same size. In some recipes the size is specified, while in others the word is open to personal interpretation because the size of the pieces doesn't matter for the success of a dish. In those cases, try not to make the pieces larger than ½ inch.

Sauerbraten

Prep time: less than 15 minutes • Minimum cooking time: 5 hours, • Makes 4 to 6
plus 1 day for marinating servings

1 cup dry red wine	½ tsp. ground ginger
1 cup beef stock	¼ cup firmly packed dark brown sugar
½ cup red wine vinegar	1 onion, peeled and thinly sliced
2 TB. tomato paste	3 garlic cloves, peeled and thinly sliced
2 TB. Worcestershire sauce	2 to 3 lb. rump or chuck roast
1 TB. Dijon mustard	10 gingersnap cookies, crushed
½ tsp. salt	Salt and black pepper to taste
½ tsp. allspice	3 cups buttered spaetzle or egg noodles

Combine wine, stock, vinegar, tomato paste, Worcestershire sauce, mustard, salt, allspice, ginger, and brown sugar in a heavy resealable plastic bag. Mix well, and add onion, garlic, and beef. Marinate in the refrigerator for 24 to 48 hours, turning the bag occasionally so meat marinates evenly.

Transfer beef and marinade to the slow cooker, and stir in gingersnap crumbs. Cook on Low for 10 to 12 hours or on High for 5 to 6 hours or until beef is very tender. Season with salt and pepper. Slice beef, spoon some gravy over it, and serve it with spaetzle or egg noodles.

Cooker Caveats

In this recipe, the marinade becomes the braising liquid, and as such, is subject to high heat, so there is no danger of contamination. But the general rule is that marinades should never be used raw. Either discard a marinade or bring it to a boil; never use raw marinade as a basting liquid for the grill or as a dipping sauce, dressing, or gravy. Also, never put cooked food on the same platter the raw food was on.

Smoked Beef Brisket with Barbecue Sauce

Prep time: less than 15 minutes • Minimum cooking time: 5 hours • Makes 4 to 6 servings

1 cup hickory or mesquite chips	Salt and black pepper to taste
2½ lb. beef brisket	2 cups beef stock
2 garlic cloves, peeled and crushed	1 cup My Favorite Barbecue Sauce (recipe in Chapter 21) or commercial barbecue sauce

Soak the wood chips in cold water for 30 minutes, and light a charcoal grill. Rub brisket with garlic, salt, and pepper. Drain the wood chips, and sprinkle the chips on the hot coals. Place brisket on the grill rack and close the grill's lid, or cover it with a sheet of heavy aluminum foil. Smoke brisket for 10 minutes per side, turning it with tongs.

Place brisket into the slow cooker and add stock. Cook brisket for 10 to 12 hours on Low or 5 to 6 hours on High or until meat is very tender. Remove brisket from the slow cooker, and slice it against the grain into thin slices. Spoon some of the pan juices over meat, and pass barbecue sauce separately.

Slow Savvy

The best way to rid meat dishes of unwanted saturated fat is to chill the dish, then remove and discard the solid layer of fat that will have formed on the top. But if you want to eat the dish the same day it's made, let the dish stand for 10 to 15 minutes, then use a shallow ladle to gather and discard the grease.

Beef Brisket in Red Wine Sauce

Prep time: less than 15 minutes • Minimum cooking time: 5 hours • Makes 4 to 6 servings

1 (2- to 2½-lb.) beef brisket

1 (1.2-oz.) pkg. dehydrated brown gravy mix

2 garlic cloves, peeled and minced

1 TB. herbes de Provence or 1 tsp. dried thyme, 1 tsp. dried oregano, and 1 tsp. dried rosemary

1 cup dry red wine

½ cup beef stock

Salt and black pepper to taste

2 cups cooked mashed potatoes or buttered egg noodles

Slow Savvy

If you want a fancier dish, use mushroom gravy instead of brown gravy, and add some sautéed mushrooms to the slow cooker for the last hour of the cooking time.

Preheat the oven broiler, and line a broiler pan with aluminum foil. Broil brisket for 3 to 5 minutes per side or until browned. Set aside. Pour gravy mix into the slow cooker, and stir in garlic, herbes de Provence, wine, and stock. Place brisket into the slow cooker.

Cook on Low for 10 to 12 hours or on High for 5 to 6 hours or until meat is tender. Turn brisket over with tongs halfway through the cooking process. Season with salt and pepper, and serve with mashed potatoes or buttered egg noodles.

Great American Meatloaf

Prep time: less than 15 minutes　•　Minimum cooking time: 3 hours　•　Makes 4 to 6 servings

2 TB. vegetable oil	½ cup grated mozzarella cheese
1 medium onion, peeled and diced	½ tsp. dried thyme
2 garlic cloves, peeled and minced	Salt and black pepper to taste
2 eggs, lightly beaten	1½ lb. lean ground beef or a combination of beef, veal, and pork
¼ cup milk	
½ cup *Italian-flavored breadcrumbs*	½ cup ketchup
	3 cups mashed potatoes

Heat oil in a small skillet over medium heat; add onion and garlic. Cook and stir for 3 minutes or until onion is translucent. Set aside.

Combine eggs, milk, breadcrumbs, cheese, thyme, salt, and pepper in a large mixing bowl, and stir well. Add meat and onion-garlic mixture and mix well.

Fold a sheet of aluminum foil in half, and place it in the bottom of the slow cooker with the sides of the foil extending up the sides of the slow cooker. Form meat mixture into an oval or round, depending on the shape of your cooker, and place it into the cooker on top of the foil. Spread ketchup on top of meat.

Ellen on Edibles
Italian-flavored bread-crumbs are flavored with herbs and cheese. If all you have is plain breadcrumbs, add 1 tablespoon chopped parsley and 1 tablespoon grated Parmesan cheese to the recipe.

Cook meatloaf on Low for 6 to 8 hours or on High for 3 to 4 hours or until a thermometer inserted into the center of loaf reads 165°F. Remove meat from the cooker by pulling it up by the sides of the foil. Drain off any grease from the foil, and slide meatloaf onto a serving platter. Serve meatloaf with mashed potatoes.

Vegetable-Stuffed Meatloaf

Prep time: less than 20 minutes • Minimum cooking time: 3 hours • Makes 4 to 6 servings

Meatloaf:

¼ cup olive oil

2 onions, peeled and chopped

3 garlic cloves, peeled and minced

1 lb. lean ground beef

½ lb. mild or hot bulk Italian sausage

1 egg, lightly beaten

¼ cup Italian-style breadcrumbs

¼ cup grated mozzarella cheese

1 TB. fresh thyme or 1 tsp. dried

1 TB. chopped fresh basil or 1 tsp. dried

Salt and black pepper to taste

Stuffing:

1 (10-oz.) box frozen chopped spinach, thawed

1 small carrot, peeled and grated

1 egg, lightly beaten

1 garlic clove, peeled and crushed

Salt and black pepper to taste

3 cups mashed potatoes

Heat oil in a small skillet over medium heat; add onion and garlic. Cook and stir for 3 minutes or until onion is translucent. Scrape the mixture into a mixing bowl. Add beef, sausage, egg, breadcrumbs, cheese, thyme, basil, salt, and pepper to the mixing bowl. Mix well to combine.

For the stuffing, place spinach into a strainer and press with the back of a spoon to extract as much water as possible. Place spinach in a mixing bowl, and add carrot, egg, garlic, salt, and pepper. Mix well to combine.

Slow Savvy

Lining a slow cooker with aluminum foil to use as handles works for any dish that you want to remove from the slow cooker in one piece. The meatloaf is fairly sturdy after it's cooked, but for more delicate foods, line the entire cooker with foil and pull the foil and the food out evenly and carefully.

Fold a sheet of aluminum foil in half, and place it in the bottom of the slow cooker with the sides of the foil extending up the sides of the slow cooker. Form half the meat mixture into an oval or round, depending on the shape of your cooker, and place it into the cooker on top of the foil. Make a trench in the center of meat with the back of a spoon. Spread spinach mixture in the trench, and top it with the remaining meat. Smooth the sides and top.

Cook meatloaf on Low for 6 to 8 hours or on High for 3 to 4 hours or until a thermometer inserted into the center of loaf reads 165°F. Remove meat from the cooker by pulling it up by the sides of the foil. Drain off any grease from the foil, and slide meatloaf onto a serving platter. Serve with mashed potatoes.

Stuffed Peppers

Prep time: less than 15 minutes   •   Minimum cooking time: 2½ hours   •   Makes 4 to 6 servings

3 medium green or red bell peppers	1 egg, lightly beaten
2 TB. vegetable oil	½ cup Italian-flavored breadcrumbs
1 onion, peeled and chopped	¼ cup grated mozzarella cheese
2 garlic cloves, peeled and minced	¼ cup milk
1 lb. lean ground beef	Salt and black pepper to taste
1 TB. Italian seasoning or 1 tsp. dried oregano, 1 tsp. dried thyme, and 1 tsp. dried basil	1 cup spaghetti sauce
	3 cups cooked pasta

Cut green bell peppers in half lengthwise. Discard the seeds, ribs, and caps. Set aside.

Heat oil in a small skillet over medium heat; add onion and garlic. Cook and stir for 3 minutes or until onion is translucent. Scrape the mixture into a mixing bowl. Add beef, Italian seasoning, egg, breadcrumbs, cheese, milk, salt, and pepper to the mixing bowl. Mix well and stuff the mixture into hollowed bell peppers.

Cooker Caveats

It's important to use the leanest ground beef possible for recipes such as this one because the grease does not drain off from browning. Ground sirloin is more expensive than ground chuck, but the extra fat in the chuck compensates.

Arrange bell peppers in the slow cooker, and pour spaghetti sauce on top of them. If bell peppers have to be layered in the slow cooker, pour half the spaghetti sauce over the bottom layer, then half over the top layer. Cook on Low for 5 to 7 hours or on High for 2½ to 3½ hours or until meat is cooked through and bell peppers have softened. Serve bell peppers with pasta.

The Least You Need to Know

◆ Slow cooking is an ideal way to cook less-expensive cuts of beef because they become wonderfully tender after their time in the slow cooker.

◆ Grease can be removed from beef dishes with a ladle once the juices have stopped bubbling or after the dish has been chilled.

◆ Foods can be removed from the slow cooker in one piece if the slow cooker is lined with aluminum foil before any food is added.

◆ To avoid extra fat in foods, use lean ground beef for recipes that do not include browning.

Chapter 14

Complementing the Cow

In This Chapter

- Ways to cook lamb and veal shanks
- Easy pork recipes for chops, roasts, and country ribs
- Making ham a star

Although beef remains the nation's favorite red meat, the other four-legged creatures have their own sets of fans as well. The recipes in this chapter give you great-tasting ways to cook lamb, pork, and veal.

Compatible Animals and Convertible Recipes

Often you can change the meat without sacrificing the quality of a recipe as long as the change is in the same flavor and texture family. For example, beef and lamb are interchangeable in recipes because both are hearty meats. In the same way, pork and veal are similar, and both can be substituted for whole pieces of chicken without changing the timing.

The question you should ask yourself is: Is it a red meat or a white meat? Even though veal is a young cow, the flavor and texture is more similar to pork or chicken than it is to beef.

Slow Savvy

One way pork differs from other meats is that browning isn't really necessary. This cuts down your prep time before the slow cooker takes over.

Chopping Roasts

If you see a recipe that calls for a roast and all you have are chops, go ahead and use the recipe as written and just substitute the cut you've got on hand. Many times it's less expensive to buy a whole roast rather than having the butcher cut it into chops. Then you can cut the chops as thick as you like.

The Least You Need to Know

- Pork roasts and chops do not have to be browned before cooking them. It is not as crucial a step as it is for the success of beef and lamb dishes.
- Lamb shanks are eaten whole, while veal shanks are cut crosswise into slices.
- Country pork ribs are a good cut to cook in the slow cooker, and they are usually less expensive than roasts.
- Pork, veal, and chicken can be substituted for each other in almost all recipes. The cooking time will be shorter for chicken.

Braised Lamb Shanks with Winter Vegetables

Prep time: less than 15 minutes   •   Minimum cooking time: 4 hours   •   Makes 4 servings

4 meaty lamb shanks (about 12 oz. each)

1 cup dry red wine

½ cup water

1 (1.2-oz.) pkg. dehydrated brown gravy mix

1 carrot, peeled and thinly sliced

1 celery stalk, peeled and thinly sliced

1 large onion, peeled and diced

3 garlic cloves, peeled and crushed

2 TB. chopped fresh parsley

1 tsp. herbes de Provence or 1 tsp. dried thyme

1 bay leaf

Salt and black pepper to taste

2 cups buttered egg noodles

Preheat the oven broiler, and line a broiler pan with aluminum foil. Broil lamb shanks for 3 to 5 minutes per side or until lightly browned.

Combine wine, water, and gravy mix in the slow cooker and stir well. Add carrot, celery, onion, garlic, parsley, herbes de Provence, and bay leaf. Stir well. Arrange lamb shanks in the cooker with meaty end down.

Cook lamb shanks on Low for 8 to 10 hours or on High for 4 to 5 hours or until lamb is very tender. Remove lamb shanks from the cooker, and keep them warm by covering them with aluminum foil. Discard bay leaf, and season sauce with salt and pepper. Serve sauce with shanks with buttered egg noodles.

Slow Savvy

Frequently, lamb shanks have a membrane over the lower part of the bone. It's not really necessary to trim this off. It will become tender after the long hours of cooking.

Chinese Roast Pork

Prep time: less than 15 minutes • Minimum cooking time: 3 hours • Makes 4 to 6 servings

2 lb. boneless pork loin or 2 lb. boneless country ribs

2 TB. Asian sesame oil

2 TB. vegetable oil

6 scallions, trimmed and thinly sliced

2 TB. grated fresh ginger

4 garlic cloves, peeled and minced

½ cup hoisin sauce

¼ cup rice wine vinegar

¼ cup chicken stock

1 TB. soy sauce

1 TB. Asian chili sauce

2 cups cooked white rice or fried rice

Remove any visible fat from pork. Heat Asian sesame and vegetable oils in a medium skillet over medium-high heat. Brown pork on all sides, and place it in the slow cooker. Reduce the heat to medium, and add scallions, ginger, and garlic. Cook and stir for 3 minutes or until scallions are soft. Scrape the mixture into the slow cooker.

Combine hoisin sauce, vinegar, stock, soy sauce, and Asian chili sauce in a small bowl. Stir well and pour the liquid over meat in the slow cooker. Cook on Low for 6 to 8 hours or on High for 3 to 4 hours or until a thermometer inserted into the center of meat reads 165°F. If using a pork loin, turn meat upside down halfway through the cooking time if one part of meat is out of the liquid. Serve pork with white or fried rice.

Cooker Caveats

Even though today's pork does not have to be cooked to well done, as does poultry, the U.S. Department of Agriculture still believes pork should be cooked to 165°F. There is no risk of bacterial contamination at this temperature.

Pork Loin with Mushroom Stuffing

Prep time: less than 15 minutes   •   Minimum cooking time: 6 hours   •   Makes 4 to 6 servings

3 TB. butter

1 large onion, peeled and diced

1 celery stalk, thinly sliced

½ lb. mushrooms, rinsed, stemmed, and thinly sliced

3 cups dried herb stuffing

¼ cup chicken stock

3 garlic cloves, peeled and crushed

1 TB. dried sage leaves

1 tsp. dried thyme

½ teaspoon salt

Black pepper to taste

2 lb. boneless pork loin roast

Heat butter in a medium skillet over medium heat; add onion, celery, and mushrooms. Cook and stir for 3 to 5 minutes or until onion is translucent and mushrooms are soft. Remove the pan from the heat, and stir in stuffing and stock. Scrape the mixture into a greased slow cooker.

Combine garlic, sage, thyme, salt, and pepper in a small bowl. Rub this mixture onto pork roast. Place roast on top of stuffing. Cook on Low for 6 to 8 hours or until a thermometer inserted into center of meat reads 165°F.

Slow Savvy _____

This stuffing will seem dry when you put it in the slow cooker, but don't worry. Both the juices that escape from the meat as it cooks as well as the steam that forms from the heat of the slow cooker will moisten it sufficiently.

Peking Meatloaf

Prep time: less than 15 minutes • Minimum cooking time: 3 hours • Makes 4 to 6 servings

1½ lb. lean ground pork	1 TB. dry sherry
1 egg, lightly beaten	½ cup chopped water chestnuts
5 scallions, trimmed and chopped	Black pepper to taste
3 garlic cloves, peeled and minced	¼ cup Dijon mustard
3 TB. grated fresh ginger	¼ cup hoisin sauce
3 TB. finely chopped cilantro	2 cups fried rice or cooked Chinese noodles
2 TB. soy sauce	

Combine pork, egg, scallions, garlic, ginger, cilantro, soy sauce, sherry, water chestnuts, and pepper in a mixing bowl. Mix well to combine.

Fold a sheet of aluminum foil in half, and place it in the bottom of the slow cooker, with the sides of the foil extending up the sides of the slow cooker. Form meat mixture into an oval or round, depending on the shape of your cooker, and place it in the cooker on top of the foil. Mix mustard and hoisin sauce in a small mixing bowl. Spread the mixture on top of meatloaf.

Slow Savvy

One way to serve this meatloaf is as wraps in flour tortillas. Spread a mixture of hoisin sauce and mustard on the tortilla, then add some crunchy bean sprouts along with a slice of the meatloaf.

Cook meatloaf on Low for 6 to 8 hours or on High for 3 to 4 hours or until a thermometer inserted into the center of meat reads 165°F. Remove meat from the cooker by pulling it up by the sides of the foil. Drain off any grease from the foil, and slide meatloaf onto a serving platter. Serve meatloaf with fried rice or Chinese noodles.

Norman Pork Chops with Apples and Cream

Prep time: less than 15 minutes   •   Minimum cooking time: 3 hours   •   Makes 4 servings

4 (1-inch-thick) pork chops (about 1½ lb.)	1 TB. fresh chopped sage or 1 tsp. dried
2 Granny Smith apples	2 TB. cornstarch
1 cup chicken stock	½ cup heavy cream
¼ cup dry white wine	Salt and black pepper to taste
2 TB. *Calvados*	2 cups cooked white or brown rice
2 TB. firmly packed light brown sugar	

Preheat the oven broiler, and line a broiler pan with aluminum foil. Brown chops for 3 to 5 minutes per side or until lightly browned. Transfer chops to the slow cooker, and pour in any juices that accumulated in the pan.

Peel and core apples. Cut each apple into 6 pieces. Place apples around pork chops into the slow cooker. Combine stock, wine, Calvados, brown sugar, and sage in a mixing bowl. Stir well to dissolve sugar. Pour the mixture over pork chops and apples. Cook on Low for 6 to 8 hours or on High for 3 to 4 hours or until pork chops are tender. If cooking on Low, raise the heat to High. Stir cornstarch into cream, and stir cornstarch mixture into the slow cooker. Cook for an additional 15 to 20 minutes or until the juices are bubbly and have thickened. Season with salt and pepper, and serve with white or brown rice.

Ellen on Edibles

Calvados is an apple brandy that is one of Normandy's culinary claims to fame. It's frequently bottled with a small apple in the bottom. Although it's expensive, it's well worth the money, even for cooking.

Cuban Pork Chops

Prep time: less than 15 minutes • Minimum cooking time: 3½ hours • Makes 4 servings

3 TB. vegetable oil

4 (8-oz.) boneless pork chops or 2 lb. boneless country pork ribs

2 large onions, peeled and thinly sliced

3 garlic cloves, peeled and minced

3 TB. grated fresh ginger

¾ cup chicken stock

⅓ cup cider vinegar

⅓ cup dark rum

⅓ cup firmly packed dark brown sugar

Salt and black pepper to taste

2 TB. cornstarch

2 TB. cold water

2 cups cooked white or brown rice

Heat oil in a large skillet over medium-high heat. Add pork chops, and brown them on both sides. Place pork chops in the slow cooker. Reduce the heat to medium. Add onion, garlic, and ginger. Cook and stir for 3 minutes or until onion is translucent. Arrange the mixture on top of pork chops.

Slow Savvy

Have you ever had brown sugar turn into a rock in the cupboard? Don't throw it out. Add a few slices of apple and close the bag securely. In a day or so, the sugar will have softened again. If you need to use some immediately, chip off some of the hard sugar and dissolve it in water.

Combine stock, vinegar, rum, and brown sugar in a small bowl. Stir well to dissolve sugar. Pour the liquid into the slow cooker. Cook on Low for 6 to 8 hours or on High for 3 to 4 hours or until chops are tender.

If cooking on Low, increase the temperature to High. Season with salt and pepper. Mix cornstarch with water in a small cup, and stir cornstarch mixture into the juices in the slow cooker. Cook for an additional 15 to 20 minutes or until the juices are bubbly and have thickened. Serve chops with white or brown rice.

Spicy Chinese Pork Ribs

Prep time: less than 15 minutes   •   Minimum cooking time: 3 hours   •   Makes 4 to 6 servings

3½ lb. meaty country pork ribs

1 cup water

5 TB. *Chinese preserved black beans*, coarsely chopped

10 garlic cloves, peeled and minced

2 TB. soy sauce

2 TB. sesame oil

1 TB. firmly packed dark brown sugar

2 TB. cornstarch

2 TB. cold water

½ to 1 tsp. red pepper flakes

2 cups steamed white rice

1 bunch scallions, trimmed and thinly sliced

Arrange pork ribs in the slow cooker. Combine water, black beans, garlic, soy sauce, oil, and brown sugar in a small bowl, and stir well. Pour the mixture over ribs.

Cook on Low for 6 to 8 hours or on High for 3 to 4 hours or until meat is tender. If cooking on Low, raise the heat to High. Mix cornstarch with cold water in a small cup, and stir cornstarch mixture into the slow cooker along with red pepper flakes. Cook for an additional 15 to 20 minutes or until the sauce is bubbly and thickened. Serve over white rice, and sprinkle each serving with some scallions.

Ellen on Edibles
Chinese preserved black **beans** are soybeans that have been packed in salt. They have a wonderful pungent and earthy flavor when they're used in dishes. They should be chopped but not rinsed because much of the flavor is in the salt.

Mexican Country Spareribs

Prep time: less than 15 minutes • Minimum cooking time: 3 hours • Makes 4 to 6 servings

3½ lb. meaty country pork ribs

½ cup chicken or beef stock

1 (14½-oz.) can diced tomatoes

1 (4-oz.) can diced mild green chilies

3 garlic cloves, peeled and minced

3 TB. tomato paste

2 TB. chili powder

1 TB. dried oregano

Salt and black pepper to taste

2 cups steamed white or brown rice

Cooker Caveats

Be careful when selecting canned chilies at the market. The cans of mild green chilies look almost exactly like the cans of chopped jalapeño chilies. A whole can of these hot peppers in any dish would be enough to make your mouth feel on fire.

Arrange pork ribs in the slow cooker. Combine stock, tomatoes, green chilies, garlic, tomato paste, chili powder, and oregano in a mixing bowl. Stir well and pour the mixture over ribs.

Cook on Low for 6 to 8 hours or on High for 3 to 4 hours or until meat is tender. Season with salt and pepper, and serve ribs over white or brown rice.

Swedish Meatballs

Prep time: less than 20 minutes   •   Minimum cooking time: 2 hours   •   Makes 4 to 6 servings

2 TB. butter

1 small onion, peeled and finely chopped

2 garlic cloves, peeled and minced

1 lb. ground pork

1 lb. ground veal or an additional 1 lb. ground pork

2 eggs, lightly beaten

¼ cup milk

½ cup plain breadcrumbs

¼ tsp. nutmeg

Salt and black pepper to taste

1 (12-oz.) can evaporated milk

½ cup beef or chicken stock

¼ cup chopped fresh dill or 1 TB. dried

1 TB. cornstarch

1 TB. cold water

2 cups buttered egg noodles

Preheat the oven to 500°F, line a baking sheet with aluminum foil, and spray the foil with vegetable oil spray. Melt butter in a small skillet over medium heat; add onion and garlic. Cook and stir for 3 minutes or until onion is translucent. Scrape the mixture into a mixing bowl. Add pork, veal, eggs, milk, breadcrumbs, nutmeg, salt, and pepper. Mix well and form heaping tablespoons of the mixture into meatballs. Place meatballs on the baking sheet, and brown them in the oven for 10 minutes or until lightly browned.

While meatballs are baking, combine evaporated milk, stock, and dill in the slow cooker and stir well. Transfer meatballs to the slow cooker with a slotted spoon.

Cook on Low for 4 to 6 hours or on High for 2 to 3 hours or until meatballs are cooked through. Then, if cooking on Low, raise the heat to High. Combine cornstarch and cold water in a small cup, and stir cornstarch mixture into the slow cooker. Cook for 10 to 15 minutes or until the liquid is bubbly and has thickened. Serve meatballs over buttered noodles.

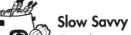

Slow Savvy

Oven-browning meatballs is a great trick to use for all meatball recipes. One of the pitfalls of meatballs is that they tend to fall apart when browned in a skillet, and this oven-browning method retains their shape. Another bonus is that you don't have a messy skillet to wash.

Ham Steaks with Italian Vegetables

Prep time: less than 15 minutes • Minimum cooking time: 3 hours • Makes 4 to 6 servings

3 TB. olive oil

2 onions, peeled and thinly sliced

3 garlic cloves, peeled and minced

1 green bell pepper, seeds and ribs removed, and thinly sliced

1 TB. *Italian seasoning* or herbes de Provence

2 lb. ham steaks, cut into serving pieces

1 (14½-oz.) can crushed tomatoes in tomato purée

2 TB. chopped fresh parsley

1 bay leaf

Salt and black pepper to taste

2 cups cooked small pasta, such as penne or shells

Ellen on Edibles

Italian seasoning is another great pre-mixed herb blend available in almost every market. It's a blend of marjoram, thyme, rosemary, savory, sage, oregano, and basil. If you don't have any, see what you've got from this list and make your own blend.

Heat olive oil in a medium skillet over medium heat; add onion, garlic, and green bell pepper. Cook and stir for 3 minutes or until onion is translucent. Stir in Italian seasoning, and cook for 1 minute, stirring constantly. Scrape the mixture into the slow cooker. Arrange ham slices over vegetables, and add tomatoes, parsley, and bay leaf.

Cook on Low for 6 to 8 hours or on High for 3 to 4 hours or until ham is tender. Discard bay leaf, and season with salt and pepper to taste. Serve ham steaks and vegetables with cooked pasta.

Madeira-Braised Ham Slices

Prep time: less than 15 minutes   •   Minimum cooking time: 3 hours   •   Makes 4 to 6 servings

2 TB. butter	½ cup raisins
1 onion, peeled and diced	½ tsp. ground cinnamon
2 garlic cloves, peeled and minced	½ tsp. dried thyme
1 small carrot, peeled and sliced	1 TB. cornstarch
2 lb. ham steaks, cut into serving pieces	2 TB. cold water
1 cup apple cider	2 cups buttered egg noodles or cooked white or brown rice
1 cup Madeira	

Heat butter in a medium skillet over medium heat; add onion, garlic, and carrot. Cook and stir for 3 minutes or until onion is translucent. Scrape the mixture into the slow cooker, and arrange ham slices on top of vegetables. Pour cider and Madeira into the slow cooker, and stir in raisins, cinnamon, and thyme.

Cook on Low for 6 to 8 hours or on High for 3 to 4 hours or until ham is tender. Then, if cooking on Low, raise the heat to High. Mix cornstarch and water, and stir cornstarch mixture into the slow cooker. Cook for 15 to 20 minutes or until the juices are bubbly and thickened. Serve ham steaks with buttered egg noodles.

Slow Savvy

Madeira is a wonderfully aromatic and flavorful wine from Portugal, but it's not as commonly used in cooking as other wines are. Dry Marsala or dry sherry are good substitutions.

Osso Buco alla Milanese (Veal Shanks Milanese-Style)

Prep time: less than 30 minutes • Minimum cooking time: 3 hours • Makes 6 servings

6 meaty veal shanks, about 2 inches thick

All-purpose flour for dredging

½ cup olive oil or as needed

4 TB. (½ stick) butter

4 large onions, peeled and diced

4 garlic cloves, peeled and minced

2 carrots, peeled and diced

2 celery stalks, peeled and diced

½ cup dry white wine

1 (14½-oz.) can crushed tomatoes in tomato purée

1 cup beef or chicken stock

1 TB. herbes de Provence or 1 tsp. dried thyme, 1 tsp. dried oregano, and 1 tsp. dried rosemary

1 bay leaf

Salt and black pepper to taste

Gremolata:

5 TB. chopped fresh parsley

2 TB. finely minced garlic

2 TB. grated lemon zest

1 TB. grated orange zest

3 cups cooked arborio rice or orzo

Rub veal shanks with flour, shaking off any extra over the sink or a plate. Heat ¼ cup oil in a large skillet over medium-high heat. Add as many veal shanks as will fit in a single layer, and brown them for 3 to 4 minutes per side or until lightly browned. Work in batches if necessary. Place shanks into the slow cooker.

Reduce the heat to medium, and add the remaining ¼ cup olive oil and butter. Add onion, garlic, carrots, and celery. Cook and stir for 3 minutes or until onion is translucent. Scrape the mixture into the slow cooker. Stir in wine, tomatoes, stock, herbes de Provence, and bay leaf.

> ### Crock Tales
> *Osso buco* has become synonymous with "veal shank" in this country as well as in Italy. Unlike lamb shanks, which are almost always braised whole, veal shanks are cut into crosswise slices. *Osso buco* means "pierced bone," and the marrow from the bone is considered such a delicacy that special marrow spoons are served with the dish.

Cook on Low for 7 to 8 hours or on High for 3 to 4 hours or until meat is very tender. Remove as much fat as possible from the surface of the slow cooker with a soup ladle. Discard bay leaf, and season with salt and pepper.

For the gremolata, combine parsley, garlic, lemon zest, and orange zest in a small mixing bowl. Serve veal shanks with a sprinkling of the gremolata. If desired, serve over rice or orzo.

Asian Veal Shanks

Prep time: less than 15 minutes • Minimum cooking time: 3½ hours • Makes 6 servings

6 meaty veal shanks

2 TB. sesame oil

4 scallions, trimmed and chopped

4 garlic cloves, peeled and minced

2 TB. grated fresh ginger

¾ cup beef or chicken stock

¾ cup dry sherry

¼ cup soy sauce

3 TB. chopped fresh cilantro

4 star anise pods

1 TB. *Szechwan peppercorns*

Red pepper flakes to taste

2 TB. cornstarch

2 TB. cold water

3 cups cooked white or brown rice

Preheat the oven broiler, and line a broiler pan with aluminum foil. Broil veal shanks for 3 to 5 minutes per side or until lightly browned. Arrange veal shanks in the slow cooker, and pour in any juices that have collected in the pan. Heat oil in a small skillet over medium heat; add scallions, garlic, and ginger. Cook and stir for 3 minutes or until the mixture is fragrant. Scrape the mixture into the slow cooker. Stir in stock, sherry, soy sauce, cilantro, star anise pods, and peppercorns.

Cook on Low for 7 to 8 hours or on High for 3 to 4 hours or until veal shanks are very tender. Remove veal shanks from the slow cooker with a slotted spatula and keep warm. Strain the sauce through a sieve, and discard the solids. Return the sauce to the slow cooker, and season it with red pepper flakes. Mix cornstarch with cold water, and stir cornstarch mixture into the slow cooker. Cook on High for 20 to 30 minutes or until the sauce is bubbly and thickened. Return veal shanks to the slow cooker to reheat, if necessary. Serve shanks over rice.

Ellen on Edibles

Szechwan peppercorns are a cousin of the Western black, white, and green peppercorns. They come from a prickly ash tree, are mildly hot, and have a distinctive flavor and aroma.

Chapter 15

Global Comfort Foods

In This Chapter

- Easy recipes for entertaining
- One-dish meals
- Traditional foods from many cultures

One-dish dinners are common to all the world's cuisines, and many of them are related by the way people moved around the world. There's a strong relationship between the jambalaya eaten in Louisiana and Spain's paella. It was the Spanish who brought the concept to the New World, after all.

What unites the recipes in this chapter is the fact that they are all quintessential comfort foods. And the slow cooker is a great tool for cooking these dishes. The low heat cooks them gently, so you don't have to worry that the bottom of the pot is burning before what's on top is done.

Steps to Success

Many of the recipes in this chapter are easy to prepare if you're going to be gone for the whole day because all the ingredients cook at the same rate in the same time. But there are some others that need a bit more tending to. Some need rice added before the end of the cooking because the rice cooks faster than the chicken, while others need a topping that requires time to cook.

Cooking Strategies

If foods have to be added sequentially, one part of the recipe always represents the bulk of the cooking time. You can do that part one day (or in the morning), then finish the dish the next day (or in the evening). Reheat the first day's cooked foods on the stove or in a microwave before continuing with the rest of the recipe.

Layering the Toppings

The Greeks are famous for making casseroles with custard toppings. These dishes are easy to do in the slow cooker. The key is to level the mixture that's cooking in the slow cooker so the custard topping cooks level and evenly. Before you add the custard topping, try to remove as much grease as possible from the under layer.

The Least You Need to Know

- Pasta should always be cooked before adding it to the slow cooker.
- Many cultures around the world enjoy one-dish meals that combine rice with a variety of meats and seafood.
- The rice used in slow cooked recipes should be converted long-grain rice.
- Some one-dish meals have to be cooked in stages because either there are ingredients that need less cooking time or there is a custard topping that cooks for a short amount of time.

Chicken Jambalaya

Prep time: less than 30 minutes • Minimum cooking time: 3½ to 4½ hours • Makes 6 to 8 servings

1 (3- to 4-lb.) chicken, cut into serving pieces, with breasts cut into 2 sections, or 6 to 8 chicken pieces of your choice (breasts, thighs, legs) with bones, rinsed and patted dry with paper towels

½ lb. kielbasa, or other smoked sausage, cut into ½-inch slices

3 TB. olive oil

2 celery stalks, chopped

1 onion, peeled and diced

½ green bell pepper, seeds and ribs removed, and diced

4 garlic cloves, peeled and minced

1 (14½-oz.) can diced tomatoes

1½ cups chicken stock

1 TB. fresh thyme or 1 tsp. dried

1 bay leaf

2 (5-oz.) pkg. yellow rice

½ lb. raw shrimp, peeled and deveined

Salt and black pepper to taste

Preheat the oven broiler, and line a broiler pan with aluminum foil. Broil chicken for 3 to 4 minutes or until lightly browned. Turn chicken pieces with tongs, add sausage to the broiler pan, and broil for an additional 3 to 4 minutes. Set aside.

Heat oil in a medium skillet over medium heat; add celery, onion, green bell pepper, and garlic. Cook and stir for 3 minutes or until onion is translucent. Scrape the mixture into the slow cooker, and stir in tomatoes, stock, thyme, and bay leaf. Arrange chicken pieces and sausage in the slow cooker. Cook on Low for 6 to 8 hours or on High for 3 to 4 hours or until chicken is cooked through, tender, and no longer pink.

Then, if cooking on Low, raise the heat to High. Stir in rice, and cook on High for 20 to 30 minutes or until rice is almost soft. Add shrimp, and cook on High for an additional 10 to 15 minutes or until shrimp are pink. Discard bay leaf, and season jambalaya with salt and pepper.

Crock Tales

Jambalaya is a staple of Louisiana cooking, where culinary traditions of France, Spain, Italy, the New World, and other cultures blended. Jambalaya was the local adaptation of the Spanish rice dish paella and became a favorite among the Cajuns, French transplants who settled in the Louisiana bayous. Some say the name of the dish comes from *jamon*, which is Spanish for "ham." Others say it is from *jambon*, the French word for "ham." Either way, ham, sausage, chicken, seafood, and rice are all included in contemporary versions of jambalaya.

Arroz con Pollo (Mexican Chicken and Rice)

Prep time: less than 20 minutes   •   Minimum cooking time: 4 hours   •   Makes 4 to 6 servings

1 (3- to 4-lb.) chicken, cut into serving pieces, rinsed and patted dry with paper towels

⅓ cup olive oil

1 large onion, peeled and diced

4 garlic cloves, peeled and minced

½ green or red bell pepper, seeds and ribs removed, and diced

1 TB. paprika

1 TB. chili powder or to taste

2 tsp. dried oregano

1 cup uncooked converted long-grain rice

1 (14½-oz.) can diced tomatoes

½ cup dry white wine

½ cup chicken stock

1 bay leaf

½ cup sliced pimiento-stuffed green olives

1 cup frozen peas, thawed

Salt and black pepper to taste

Preheat the oven broiler, and line a broiler pan with aluminum foil. Place chicken pieces into the pan, and brown them for 3 to 5 minutes per side or until lightly browned, turning the pieces with tongs. Arrange chicken pieces in the slow cooker.

Heat 2 tablespoons oil in a medium skillet over medium heat; add onion, garlic, and green or red bell pepper. Cook and stir for 3 minutes or until onion is translucent. Add paprika, chili powder, and oregano. Cook for 1 minute, stirring constantly. Scrape the mixture into the slow cooker. Add remaining oil to the skillet. Cook rice for 3 to 4 minutes, stirring frequently, or until grains are opaque and lightly browned. Remove the pan from the heat and set aside.

![Cooker Caveats] **Cooker Caveats**

It's important for the success of this dish and other dishes that include rice that you use long-grain converted rice such as Uncle Ben's. A shorter-grain rice will turn to mush. Converted white rice has undergone a steam-pressure process that makes the grains fluffier and keep separate when cooked.

Add tomatoes, wine, stock, and bay leaf to the slow cooker. Cook on Low for 4 to 6 hours or on High for 2 to 3 hours or until chicken is cooked through. Then, if cooking on Low, raise the heat to High. Add rice to the slow cooker. Cook for 1 hour or until rice is almost tender and chicken is no longer pink. Add olives and peas to the slow cooker. Cook for 10 to 15 minutes or until peas are hot. Discard bay leaf, and season with salt and pepper.

Party Paella

Prep time: less than 20 minutes • Minimum cooking time: 2½ hours • Makes 6 to 8 servings

2 TB. olive oil

1 onion, peeled and diced

3 garlic cloves, peeled and minced

½ red or green bell pepper, seeds and ribs removed, and cut into ½-inch dice

3 boneless, skinless chicken breast halves, cut into 1-inch cubes

½ lb. smoked ham, cut into ½-inch dice

2 cups long-grain converted rice

4 cups chicken stock

1 tsp. dried oregano

1 tsp. dried thyme

1 bay leaf

½ tsp. crushed saffron threads

Salt and black pepper to taste

1 cup frozen peas, thawed

¾ lb. medium shrimp, peeled and deveined

Heat oil in a medium skillet over medium heat; add onion, garlic, and red or green bell pepper. Cook and stir for 3 minutes or until onion is translucent. Scrape the mixture into the slow cooker. Add chicken, ham, rice, stock, oregano, thyme, bay leaf, and saffron to the slow cooker. Stir well.

Cook on Low for 4 to 6 hours or on High for 2 to 3 hours or until rice is almost tender. Then, if cooking on Low, raise the heat to High. Season the mixture with salt and pepper, discard bay leaf, and stir in peas and shrimp. Cook for an additional 30 to 45 minutes or until shrimp are pink.

Crock Tales

If you want to win a trivia contest, know that, ounce-for-ounce, saffron is the most expensive food in the world. All the individual threads are harvested by hand from the purple crocus. Saffron was once used not only for cooking but also in making medicines and dyeing cloth that characteristic yellow color.

Pastitsio (Greek Beef and Pasta)

Prep time: less than 30 minutes • Minimum cooking time: 4½ hours • Makes 4 to 6 servings

Meat layer:

2 TB. vegetable oil

1 large onion, peeled and diced

3 garlic cloves, peeled and minced

1 lb. lean ground beef or lamb

1 (28-oz.) can diced tomatoes

2 TB. tomato paste

1 TB. dried oregano

1 TB. dried basil

2 tsp. dried sage

½ tsp. ground cinnamon

Topping:

3 TB. butter

3 TB. all-purpose flour

2 cups whole milk

½ cup grated Parmesan cheese

2 eggs, lightly beaten

Salt and black pepper to taste

2 cups cooked small pasta, such as macaroni or small shells

Heat oil in a medium skillet over medium heat; add onion and garlic. Cook and stir for 3 minutes or until onion is translucent. Scrape the mixture into the slow cooker, and return the pan to the stove. Add ground beef to the pan, breaking up any lumps with a fork. Brown beef for 3 to 5 minutes. Remove beef from the pan with a slotted spoon, and add it to the slow cooker.

Stir tomatoes, tomato paste, oregano, basil, sage, and cinnamon into the slow cooker. Cook on Low for 6 to 7 hours or on High for 3 to 4 hours or until beef is cooked.

Slow Savvy

You'll find that liquid accumulates on top of custard mixtures as they set. This is natural when cooking a topping in the slow cooker. The good news is that the low temperature leads to a silky, creamy custard. To remove the accumulated liquid, gently spoon it off before serving the dish.

While the mixture is cooking, prepare the topping. Melt butter in a small saucepan over low heat. Stir in flour; cook and stir for 3 minutes to cook flour. Raise the heat to medium, and whisk in milk. Bring the mixture to a boil, stirring frequently. Add Parmesan cheese, and stir to melt it into the topping. Remove the pan from the heat, and whisk for 1 minute. Add eggs to the topping, and whisk it well. Season the topping with salt and pepper.

When beef is cooked, if cooking on Low, raise the heat to High. Stir cooked pasta into beef mixture, and season it with salt and pepper. Pour the topping evenly over beef mixture. Cook on High for 1 to 1½ hours or until the mixture is bubbly around the sides and the topping is firm in the center.

Moussaka

Prep time: less than 30 minutes   •   Minimum cooking time: 4 hours   •   Makes 4 to 6 servings

Meat:

1 (1-lb.) *eggplant*, peeled and cut into 1-inch cubes

Salt

⅓ cup olive oil

1 onion, peeled and diced

2 garlic cloves, peeled and minced

1 cup lean ground lamb or beef

⅓ cup dry red wine

1 (8-oz.) can tomato sauce

2 TB. chopped fresh parsley

1 tsp. dried oregano

¼ tsp. ground cinnamon

Topping:

2 TB. butter

2 TB. all-purpose flour

1 cup milk

2 eggs, lightly beaten

¼ cup grated Parmesan cheese

1 TB. chopped fresh dill or 1 tsp. dried

Salt and black pepper to taste

Place eggplant into a colander, and sprinkle it liberally with salt. Place a plate on top of eggplant, and weight it with cans. Let eggplant sit for 30 minutes, then rinse it well, and dry it with paper towels. Heat half the oil in a large skillet over medium heat; add eggplant cubes. Cook and stir for 5 minutes or until eggplant begins to soften. Transfer eggplant to the slow cooker.

Heat remaining oil in the skillet; add onion and garlic. Cook and stir for 3 minutes or until onion is translucent. Scrape the mixture into the slow cooker. Place lamb into the skillet. Brown lamb for 3 to 5 minutes, breaking up any lumps with a fork. Transfer lamb to the slow cooker with a slotted spoon. Stir in wine, tomato sauce, parsley, oregano, and cinnamon. Stir well. Cook on Low for 5 to 7 hours or on High for 2½ to 3 hours or until eggplant is tender.

While the mixture is cooking, prepare the topping. Heat butter in a small saucepan over low heat. Stir in flour and cook for 2 minutes, stirring constantly. Gradually add milk, whisking constantly. Bring the mixture to a boil, and remove the pan from the heat. Stir in eggs, cheese, and dill. Stir well and season with salt and pepper.

When the meat is cooked, if cooking on Low, raise the heat to High. Level meat filling, and pour the topping evenly over the top. Cook for 1 to 1½ hours until custard is set.

Ellen on Edibles

Like tomatoes, **eggplants** are classified as fruits in botany, but we treat them as vegetables. Eggplants have male and female gender, and the males are preferable because they are less bitter and have fewer seeds. To tell a male from a female, look at the nonstem end. The male is rounded and has a more even hole; the female hole is indented.

Tamale Casserole

Prep time: less than 15 minutes • Minimum cooking time: 3½ hours • Makes 4 to 6 servings

2 TB. olive oil	1 cup whole milk
1 onion, peeled and diced	¾ cup yellow cornmeal
2 garlic cloves, peeled and diced	1 cup chunky tomato salsa, plus additional for garnish
1 TB. chili powder	1 (10-oz.) box frozen corn, thawed
1 tsp. ground cumin	Salt and black pepper to taste
1 lb. lean ground beef	1 cup grated Cheddar cheese
1 egg, lightly beaten	

Heat olive oil in a medium skillet over medium heat; add onion and garlic. Cook and stir for 3 minutes or until onion is translucent. Stir in chili powder and cumin. Cook for 1 minute, stirring constantly. Scrape the mixture into a mixing bowl. Add ground beef to the skillet. Brown meat for 5 to 7 minutes, breaking up any lumps with a fork. Transfer meat to the mixing bowl with a slotted spoon.

Stir egg, milk, cornmeal, salsa, and corn. Season the mixture with salt and pepper. Line the bottom and sides of the slow cooker with aluminum foil, and grease the foil with vegetable oil spray or vegetable oil. Scrape the mixture into the slow cooker. Cook on High for 3 to 4 hours or until the mixture is solid. Sprinkle cheese on top of the pie, and cook for an additional 10 to 15 minutes or until cheese is melted. Remove the dish from the slow cooker by pulling up on the foil. Cut the casserole into wedges, and pass extra salsa separately.

Crock Tales

Authentic tamales date back to the Aztecs, and they are still served in both Mexico and the American Southwest. The tradition is to serve them on Sunday nights and as a ceremonial food on All Saint's Day. Real tamales are bits of food surrounded by a cornmeal mush and steamed in individual cornhusks. This casserole incorporates all the same elements without the husks.

Sweet and Sour Stuffed Cabbage

Prep time: less than 30 minutes   •   Minimum cooking time: 5 to 6 hours   •   Makes 4 to 6 servings

1 small head (about 1 lb.) green cabbage	2 McIntosh or Rome apples, peeled and diced
1½ lb. lean ground beef	½ cup raisins
1 cup cooked white rice	1 (8-oz.) can tomato sauce
1 small onion, peeled and grated	½ cup cider vinegar
Salt and black pepper to taste	½ cup firmly packed dark brown sugar

Bring a 4-quart saucepan of water to a boil. Remove the core from cabbage by cutting around it with a sharp knife. Pull off 10 to 12 large leaves from the outside and set aside. Cut remaining cabbage in half, and cut off 2 cups thin shreds. *Blanch* the leaves and shreds in the boiling water for 5 minutes and then drain. Combine ground beef, rice, onion, salt, and pepper in a mixing bowl. Mix well.

Place half the drained cabbage shreds into the bottom of the slow cooker. Top with half the apples and half the raisins. Place ¼ cup beef mixture at the root end of a cabbage leaf. Tuck in the sides, and roll up the leaf into a cylinder. Repeat for the remaining cabbage leaves and beef filling. Place the rolls seam side down in the slow cooker in a single layer. Top with the remaining cabbage shreds, apple, and raisins, and start a new layer of cabbage rolls. Mix tomato sauce, vinegar, and brown sugar in a mixing bowl. Stir well to dissolve sugar. Pour the sauce over cabbage rolls. Cook on Low for 10 to 12 hours or on High for 5 to 6 hours or until the sauce is bubbly and an instant-read thermometer inserted into beef filling reads 165°F.

Ellen on Edibles _____

Blanch literally means "to whiten," but that's not how the word is used in cooking. In the kitchen it means "to boil for a short period of time." Foods such as peaches and tomatoes are blanched to loosen the skins so you can peel them more easily, and foods like cabbage are blanched to make them milder and to soften them so they're easier to roll. Green vegetables are often blanched to set their color.

Spaghetti with Meat Sauce

Prep time: less than 20 minutes   •   Minimum cooking time: 4 to 5 hours   •   Makes 6 to 8 servings

¼ cup olive oil

1 large onion, peeled and diced

6 garlic cloves, peeled and minced

½ lb. white mushrooms, rinsed, stemmed, and sliced

1½ lb. lean ground beef or some combination of beef and Italian sausage

2 TB. dried oregano

1 TB. dried basil

1 TB. granulated sugar

2 tsp. dried thyme

1 bay leaf

3 (14½-oz.) cans diced tomatoes

1 (8-oz.) can tomato sauce

½ cup dry red wine

Salt and black pepper or red pepper flakes to taste

4 to 6 cups cooked spaghetti or other cooked pasta

Heat oil in a large skillet over medium heat. Add onion, garlic, and mushrooms. Cook and stir for 3 to 5 minutes or until onion is translucent and mushrooms are soft. Scrape the mixture into the slow cooker. Place meat into the skillet, and break up any lumps with a fork. Brown meat for 3 to 5 minutes, stirring occasionally. Remove meat from the skillet with a slotted spoon, and place it in the slow cooker.

Add oregano, basil, sugar, thyme, bay leaf, tomatoes, tomato sauce, and wine to the slow cooker and stir well. Cook on Low for 8 to 10 hours or on High for 4 to 5 hours. Discard bay leaf, and season the sauce with salt and pepper. Serve the sauce over cooked spaghetti.

Slow Savvy

It's easy to personalize this dish to your own taste. You can use a proportion of mild or hot Italian sausage in place of some of the ground beef. Or you can transform it into spaghetti with meatballs instead of meat sauce. Form the meat into balls and brown them in a 500°F oven for 10 minutes. Then drop them into the liquid in the slow cooker.

Tsimmis
(Eastern European Beef and Carrots with Dried Fruits)

Prep time: less than 15 minutes • Minimum cooking time: 5 hours • Makes 6 to 8 servings

2 lb. boneless short ribs or chuck roast, cut into 2-inch cubes

1½ lb. carrots, peeled and cut into ½-inch slices

1½ lb. sweet potatoes, peeled and cut into 1-inch cubes

1 large onion, peeled and diced

1 cup dried apricots

1 cup pitted prunes

1 cup apple cider

1 cup beef stock

½ tsp. grated nutmeg

½ to 1 tsp. ground cinnamon

Salt and black pepper to taste

Preheat the oven broiler, and line a broiler pan with aluminum foil. Brown short ribs for 3 to 5 minutes per side or until lightly browned. Transfer beef to the slow cooker. Add carrots, sweet potatoes, onion, apricots, and prunes to the slow cooker. Combine cider, stock, nutmeg, and cinnamon in a mixing bowl, and pour the liquid into the slow cooker.

Cook on Low for 10 to 12 hours or on High for 5 to 6 hours or until carrots and beef are very tender. Season with salt and pepper to taste.

Crock Tales

Tsimmis is a traditional dish served by Eastern European Jews, and its name also has slang meaning in Yiddish: "What's the big tsimmis" means "What's the big deal?"

Corned Beef and Cabbage

Prep time: less than 15 minutes • Minimum cooking time: 5 to 6 hours • Makes 4 to 6 servings

1 (2½- to 3-lb.) corned beef brisket

1 onion, peeled and sliced

1 celery stalk, sliced

1 carrot, peeled and sliced

4 garlic cloves, peeled and minced

1 bay leaf

½ small green cabbage

Cut off as much fat as possible from the top of corned beef. Rinse and set aside. Place onion, celery, carrot, garlic, and bay leaf into the slow cooker. Place corned beef on top of vegetables. Add enough water to come halfway up the side of corned beef.

Cut cabbage in half. Cut the core from one half, and slice the half into wedges. Arrange wedges on top of corned beef. Cook on Low for 10 to 12 hours or on High for 5 to 6 hours or until corned beef is tender. Discard bay leaf, and thinly slice corned beef. Serve it with cabbage and other vegetables.

Cooker Caveats

Corned beef is cured in salt, so no additional salt should ever be added when cooking it. There is sufficient salt in the brisket to season all the vegetables in the slow cooker as well. As curing is not really necessary for preserving the meat anymore, there are many reduced-sodium brands of corned beef on the market today. They're a good bet for any corned beef dish.

New England Boiled Dinner

Prep time: less than 20 minutes • Minimum cooking time: 6 hours • Makes 6 to 8 servings

3 large red-skinned potatoes, scrubbed, and each cut into 8 pieces

2 carrots, peeled and cut into 1-inch pieces

2 onions, peeled and quartered

1 (3- to 4-lb.) flat-cut corned beef, trimmed of all visible fat

½ small head green cabbage, cored and cut into thin wedges

2 cups chicken stock

1 cup dry white wine

1 TB. fresh thyme or 1 tsp. dried

1 bay leaf

Black pepper to taste

Dijon mustard

Arrange potatoes, carrots, and onions in the bottom of the slow cooker. Place corned beef on top of vegetables, and arrange cabbage on top of corned beef. Add stock, wine, thyme, and bay leaf to the slow cooker. Do not worry if cabbage is not covered; it will become tender from the steam.

Cook on Low for 12 to 14 hours or on High for 6 to 7 hours or until meat and vegetables are very tender. Arrange vegetables on a platter, and slice corned beef into thin slices against the grain. Season with pepper, and pass a dish of mustard on the side.

Slow Savvy

It's easy to turn any leftovers from this recipe into corned beef hash. Sauté some onions and green pepper; then chop the corned beef and potatoes. Mix it all together, and you've got hash.

Macaroni and Cheese with Diced Ham

Prep time: less than 20 minutes • Minimum cooking time: 1½ hours • Makes 4 to 6 servings

½ lb. macaroni, cooked al dente according to package directions

¾ lb. (about 3 cups) grated sharp cheddar cheese

1 (12-oz.) can evaporated milk

1½ cups whole milk

1 tsp. dry mustard

1 lb. ham steak, cut into ½-inch cubes

Salt and black pepper to taste

Grease the inside of the slow cooker liberally with vegetable oil spray or melted butter. Combine macaroni, cheese, evaporated milk, milk, mustard, ham, salt, and pepper in the slow cooker. Cook on Low 3 to 4 hours or on High for 1½ to 2 hours or until the mixture is hot and bubbly.

Slow Savvy

Macaroni and cheese is one dish that is so easy to personalize and make many ways. Any small pasta can take the place of the macaroni. Any semi-hard cheese, like Swiss or Gruyère, can be used instead of cheddar. You can omit the mustard and add some fresh or dried herbs, too.

Cassoulet

Prep time: less than 30 minutes • Minimum cooking time: 5½ hours • Makes 6 to 8 servings

1 lb. flageolet or other small beans such as navy beans	1 TB. herbes de Provence or 1 tsp. dried thyme and 1 tsp. dried rosemary
2 TB. olive oil	1 bay leaf
2 large onions, peeled and diced	1½ lb. stewing lamb, cut into 1-inch cubes
5 garlic cloves, peeled and minced	1 lb. kielbasa or other smoked pork sausage, cut into ½-inch slices
2 cups chicken stock	
1 cup dry white wine	2 duck legs from Duck Confit (recipe in Chapter 12), skinned, boned, and diced or ½ lb. roasted duck, boned and diced
1 (14½-oz.) can diced tomatoes	
3 TB. tomato paste	Salt and black pepper to taste

Rinse beans in a colander, and place them into a mixing bowl covered with cold water. Allow beans to soak overnight. Or place beans into a saucepan, and bring to a boil over high heat. Boil 1 minute. Turn off the heat, cover the pan, and soak beans for 1 hour. Drain beans; discard the soaking water, and place beans in the slow cooker.

Heat oil in a medium skillet over medium heat; add onion and garlic. Cook and stir for 3 minutes or until onion is translucent. Scrape the mixture into the slow cooker. Stir in stock, wine, tomatoes, tomato paste, herbes de Provence, and bay leaf. Cook bean mixture for 4 hours on Low or 2 hours on High.

Preheat the oven broiler, and line a broiler pan with aluminum foil. Broil lamb and kielbasa for 3 minutes per side or until browned. Stir meats into the slow cooker along with any juices that have collected in the pan. Cook for 5 to 7 hours on Low or 3 to 4 hours on High or until lamb is tender. Stir duck meat into the slow cooker. Cook for an additional 15 to 20 minutes or until duck is hot. Discard bay leaf, and season with salt and pepper.

Crock Tales

Cassoulet goes back centuries and is one of the culinary triumphs of southwest France, with most authorities citing Castelnaudary in the Languedoc province as its birthplace. Beans and a variety of meats are always part of the dish, but there are many versions. Duck or goose confit (in which the meat is cured in its own fat) is a traditional ingredient, because confit is popular in southwestern France. Other traditional ingredients, such mutton, partridge, various cuts of pork and sausages, are a matter of regional debate.

Choucroute Garnie
(Alsatian Sauerkraut and Meats)

Prep time: less than 30 minutes   •   Minimum cooking time: 4 to 5 hours   •   Makes 6 to 8 servings

3 lb. sauerkraut

1 large onion, peeled and thinly sliced

1 carrot, peeled and thinly sliced

1 cup dry white wine

¼ cup gin (or 10 whole juniper berries)

1 cup beef stock

1 bay leaf

1½ lb. smoked pork butt, cut into 1-inch cubes

½ lb. kielbasa or other smoked sausage, cut into ½-inch slices

Salt and black pepper to taste

Cooker Caveats

One step you really don't want to bypass in this recipe is soaking the sauerkraut. Once it's been soaked, the pickled cabbage retains some lip-pursing flavor, but it's quite mild. If you don't soak it, your dish will taste like a pickle that's been heated.

Drain sauerkraut in a colander. Place sauerkraut into a large mixing bowl of cold water for 10 minutes. Drain and repeat the soaking. Press out as much water as possible from sauerkraut, and place it into the slow cooker.

Add onion, carrot, wine, gin, stock, and bay leaf to the slow cooker. Mix well. Add pork and kielbasa. Press the pieces down into sauerkraut. Cook on Low for 8 to 10 hours or on High for 4 to 5 hours or until meats are very tender. Discard bay leaf, and season the dish with salt and pepper.

Chapter 16

Brightening Breakfast and Brunch

In This Chapter

- ◆ Savory bread puddings for bountiful brunches
- ◆ Egg dishes to feed a crowd
- ◆ Creamy hot cereals for nourishing breakfasts

Are you one of the people who shies away from inviting people for brunch because you think it's too much work early in the day? Or do you picture yourself endlessly cooking eggs? If so, you're not alone. I used to be one of you.

The slow cooker can change all that. Many of the dishes in this chapter can be prepared ready to cook the day before, and they cook while you're setting the table.

Egg-Cetera

The slow cooker is very successful with egg dishes because eggs need to cook at a low temperature to remain tender. The protein in an egg becomes hard at 165°F, which is just about what the slow cooker heats to on Low. Eggs should be cooked to that temperature to make them totally safe and bacteria-free.

The scientific reality is that if eggs are cooked at a high temperature, they toughen. That might be the objective if you're making fried eggs, because you need them to be hard enough that you can flip them in the pan without breaking them. But the recipes in this chapter are tender egg dishes, and the slow cooker treats them kindly.

Options from Other Chapters

Brunch is a cross between breakfast and brunch, and depending on your emphasis, you can find other appropriate dishes in this book. In Chapter 20, there are some wonderful potato, sweet potato, and grain recipes that are appropriate at any time of day. If you want more of a lunch than a breakfast, look at some of the one-dish meals in Chapter 15. And the desserts in Chapters 22 and 23 contain many homey dishes that are good for breakfast or brunch.

The Least You Need to Know

- A strata is a savory bread pudding that has eggs and cheese along with other ingredients. It can be prepared in a slow cooker as a breakfast or brunch dish.
- A frittata is an Italian omelet that is cooked until set, then served in wedges.
- Eggs should be cooked at a low temperature so they don't become tough. The slow cooker is an excellent egg cooker.
- Even oatmeal can be made in the slow cooker.

Scrambled Eggs for a Crowd

Prep time: less than 15 minutes   •   Minimum cooking time: 2 hours   •   Makes 12 to 18 servings

3 dz. eggs

1 cup sour cream

Salt and black pepper to taste

Grease the inside of the slow cooker liberally with vegetable oil spray or melted butter. Whisk eggs with sour cream, and season eggs with salt and pepper. Pour the mixture into the slow cooker.

Cook on Low for 2 to 4 hours or until eggs are set. Stir eggs after 1¹/₂ hours of cooking to break up the cooked egg portion.

Slow Savvy _____
If you're making a small amount of scrambled eggs, modify this preparation method. Melt some butter in a skillet over low heat, add the beaten eggs, and cover the pan. Cook until the eggs begin to puff, stir, and turn off the heat.

Creamy Oatmeal with Dried Fruit

Prep time: less than 15 minutes   •   Minimum cooking time: 2½ hours   •   Makes 6 to 8 servings

2 cups old-fashioned rolled oats or Irish steel-cut oats

1 (12-oz.) can evaporated milk

1½ cups apple juice

¼ cup pure maple syrup

¼ cup chopped dried apricots

¼ cup dried cranberries

¼ cup raisins

¾ tsp. ground cinnamon

½ tsp. salt

Grease the slow cooker with vegetable oil spray or melted butter, and add oats, evaporated milk, apple juice, maple syrup, apricots, cranberries, raisins, cinnamon, and salt. Stir well.

Cook on Low for 5 to 7 hours or on High for 2¹/₂ to 3 hours until oatmeal is soft and the mixture is creamy, stirring halfway through the cooking time.

Cooker Caveats _____
It's important to use old-fashioned rolled oats or Irish steel-cut oats for this recipe. Quick-cooking or instant oats will turn into mush with no texture.

Spinach and Cheese Strata

Prep time: less than 15 minutes • Minimum cooking time: 4 hours • Makes 4 to 6 servings

3 TB. butter

1 onion, peeled and diced

6 eggs, lightly beaten

2 cups whole milk

1 TB. herbes de Provence or 1 tsp. dried thyme, 1 tsp. dried rosemary, and 1 tsp. dried basil

Salt and black pepper to taste

⅔ lb. loaf white bread, broken into small pieces

1 (10-oz.) box frozen chopped spinach, thawed

1½ cups grated mozzarella cheese

Heat butter in a small skillet over medium heat; add onion. Cook and stir for 3 minutes or until onion is translucent. Remove the pan from the heat and set aside.

Ellen on Edibles

Strata is a fancy name for a savory bread pudding. The only constants are bread, eggs, and some sort of cheese. There are a few strata recipes in this chapter, but you can also use your imagination and include any fillings you'd put in an omelet.

Grease the inside of the slow cooker liberally with vegetable oil spray or melted butter. Combine eggs, milk, herbes de Provence, salt, and pepper in a large mixing bowl. Whisk well. Place bread pieces into the bowl. Stir so bread absorbs egg mixture. Place spinach into a sieve and press with the back of a spoon to extract as much liquid as possible. Add onion, spinach, and cheese to bread mixture and stir well. Transfer the mixture to a slow cooker.

Cook on Low for 4 to 6 hours or until the mixture is puffed and a thermometer inserted in the center reads 165°F.

Nantucket Strata

Prep time: less than 15 minutes • Minimum cooking time: 4 hours • Makes 6 to 8 servings

12 slices good-quality white bread	½ lb. lobster meat, cut into ½-inch dice
4 TB. (½ stick) butter, softened	2 cups whole milk
½ red bell pepper, seeds and ribs removed, finely chopped	6 eggs
3 scallions, trimmed and chopped	Salt and black pepper to taste
¼ lb. bulk linguiça or chorizo sausage	1 cup grated Swiss cheese

Toast bread and spread the slices with 2 tablespoons butter. Cut bread into 1-inch-wide strips and set aside.

Melt remaining 2 tablespoons butter in a skillet over medium heat; add red bell pepper and scallions. Cook, stirring, for 3 minutes or until scallions are soft. Scrape the mixture into a mixing bowl. Add sausage to the skillet, breaking it up with a fork. Cook and stir for 5 minutes or until sausage is browned. Remove sausage from the skillet with a slotted spoon, add it to vegetables, then add lobster.

Grease the inside of the slow cooker liberally with vegetable oil spray or melted butter. Whisk milk and eggs together, and add salt and pepper to taste. Arrange half the bread slices in the slow cooker, and sprinkle with half the sausage-lobster mixture and half the cheese. Repeat with remaining bread, lobster, and cheese, then pour egg mixture over the top. Refrigerate the strata for at least 2 hours, preferably overnight.

Cook on Low for 4 to 6 hours or until the mixture is puffed and a thermometer inserted in the center reads 165°F.

Slow Savvy

The best place to store eggs is in their cardboard carton. The carton helps prevent moisture loss, and it shields the eggs from absorbing odors from other foods. If you're not sure if your eggs are fresh, submerge them in a bowl of cool water. If they stay on the bottom, they're fine. If they float to the top, it shows they're old because eggs develop an air pocket at one end as they age.

Spanish Frittata

Prep time: less than 30 minutes • Minimum cooking time: 2 hours • Makes 4 to 6 servings

2 TB. olive oil

1 large potato, peeled and cut into ½-inch dice or 1 cup frozen hash brown potatoes, thawed

1 red bell pepper, seeds and ribs removed, thinly sliced

1 sweet onion, such as Vidalia or Bermuda, peeled and thinly sliced

2 garlic cloves, peeled and minced

1 TB. fresh thyme or 1 tsp. dried

Salt and black pepper to taste

8 eggs

¼ cup grated Parmesan cheese

¼ cup shredded mozzarella cheese

Heat oil in a skillet over medium-high heat. Add potatoes and brown them well. Reduce the heat to medium; add red bell pepper, onion, garlic, and thyme to the pan. Cook and stir for 3 minutes or until onion is translucent. Reduce the heat to low, cover the pan, and cook vegetable mixture for 15 minutes or until vegetables are tender. Season vegetables with salt and pepper, and let them cool for 10 minutes.

Whisk eggs well, stir in Parmesan and mozzarella cheeses, and season with salt and pepper. Stir cooled vegetable mixture into eggs.

Grease the inside of the slow cooker liberally with vegetable oil spray or melted butter. Pour egg mixture into the slow cooker. Cook on High for 1½ to 2 hours or until eggs are set. Run a spatula around the sides of the slow cooker and under the bottom of the frittata to release it. Slide it gently onto a serving platter, and cut it into wedges. Serve hot or at room temperature.

Crock Tales

A frittata is basically a solid Italian omelet. While we bake frittatas, Italians fry them. The Italian word *frittata* is derived from the Latin *frigere*, which means "to fry." In Spain, the same dish is called a "tortilla," which bears no relationship to the thin corn or wheat pancakes eaten in Mexico and Central America.

Vegetable Frittata with Pasta

Prep time: less than 20 minutes • Minimum cooking time: 1½ hours • Makes 4 to 6 servings

1 (6-oz.) pkg. refrigerated fresh angel-hair pasta

3 TB. olive oil

2 small zucchini, trimmed and thinly sliced

4 scallions, trimmed and thinly sliced

3 garlic cloves, peeled and minced

2 tomatoes, cored, seeded, and finely chopped

3 TB. chopped fresh basil or 1 tsp. dried

1 TB. chopped fresh oregano or 1 tsp. dried

¼ cup sliced green olives

Salt and black pepper to taste

6 eggs

½ cup grated Parmesan cheese

Cook pasta according to package directions until al dente. Drain and set aside to cool.

Heat oil in a large skillet over medium heat; add zucchini, scallions, and garlic. Cook and stir for 3 to 5 minutes, stirring constantly, until zucchini is tender. Add tomatoes, basil, oregano, and olives. Cook the mixture for 5 minutes or until the liquid from tomatoes has evaporated. Season with salt and pepper, and cool for 10 minutes.

Grease the inside of the slow cooker liberally with vegetable oil spray or melted butter. Whisk eggs with cheese, and stir in cooked pasta and vegetables. Pour the mixture into the slow cooker. Cook on High for 1½ to 2 hours or until eggs are set. Run a spatula around the sides of the slow cooker and under the bottom of the frittata cake to release it. Slide it gently onto a serving platter, and cut it into wedges. Serve hot or at room temperature.

Cooker Caveats

It's important that you cook the vegetables until they're dry. If they're not cooked to that point, the frittata will be watery and not come out of the pan easily.

Sausage and Pepper Hash

Prep time: less than 30 minutes   •   Minimum cooking time: 2 hours   •   Makes 6 servings

2 lb. bulk pork sausage

10 shallots, peeled and minced

6 garlic cloves, peeled and minced

3 yellow bell peppers, seeds and ribs removed, and finely chopped

3 red bell peppers, seeds and ribs removed, and finely chopped

3 green bell peppers, seeds and ribs removed, and finely chopped

1 jalapeño chili pepper, seeds and ribs removed, and finely chopped

1 TB. chopped fresh sage or 1 tsp. dried

1 TB. fresh thyme or 1 tsp. dried

1 TB. chopped fresh rosemary or 1 tsp. dried

1 TB. chopped fresh oregano or 1 tsp. dried

½ cup chopped fresh parsley

3 bay leaves

Salt and black pepper to taste

12 eggs

Place a large skillet over medium heat. Add sausage, breaking up any lumps with a fork, and cook, stirring frequently, for 6 to 8 minutes until sausage is browned, with no trace of pink.

Remove sausage from the pan with a slotted spoon, drain it on paper towels, and place it into the slow cooker. Add shallots, garlic, yellow bell peppers, red bell peppers, green bell peppers, and jalapeño pepper to the pan. Cook and stir for 3 minutes or until shallots are translucent.

Scrape vegetables into the slow cooker, and add sage, thyme, rosemary, oregano, parsley, and bay leaves.

Cook on Low for 4 to 6 hours or on High for 2 to 3 hours or until vegetables are very soft. Tilt the slow cooker, and skim off as much grease as possible. Discard bay leaves, and season hash with salt and pepper.

Preheat the oven to 350°F. Spread sausage mixture in a 9×13-inch baking dish. Make 12 indentations in the mixture with the back of a spoon, and break 1 egg into each. Sprinkle eggs with salt and pepper, and bake for 12 to 15 minutes or until egg whites are set. Serve immediately.

Crock Tales

Hash is a general term for food that is finely chopped. The English word first appears in the mid-seventeenth century; it comes from the French word *hacher,* which means "to chop." Because hash was frequently made with leftovers, inexpensive restaurants became known as "hash houses."

Stuffed Brunch Peppers

Prep time: less than 20 minutes • Minimum cooking time: 2½ hours • Makes 4 servings

4 bell peppers of any color that can sit evenly when placed on a flat surface	½ cup spaghetti sauce
2 TB. olive oil	4 eggs
¼ cup Italian-flavored breadcrumbs	Salt and black pepper to taste
1 lb. bulk sweet Italian sausage	3 TB. grated Parmesan cheese

Cut the tops off peppers. Discard the tops and seeds, and pull out the ribs with your fingers. Set aside.

Heat oil in a skillet over medium heat; add breadcrumbs. Cook and stir for 3 minutes or until browned. Scrape breadcrumbs into a small bowl and set aside. In the same pan, cook sausage over medium-high heat, breaking up any lumps with a fork. Cook and stir for 5 minutes, until sausage is browned, with no trace of pink. Remove sausage from the pan with a slotted spoon, and drain it on paper towels. Place sausage into a small mixing bowl, and stir in spaghetti sauce. Spoon sausage mixture into the bottom of each pepper, dividing it evenly between them.

Arrange peppers in the slow cooker. Cook on Low for 4 to 6 hours or on High for 2 to 3 hours or until peppers have softened. Then, if cooking on Low, raise the heat to High. Break an egg into each pepper, and sprinkle egg with salt, pepper, toasted breadcrumbs, and cheese. Cook for 20 to 30 minutes, until eggs are cooked.

Crock Tales _____

Author and traveler Mark Twain was a great fan of breakfast. He was quoted as saying that "nothing helps scenery like ham and eggs."

Hot Apple Granola

Prep time: less than 15 minutes • Minimum cooking time: 3 hours • Makes 4 to 6 servings

4 Granny Smith apples, peeled, cored, and diced

¾ tsp. ground cinnamon

¼ cup granulated sugar

2 TB. lemon juice

2 cups granola cereal

½ cup raisins

4 TB. melted butter

Place apples into a mixing bowl. Toss them with cinnamon, sugar, and lemon juice until evenly coated. Stir in granola cereal and raisins. Transfer the mixture to a greased slow cooker. *Drizzle* the top with melted butter.

Cook on Low for 6 to 8 hours or on High for 3 to 4 hours or until apples are tender.

Ellen on Edibles

Drizzle is a way of pouring a small amount of liquid over a large area. Rather than pouring all the liquid in one place, the idea is to spoon small amounts over as much surface area as possible. If you're sure of hand, you can do it with a measuring cup, but it's a safer bet that you'll be more successful if you do it with a teaspoon.

Part

Healthful but Homey

If you're trying to eat heathfully, don't leave your slow cooker in the box. There are myriad dishes of the simmered set that have an excellent nutritional profile.

Fish and seafood dishes cooked in the slow cooker take a slightly different approach than other types of food because most of the slow cooker's work is done before the fish is added.

In this part, you'll also find a treasure trove of side dish recipes. There are vegetables, beans, and creative looks at carbohydrates such as potatoes and grains.

Chapter 17

Sensational Seafood

In This Chapter

- ◆ Chowders as starters and for supper
- ◆ Main meal fish soups and stews
- ◆ Slow cooked vegetable sauces for delicate fish dishes

Unlike meats, which can take a whole workday to cook in the slow cooker, fish and seafood need only a few minutes to cook. In fact, overcooking seafood is more of a risk than undercooking. That's why the slow cooker plays a background role in creating delicious fish dishes.

The soups in this chapter are meals in a bowl. All you need to complete dinner is a tossed green salad. In this chapter, you'll find recipes for soup entrées for all seasons and from all over the globe. Every culture with a coastline has a fish soup that's a national favorite. From the sun-drenched shores of the Mediterranean coast of France to the rocky coastline of New England, wherever you find water, you'll find great fish soups.

What makes these dishes different from those in other parts of this book is that the seafood is cooked for a very brief time at the end of the cooking cycle.

Fish as the Finale

When using the slow cooker for seafood dishes, the actual star of the show is a late-comer. The trick is to cook the background ingredients—the vegetables or sauces—for hours so they are tender. Then the fish gets added and usually cooks for no more than 30 minutes. The exact cooking time depends on how much fish you are using and if other ingredients are added at the same time.

The timing of these recipes takes into account the cooking time for the fish used in the recipe. If you fear that the carrots in a soup might not be tender when the fish is added, they will be by the time the fish is done.

If you use the Low setting for the majority of the cooking, you'll be instructed to increase the temperature to High before adding the seafood. The seafood should cook quickly once the dish is ready for its entrance.

Substituting Species

Fish fall into basic families, and depending on where you live, you can always find something fresh. The biggest group is the "firm-fleshed white fish." The cod family, including scrod, haddock, and whiting, are native to the North Atlantic. Grouper comes from southern waters, as does red snapper. Other options are sea bass, striped bass, turbot, and orange roughy.

All these species of fish are mildly flavored and thick enough to hold together in the slow cooker. Species such as sole and flounder are too thin, although their taste is in the same family. Fish for the slow cooker should be at least three-quarters of an inch thick.

The Least You Need to Know

- Seafood should be added to the slow cooker at the end of the cooking time so it does not overcook.
- Firm-fleshed white fish such as cod, halibut, and grouper are the best choices for most slow cooker recipes.
- The test of doneness for fish is when it flakes easily and the center of the fish is not translucent. Shrimp is done when it turns bright pink.
- Most clam chowders are either cream- or tomato-based.

Nantucket Clam Chowder

Prep time: less than 20 minutes   •   Minimum cooking time: 3 hours   •   Makes 4 to 6 servings

3 TB. butter

1 large onion, peeled and diced

3 TB. all-purpose flour

2 (8-oz.) bottles clam juice

2 (6½-oz.) cans chopped or minced clams

2 celery stalks, trimmed and sliced

2 large red-skinned potatoes, scrubbed and cut into ½-inch dice

3 TB. chopped fresh parsley

1 TB. fresh thyme or ½ tsp. dried

1 bay leaf

1 cup half-and-half

Salt and black pepper to taste

Heat butter in a small skillet over medium heat; add onion. Cook and stir for 3 minutes or until onion is translucent. Reduce the heat to low, and stir in flour. Cook *roux* for 2 minutes, stirring constantly. Raise the heat to medium high, and stir in 1 bottle of clam juice. Bring to a boil, and simmer for 1 minute.

Pour the mixture into the slow cooker. Stir in the remaining bottle of clam juice, clams and their juice, celery, potatoes, parsley, thyme, and bay leaf. Cook on Low for 6 to 8 hours or on High for 3 to 4 hours or until potatoes are tender.

Then, if cooking on Low, raise the heat to High. Stir in half-and-half, season with salt and pepper, and discard bay leaf. Cook the soup for an additional 15 to 20 minutes or until bubbling.

Ellen on Edibles

Roux (pronounced *roo*, like kangaroo) is the French term for flour that is cooked in fat and is used to thicken sauces and soups. For delicate cream sauces, the goal is to keep the mixture white, but it's the deep brown roux that gives Cajun and Creole foods their characteristic nutty taste. A dark roux is made with oil or lard instead of butter because butter would burn long before the right color is reached.

Manhattan Clam Chowder

Prep time: less than 15 minutes • Minimum cooking time: 3 hours • Makes 6 to 8 servings

2 TB. bacon fat or vegetable oil

1 large onion, peeled and diced

2 celery stalks, diced

1 carrot, peeled and finely chopped

½ green bell pepper, seeds and ribs removed, and finely chopped

3 large red-skinned potatoes, scrubbed and diced

6 bacon slices, cooked and crumbled (optional)

1 (28-oz.) can crushed tomatoes

2 (8-oz.) bottles clam juice

2 (6½-oz.) cans chopped or minced clams

3 TB. chopped fresh parsley

1 TB. fresh thyme or 1 tsp. dried

2 tsp. fresh oregano or ½ tsp. dried

1 bay leaf

Salt and black pepper to taste

Crock Tales

In Melville's *Moby Dick*, Ishmael and Queequeg land on Nantucket and are sent to Hosea Hussey's Try Pots Inn. The name of the inn comes from the iron cauldrons used to melt blubber into whale oil. Melville writes that the two had "chowder for breakfast, chowder for dinner, and chowder for supper."

Heat bacon fat in a medium skillet over medium heat; add onion, celery, carrot, and green bell pepper. Cook and stir for 3 minutes until onion is translucent and pepper has begun to soften. Scrape the mixture into the slow cooker.

Add potatoes, bacon (if using), tomatoes, clam juice, clams with their juice, parsley, thyme, oregano, and bay leaf to the slow cooker. Cook on Low for 6 to 8 hours or on High for 3 to 4 hours or until potatoes are tender. Discard bay leaf, and season chowder with salt and pepper.

Provençal Fish Soup

Prep time: less than 30 minutes   •   Minimum cooking time: 3½ hours   •   Makes 4 to 6 servings

¼ cup olive oil

1 large onion, peeled and diced

2 garlic cloves, peeled and minced

1 TB. paprika

1 celery stalk, trimmed and sliced

1 carrot, peeled and sliced

2 large potatoes, peeled and cut into ½-inch dice

1 (14½-oz.) can diced tomatoes

3 cups seafood stock or bottled clam juice

1 cup dry white wine

½ cup orange juice

2 TB. chopped fresh parsley

1 TB. fresh thyme or ½ tsp. dried

1 TB. grated orange zest

1½ lb. halibut, swordfish, or any firm-fleshed white fish, cut into 1-inch cubes

½ lb. medium shrimp, peeled and deveined

Salt and black pepper to taste

Thick slices of toasted French or Italian bread

Heat oil in a medium skillet over medium heat; add onion and garlic. Cook and stir for 3 minutes or until onion is translucent. Reduce the heat to low, and stir in paprika. Stir for 1 minute, and scrape the mixture into the slow cooker.

Add celery, carrot, potatoes, tomatoes, stock, wine, orange juice, parsley, thyme, and orange zest to the slow cooker. Cook on Low for 6 to 8 hours or on High for 3 to 4 hours or until vegetables are tender.

Then, if cooking on Low, raise the heat to High. Add fish and shrimp to the slow cooker, and season with salt and pepper. Cook for 20 to 40 minutes or until fish is just cooked through. Ladle the soup over slices of toast.

Slow Savvy

Feel free to substitute the species of fish used for this or any other recipe in this chapter. Clams, oysters, scallops, shrimp, and stronger fish such as tuna all work well. It's up to you. Just make sure the fish is at least ¾-inch thick.

Curried Fish Soup

Prep time: less than 15 minutes • Minimum cooking time: 3½ hours • Makes 4 to 6 servings

2 TB. sesame oil

1 large onion, peeled and chopped

½ red bell pepper, seeds and ribs removed, and chopped

2 garlic cloves, peeled and minced

2 TB. grated fresh ginger

2 TB. lemon juice

1 TB. ground coriander

1 TB. turmeric

1 TB. *curry powder*

3 cups seafood stock or bottled calm juice

1 cup canned unsweetened coconut milk

1½ lb. cod, halibut, swordfish, seas bass, or any firm-fleshed white fish, cut into 1-inch pieces

1 (10-oz.) box frozen green beans, thawed

Salt and cayenne to taste

3 cups cooked white rice

Condiments:

Chutney

Raisins

Scallions, trimmed and thinly sliced

Grated sweetened coconut

Slivered almonds, toasted in a 350°F oven for 5 minutes or until browned

Heat oil in a medium skillet over medium heat; add onion, red bell pepper, and garlic. Cook and stir for 3 minutes or until onion is translucent. Scrape the mixture into the slow cooker. Stir ginger, lemon juice, coriander, turmeric, curry powder, and stock into the slow cooker.

Ellen on Edibles

Curry powder is actually a blend of up to 20 spices; the yellow color comes from turmeric. Some of the other ingredients are dried red chilies, coriander seed, fenugreek seed, mustard seed, ground ginger, and cinnamon.

Cook on Low for 5 to 6 hours or on High for 2½ to 3 hours or until the mixture is bubbly and onions are soft. Then, if cooking on Low, raise the heat to High. Stir in coconut milk, fish, and green beans. Cook on High for 1 hour or until soup is simmering and fish is cooked through. Season with salt and cayenne. Serve spooned over rice. Pass chutney, raisins, scallions, coconut, and toasted almonds separately.

Caldo de Perro
(Spanish Fish Soup with Potatoes, Greens, and Aioli)

Prep time: less than 20 minutes • Minimum cooking time: 3½ hours • Makes 4 to 6 servings

Soup:

2 TB. olive oil

2 onions, peeled and diced

3 garlic cloves, peeled and minced

4 cups fish stock or bottled clam juice

½ cup dry white wine

2 TB. lemon juice

1 lb. red-skinned potatoes, scrubbed and cut into ¾-inch pieces

2 TB. chopped fresh parsley

1 tsp. dried thyme

1 bay leaf

½ lb. Swiss chard

1½ lb. halibut, cod, monkfish, snapper, sea bass, or any firm-fleshed white fish, cut into 1-inch cubes

Salt and black pepper to taste

Aioli:

½ cup mayonnaise

4 garlic cloves, peeled and crushed

1 tsp. grated lemon zest

Thick slices of toasted French or Italian bread

Heat oil in a small skillet over medium heat; add onion and garlic. Cook and stir for 3 minutes or until onion is translucent. Scrape the mixture into the slow cooker.

Add stock, wine, lemon juice, potatoes, parsley, thyme, and bay leaf to the slow cooker. Cook on Low for 6 to 8 hours or on High for 3 to 4 hours or until potatoes are tender. While the soup is cooking, prepare Swiss chard. Rinse the leaves, and discard the stems. Cut the leaves crosswise into ½-inch slices.

When the potatoes are ready, if cooking on Low, increase the heat to High. Add fish and Swiss chard. Cook for 20 to 45 minutes or until fish is just cooked through. Season the soup with salt and pepper, and discard bay leaf.

Mix mayonnaise with garlic and lemon zest. Ladle the soup over toast slices, and pass aioli separately.

Slow Savvy

Aioli is a garlicky mayonnaise sauce that hails from Provence. As well as passing aioli to add some garlicky goodness to the soup, you can also use it to top the toast. Mix equal parts aioli and grated Parmesan cheese, and spread the mixture on the bread. Then broil the slices until browned and bubbly.

New England Seafood Chowder

Prep time: less than 20 minutes • Minimum cooking time: 2½ hours • Makes 4 to 6 servings

2 TB. bacon fat or vegetable oil

1 large onion, peeled and diced

4 cups seafood stock or bottled clam juice

1 lb. red-skinned potatoes, scrubbed and cut into ½-inch cubes

2 TB. chopped fresh parsley

½ tsp. dried thyme

1 bay leaf

1 lb. cod, halibut, or other firm-fleshed white fish, cut into 1-inch cubes

½ lb. bay scallops

1 (10-oz.) box frozen corn kernels, thawed

1 cup heavy cream

6 slices bacon, cooked until crisp and crumbled (optional)

Salt and black pepper to taste

Heat bacon fat in a small skillet over medium heat; add onion. Cook and stir for 3 minutes or until onion is translucent. Scrape onion into the slow cooker, and add stock, potatoes, parsley, thyme, and bay leaf. Cook on Low for 4 to 6 hours or on High for 2 to 3 hours or until potatoes are tender.

Then, if cooking on Low, raise the heat to High. Add fish, scallops, corn, cream, and bacon (if using). Cook for 40 to 60 minutes or until fish is cooked through. Discard bay leaf, and season with salt and pepper.

Cooker Caveats

There are many theories as to the derivation of the word *chowder*. One theory is that is comes from the French word *chaudière*, which is the large cauldron into which Breton fishermen threw their catch to create a communal stew. There is also an English ancestry that maintains that *chowder* is a variation of an old Cornwall word, *jowter*, a fish peddler.

Shrimp Creole

Prep time: less than 20 minutes   •   Minimum cooking time: 3½ hours   •   Makes 4 to 6 servings

3 TB. olive oil

6 scallions, trimmed and chopped

2 celery stalks, trimmed and chopped

½ green bell pepper, seeds and ribs removed, and finely chopped

3 garlic cloves, peeled and minced

1 TB. dried oregano

1 TB. paprika

1 tsp. ground cumin

½ tsp. dried basil

2 (8-oz.) cans tomato sauce

½ cup seafood stock or bottled clam juice

2 bay leaves

1½ lb. raw medium shrimp, peeled and deveined

Salt and cayenne to taste

2 to 3 cups cooked white rice

Heat oil in a medium skillet over medium heat; add scallions, celery, green bell pepper, and garlic. Cook and stir for 3 minutes until scallions are soft. Reduce the heat to low, and stir in oregano, paprika, cumin, and basil. Cook 1 minute, stirring constantly. Scrape the mixture into the slow cooker.

Stir tomato sauce, stock, and bay leaves into the slow cooker. Cook on Low for 6 to 8 hours or on High for 3 to 4 hours or until vegetables are soft. Then, if cooking on Low, raise the heat to High. Discard bay leaves, and stir in shrimp. Cook for 15 to 30 minutes or until shrimp are pink and cooked through. Season with salt and cayenne, and serve over white rice.

Cooker Caveats

It's a great time-saver to double or triple many of the recipes in this chapter—including this one—to freeze some of the base for a future meal. However, do not freeze the seafood. It will fall apart when it's thawed and reheated. Freezing makes all liquids expand, and when this happens to fish, it breaks down its delicate cell walls.

Seafood Gumbo

Prep time: less than 20 minutes • Minimum cooking time: 3½ hours • Makes 6 servings

¼ cup plus 3 TB. vegetable oil (divided use)

¼ cup all-purpose flour

1 cup water

3 onions, peeled and diced

1 green or red bell pepper, seeds and ribs removed, and diced

2 celery stalks, trimmed and sliced

4 garlic cloves, peeled and minced

1 (10-oz.) box frozen sliced okra, thawed

1 (14½-oz.) can diced tomatoes

3 cups seafood stock or bottled clam juice

1 TB. fresh thyme or 1 tsp. dried

1 TB. fresh chopped basil or 1 tsp. dried

2 bay leaves

1 lb. snapper, cod, halibut, or other firm-fleshed white fish, cut into 1-inch cubes

¾ lb. raw medium shrimp, peeled and deveined

½ pint shucked oysters or ¼ lb. additional shrimp

Salt and cayenne to taste

3 cups cooked white rice

Heat ¼ cup oil in a small saucepan over medium-high heat. Whisk in flour, and reduce the heat to medium. Whisk flour constantly for 5 to 7 minutes or until roux is walnut brown. Whisk in water, and whisk until the mixture is thick and smooth. Scrape roux into the slow cooker.

Heat remaining 3 tablespoons oil in a medium skillet over medium heat; add onion, green bell pepper, celery, and garlic. Cook and stir for 3 minutes or until onion is translucent. Scrape the mixture into the slow cooker, and add okra, tomatoes, stock, thyme, basil, and bay leaves. Cook on Low for 6 to 8 hours or on High for 3 to 4 hours or until vegetables are tender. Then, if cooking on Low, raise the heat to High. Add fish, shrimp, and oysters to the slow cooker, and cook for 15 to 30 minutes or until fish is cooked through and oyster edges have curled. Discard bay leaves, and season gumbo with salt and cayenne. Serve over white rice.

Crock Tales

Gumbo is a Louisiana culinary classic that dates back to the French and Spanish settlers and the African slaves who served them. Although it can contain fish, meats, or poultry, the constant that gives it its name is okra. Okra is what thickens the dish, and the word *gumbo* comes from the African word *gombo*, which means "okra."

Sweet and Sour Fish Stew

Prep time: less than 20 minutes   •   Minimum cooking time: 3½ hours   •   Makes 4 to 6 servings

2 TB. sesame oil

1 large red onion, peeled, halved, and sliced

3 scallions, trimmed and thinly sliced

4 garlic cloves, peeled and minced

2 TB. grated fresh ginger

½ tsp. red pepper flakes plus more to taste

1½ cups seafood stock or bottled clam juice

2 TB. balsamic vinegar

2 TB. soy sauce

2 TB. firmly packed dark brown sugar

4 bok choy stalks, trimmed and sliced

2 celery stalks, trimmed and sliced

2 carrots, peeled and thinly sliced

¼ lb. fresh shiitake mushrooms, stemmed and sliced, if large

½ lb. raw shrimp, peeled and deveined

½ lb. bay scallops, rinsed, or sea scallops, cut in half

½ lb. snapper, cod, halibut, or other firm-fleshed white fish, cut into 1-inch cubes

½ lb. snow peas, rinsed and trimmed

2 TB. cornstarch

2 TB. cold water

Salt to taste

2 to 3 cups cooked white rice or jasmine rice

Heat oil in a medium skillet over medium heat; add onion, scallions, garlic, ginger, and ½ teaspoon red pepper flakes. Cook and stir for 3 minutes or until onion is translucent. Scrape the mixture into the slow cooker. Stir in stock, vinegar, soy sauce, and brown sugar. Add bok choy, celery, carrots, and mushrooms.

Cook the stew on Low for 6 to 8 hours or on High for 3 to 4 hours or until vegetables are tender-crisp. Then, if cooking on Low, increase the heat to High. Add shrimp, scallops, fish, and snow peas to the slow cooker. Cook for 30 to 45 minutes or until fish is cooked through. Mix cornstarch and cold water in a small cup, and stir cornstarch mixture into the stew. Cook for an additional 5 to 10 minutes or until the stew is bubbly and has thickened. Season with salt and additional red pepper flakes, and serve the stew over rice.

Slow Savvy

For this or any Chinese dish, you can vary the cooking time to make the vegetables the texture you like them. This timing renders the vegetables soft, but if you want them crisper, cut back by as much as an hour or two.

Italian-Style Baked Bluefish

Prep time: less than 30 minutes • Minimum cooking time: 2½ hours • Makes 4 to 6 servings

¼ cup olive oil

2 celery stalks, trimmed and sliced

1 onion, peeled and diced

6 garlic cloves, peeled and minced

1 (14½-oz.) can diced tomatoes

½ cup dry white wine

¼ cup chopped kalamata olives

4 TB. small capers, rinsed and drained

2 TB. chopped fresh parsley

2 tsp. fresh thyme or ½ tsp. dried

2 lb. bluefish fillets, skinned and cut into serving pieces

Salt and black pepper to taste

2 cups cooked white rice or pasta

 Cooker Caveats

Many people think of bluefish as being a strong-smelling fish, but that is not the case when it's freshly caught. When buying bluefish, there should be no "fishy" smell to the fillets at all. If you don't live in a bluefish part of the country, try mackerel for this recipe instead.

Heat oil in a medium skillet over medium heat; add celery, onion, and garlic. Cook and stir for 3 minutes or until onion is translucent. Scrape the mixture into the slow cooker, and add tomatoes, wine, olives, capers, parsley, and thyme. Cook on Low for 4 to 5 hours or on High for 2 to 3 hours or until vegetables are tender.

Then, if cooking on Low, increase the heat to High. Pour the vegetable mixture into a mixing bowl. Season bluefish pieces with salt and pepper. Place half the bluefish pieces into the slow cooker, and top with half the vegetable mixture. Repeat with the other half of bluefish and vegetable mixture. Cook fish on High for 20 to 30 minutes or until it is cooked through and flakes easily. Serve fish with rice or pasta.

Cod with Tomatoes and Fennel

Prep time: less than 15 minutes   •   Minimum cooking time: 2½ hours   •   Makes 4 to 6 servings

¼ cup olive oil

1 large onion, peeled and thinly sliced

3 garlic cloves, peeled and minced

2 fennel bulbs, cored and thinly sliced

1 (28-oz.) can diced tomatoes, drained

½ cup dry white wine

½ cup orange juice

2 TB. Pernod, ouzo, or other anise-flavored liqueur

1 TB. grated orange zest

2 lb. thick cod fillets, cut into serving pieces

Salt and black pepper to taste

Heat oil in a large saucepan over medium heat; add onion and garlic. Cook and stir for 3 minutes or until onion is translucent. Add fennel and cook for an additional 2 minutes. Scrape the mixture into the slow cooker. Add tomatoes, wine, orange juice, Pernod, and orange zest to slow cooker. Cook on Low for 4 to 6 hours or on High for 2 to 3 hours or until fennel is tender-crisp.

Then, if cooking on Low, increase the heat to High. Season cod with salt and pepper, and place it on top of vegetables. Cook for 30 to 45 minutes or until fish is cooked through and flakes easily.

Slow Savvy

This is one dish that can be started the day before you want to serve it. Cook the vegetables, then refrigerate the mixture. The next day, arrange the vegetables in a baking pan and place the cod on top. By the time the fish cooks, the vegetables will have reheated.

Monkfish with Cabbage and Bacon

Prep time: less than 30 minutes • Minimum cooking time: 2 hours • Makes 4 to 6 servings

½ head Savoy or green cabbage, shredded

¼ lb. bacon, diced

2 lb. monkfish fillets, trimmed and cut into serving pieces

3 garlic cloves, peeled and minced

1 cup fish stock or bottled clam juice

2 TB. snipped fresh chives

1 TB. chopped fresh parsley

1 TB. chopped fresh basil or 1 tsp. dried

2 tsp. fresh tarragon or ½ tsp. dried

2 tsp. grated lemon zest

Salt and black pepper to taste

2 TB. butter

1 to 1½ lb. steamed new potatoes

Bring a large pot of salted water to a boil. Add cabbage and boil for 4 minutes. Drain cabbage and place it into the slow cooker.

Cook bacon in a heavy skillet over medium heat until it becomes crisp. Remove bacon from the pan with a slotted spoon, and place it in the slow cooker. Raise the heat to high, and *sear* monkfish in the bacon fat on all sides, turning the pieces gently with tongs, until browned. Refrigerate the monkfish.

Add garlic, stock, chives, parsley, basil, tarragon, and lemon zest to the slow cooker. Cook on Low for 3 to 4 hours or on High for 1½ to 2 hours or until cabbage is almost tender.

Ellen on Edibles

Sear is a term used for quickly browning food in very hot fat. In addition to browning the food, searing seals the outer layer so its juices do not escape as readily during cooking. When searing food, always turn it with tongs rather than a meat fork, which lets all the juices escape.

Then, if cooking on Low, increase heat to High. Season monkfish with salt and pepper, and place it on top of vegetables. Cook monkfish for 15 to 30 minutes until it is cooked through. Remove monkfish from the slow cooker, and keep it warm. Add butter to cabbage, and stir to melt butter. Season with salt and pepper.

To serve, mound equal-size portions of cabbage on each plate. Slice monkfish into medallions, and arrange on top of cabbage. Serve with steamed new potatoes.

Moroccan Fish Tagine

Prep time: less than 20 minutes • Minimum cooking time: 2½ hours • Makes 4 to 6 servings

2 lb. cod, halibut, or other firm-fleshed white fish, cut into serving pieces

Marinade:

½ cup olive oil

¼ cup lemon juice

¼ cup dry white wine

2 TB. chopped fresh cilantro

1 TB. paprika

1 tsp. ground cumin

1 tsp. ground ginger

½ tsp. salt

¼ tsp. cayenne

Tagine:

2 TB. olive oil

2 large onions, peeled and diced

3 garlic cloves, peeled and minced

1 cup fish stock or bottled clam juice

½ cup sliced green olives

Salt and black pepper to taste

2 to 3 cups hot cooked couscous

Rinse fish fillets and set aside. Combine oil, lemon juice, wine, cilantro, paprika, cumin, ginger, salt, and cayenne in a heavy, resealable plastic bag. Mix well and add fish. Marinate fish in the refrigerator for 2 to 4 hours, turning the bag occasionally so fish marinates evenly.

Heat oil in a medium skillet over medium heat; add onions and garlic. Cook and stir for 3 minutes or until onion is translucent. Scrape the mixture into the slow cooker. Drain marinade from fish, and add liquid to the slow cooker, along with stock and olives. Return fish to the bag and refrigerate. Cook on Low for 4 to 5 hours or on High for 2 to 3 hours or until onion is tender.

Then, if cooking on Low, increase the heat to High. Add fish to the slow cooker, and cook for 30 to 40 minutes until fish is cooked through and flakes easily. Season with salt and pepper, and serve fish with hot couscous.

Crock Tales _____

A tagine might sound exotic, but it's basically a Moroccan stew that can feature just about any sort of fish, meat, or poultry as long as there are olives and spices such as cumin.

Mexican Snapper

Prep time: less than 15 minutes • Minimum cooking time: 2½ hours • Makes 4 to 6 servings

2 TB. olive oil

2 onions, peeled and thinly sliced

4 garlic cloves, peeled and minced

1 jalapeño chili pepper, seeds and ribs removed, and finely chopped

1 TB. chili powder

2 tsp. dried oregano

1 (14½-oz.) can diced tomatoes

1 cup fish stock or bottled clam juice

2 TB. lemon juice

2 TB. tomato paste

1 tsp. grated lemon zest

¼ cup sliced green olives

2 lb. red snapper or other firm-fleshed white fish fillets, cut into serving pieces

Salt and black pepper to taste

2 cups cooked white or brown rice

Heat oil in a medium skillet over medium heat; add onion, garlic, and jalapeño pepper. Cook and stir for 3 minutes or until onion is translucent. Stir in chili powder and oregano. Cook for 1 minute, stirring constantly. Scrape the mixture into the slow cooker. Add tomatoes, stock, lemon juice, tomato paste, and lemon zest to the slow cooker. Stir well.

Cook for 4 to 6 hours on Low or for 2 to 3 hours on High or until vegetables are tender. Then, if cooking on Low, increase the heat to High. Stir in olives, and gently add fish. Cook for 20 to 40 minutes until fish is cooked through and flakes easily. Season with salt and pepper, and serve fish with rice.

Slow Savvy

It's a chili pepper's seeds and ribs that contain almost all the capsaicin, the chemical compound that delivers the peppers' punch. Because small chilies have proportionately more seeds and ribs to flesh, a general rule is the smaller the chili, the hotter the pepper.

Lobster Bread Pudding

Prep time: less than 30 minutes   •   Minimum cooking time: 2 hours   •   Makes 4 to 6 servings

Pudding:

12 slices white bread, toasted

4 TB. (½ stick) butter

2 shallots, peeled and minced

1 garlic clove, peeled and minced

½ lb. fresh shiitake or crimini mushrooms, rinsed, stemmed, and sliced

¼ cup brandy

1 lb. cooked lobster meat, cut into ½-inch cubes

3 eggs

1 cup heavy cream

½ cup lobster stock or bottled clam juice

2 tsp. fresh chopped tarragon or ½ tsp. dried

Salt and black pepper to taste

Sauce:

½ cup dry white wine

1 (8-oz.) pkg. refrigerated Alfredo sauce

1 TB. tomato paste

2 TB. chopped fresh chives or 2 tsp. dried

Salt and black pepper to taste

Break bread into small cubes, and place them into a well-greased slow cooker. Heat butter in a medium skillet over medium heat; add shallots, garlic, and mushrooms. Cook and stir for 3 to 5 minutes until shallots are translucent. Raise the heat to high and add brandy. Cook for 2 to 3 minutes or until brandy has evaporated. Scrape the mixture into the slow cooker. Add lobster to the slow cooker. Whisk together eggs, cream, stock, tarragon, salt, and pepper. Pour the mixture into the slow cooker and stir well. Press bread into the liquid with the back of a spoon so it absorbs the custard. Cook on Low for 4 to 6 hours or on High for 2 to 3 hours or until a toothpick inserted into the center comes out clean.

Slow Savvy

The oven broiler is the best way to toast large amounts of bread at the same time. Place the oven rack about one third the way down, then arrange the bread on baking sheets. Do watch the bread carefully, though. There are only a few seconds between nicely toasted and burned.

While pudding is cooking, make sauce. Pour wine into a small saucepan, and boil over high heat until it is reduced in volume by half. Add Alfredo sauce, tomato paste, and chives. Stir until smooth, and season the sauce with salt and pepper. Pass the sauce separately.

Chapter 18

Vegetarian and Versatile

In This Chapter

◆ Great recipes for both summer and winter squash
◆ Sprucing up winter vegetables
◆ International vegetable medleys

Planning a menu is like getting dressed for a party. If you're wearing a simple black dress, the accessories make the fashion statement. But if you're in a bright print, you'll keep the shoes and purse simple.

In the same way, only one food on an entrée plate should be the star. If you're cooking an elaborate entrée, probably the best side dish to serve is a simply prepared steamed vegetable to add contrasting color and texture as well as its nutrition to the plate. But if your entrée is a simple grilled or broiled dish, the vegetable and other side dishes can be a bit more elaborate.

This chapter presents some of those vegetable dishes that are meant to be dazzlers.

The Root of the Matter

The slow cooker is ideal for root vegetables and other hard vegetables we associate with winter. When those ingredients are called for, so is a longer cooking time—regardless of the method used to cook them.

A root vegetable is just what it sounds like. The vegetable part grows in the ground, and its green leaves are all you see in the garden rows. The most common root vegetable is the ubiquitous carrot. Others are parsnips, which look like white carrots, beets, and turnips.

The Least You Need to Know

- The root vegetables family includes carrots, parsnips, turnips, and beets. These vegetables actually grow in the dirt beneath the soil level.
- Root vegetables, winter squash, and cabbage all require long cooking times to make them tender.
- Zucchini and yellow squash can be substituted for one another in any recipe.
- Herbs, spices, vinegars, cheeses, and other seasonings infuse vegetable dishes with the flavors of the world's cuisines.

Baked Acorn Squash

Prep time: less than 15 minutes • Minimum cooking time: 3 hours • Makes 4 servings

1 (1½-lb.) acorn squash

2 TB. butter, melted

¼ cup firmly packed dark brown sugar

¼ tsp. ground cinnamon

Pinch of salt

Cut squash into quarters with a sharp knife, and scrape out the seeds. Place the quarters into the slow cooker, skin side down, so the hollow in the flesh faces upward. Combine butter, brown sugar, cinnamon, and salt. Divide the mixture into four quarters, and spoon it into the hollows in the squash pieces.

Cook on Low for 5 to 7 hours or on High for 3 to 4 hours or until squash is tender when pierced with the tip of a knife.

Slow Savvy

Picking the best produce is half of winning the game. In the case of acorn squash, they should be heavy for their size and the rind should be deeply colored, hard, and blemish-free.

Turnip Purée

Prep time: less than 15 minutes • Minimum cooking time: 2½ hours • Makes 4 to 6 servings

2 lb. turnips, peeled and cut into ½-inch cubes

3 TB. butter, cut into small pieces

½ cup vegetable or chicken stock

¼ cup heavy cream

Salt and white pepper to taste

Place turnips into the slow cooker, and dot the top of the cubes with butter. Pour stock over turnips.

Cook on Low for 4 to 5 hours or on High for 2 to 3 hours or until turnips are tender. Drain turnips in a colander, and return them to the slow cooker. Add cream, and mash turnips with a potato masher until smooth. Season with salt and pepper, and cook for an additional 15 to 20 minutes to heat through.

Crock Tales

Scarlett O'Hara was holding a turnip when she uttered the immortal line from *Gone with the Wind:* "With God as my witness, I'm never going to be hungry again."

Fall Tomato Gratin

Prep time: less than 15 minutes • Minimum cooking time: 2 hours • Makes 4 to 6 servings

⅓ cup olive oil

4 garlic cloves, peeled and minced

¼ loaf French or Italian bread, cut into ½-inch cubes (about 3 cups)

3 lb. tomatoes, cored, seeded, and cut into ½-inch dice

2 tsp. chopped fresh oregano or ½ tsp. dried

1 tsp. thyme or ¼ tsp. dried

⅓ cup heavy cream

¼ cup freshly grated Parmesan cheese

Salt and black pepper to taste

Ellen on Edibles

Gratin is any dish that's topped with cheese. Like many French cooking terms, this one comes from the name of the gratin pan. It's shallow so there is a larger top surface area for the topping.

Grease the inside of the slow cooker liberally with vegetable oil spray. Heat oil in a large skillet over medium heat; add garlic. Cook and stir for 2 minutes. Add bread cubes, and cook for 3 to 4 minutes, stirring frequently, until they are lightly browned. Spoon garlic and bread into the slow cooker.

Add tomatoes, oregano, thyme, cream, Parmesan cheese, salt, and pepper to the slow cooker. Toss to combine, and spread out the mixture evenly in the slow cooker, patting it down with the back of a spoon. Cook on Low for 3 to 4 hours or on High for 2 to 3 hours or until tomatoes are soft.

Sweet and Sour Red Cabbage

Prep time: less than 15 minutes   •   Minimum cooking time: 3 hours   •   Makes 6 to 8 servings

1 (2-lb.) red cabbage, cored and shredded	½ cup dry red wine
2 TB. red wine vinegar	½ cup vegetable or chicken stock
2 TB. granulated sugar	1 cinnamon stick
4 TB. (½ stick) butter (divided use)	1 bay leaf
1 onion, peeled and chopped	⅓ cup red currant jelly
1 apple, peeled and chopped	Salt and black pepper to taste

Place cabbage into the slow cooker. Sprinkle it with vinegar and sugar and toss. Heat 2 tablespoons butter in a medium skillet over medium heat; add onion and apple. Cook and stir for 3 minutes or until onion is translucent. Scrape the mixture into the slow cooker, and stir in wine, stock, cinnamon stick, and bay leaf.

Cook on Low for 6 to 8 hours or on High for 3 to 4 hours or until cabbage is almost tender. Then, if cooking on Low, raise the heat to High. Discard cinnamon stick and bay leaf, and stir jelly and remaining 2 tablespoons butter into cabbage. Cook on High for an additional 30 to 40 minutes or until cabbage is tender and glazed. Season with salt and pepper.

Slow Savvy

It's important to sprinkle the red cabbage with the vinegar because that's what keeps it red while it cooks. Otherwise, the cabbage will turn purple.

Maple-Glazed Beets

Prep time: less than 15 minutes • Minimum cooking time: 3 hours • Makes 4 to 6 servings

2 bunches beets (about 1½ lb.), scrubbed, peeled, and cut into ¼-inch slices

⅓ cup balsamic vinegar

¼ cup maple syrup

2 TB. butter, melted

2 TB. chopped fresh parsley

Salt and black pepper to taste

Cooker Caveats

A good way to judge the freshness of beets when you buy them at the market is by their fresh, lively beet greens. But remember to cut them off as soon as you come home. The greens leach moisture from the beets and make them dry and bitter.

Arrange beet slices in the slow cooker. Combine vinegar, maple syrup, and melted butter in a small mixing bowl. Pour the mixture over beets.

Cook on Low for 6 to 8 hours or on High for 3 to 4 hours or until beets are tender. Sprinkle beets with parsley, and season with salt and pepper.

Asian Butternut Squash

Prep time: less than 20 minutes   •   Minimum cooking time: 3 hours   •   Makes 6 to 8 servings

2½ lb. peeled butternut squash, cut into ½-inch cubes

½ cup hoisin sauce

¼ cup orange juice

3 TB. butter, melted

1 tsp. grated orange zest

½ tsp. Chinese five-spice powder

Salt and black pepper to taste

Place squash into the slow cooker. Combine hoisin sauce, orange juice, melted butter, orange zest, and Chinese five-spice powder in a small mixing bowl. Stir well and pour the mixture over squash.

Cook on Low for 6 to 8 hours or on High for 3 to 4 hours or until squash is tender. For chunky squash, mash the cubes with a potato masher right in the slow cooker. For smooth squash, spoon the contents of the slow cooker into a food processor fitted with a steel blade. Purée until smooth. Season squash with salt and pepper.

Slow Savvy

If you can't find butternut squash, you can make this dish with other species of winter squash, such as acorn, Hubbard, or turban squash.

Ginger-Glazed Carrots

Prep time: less than 20 minutes • Minimum cooking time: 2 hours • Makes 6 servings

1½ lb. carrots, trimmed, peeled, and cut on the diagonal into ¼-inch slices

½ cup freshly squeezed orange juice

3 TB. butter, melted

3 TB. firmly packed dark brown sugar

2 TB. grated fresh ginger

1 tsp. grated orange zest

2 scallions, trimmed and finely chopped

Salt and black pepper to taste

Place carrots into the slow cooker. Combine orange juice, butter, brown sugar, ginger, and orange zest in a small mixing bowl. Pour the liquid over carrots.

Cook on Low for 4 to 6 hours or on High for 2 to 3 hours or until carrots are tender. Sprinkle carrots with chopped scallions, and season with salt and pepper.

Slow Savvy

If you're peeling one carrot, a vegetable peeler is probably the quickest way. When you're doing a whole bunch, however, there's an easier method. Boil the carrots for 2 minutes, then plunge them into a bowl of ice water. The peels will slip off when you rub the carrots with your fingers.

Braised Fennel

Prep time: less than 15 minutes   •   Minimum cooking time: 2 hours   •   Makes 4 to 6 servings

1 large fennel bulb, about 1¼ lb.

2 TB. butter

½ small onion, peeled and thinly sliced

1 garlic clove, peeled and minced

1 cup vegetable or chicken stock

½ tsp. dried thyme

Salt and black pepper to taste

Cut the stalks off fennel bulb, and cut the bulb in half through the root. Trim out the root, then slice the fennel thinly across the bulb. Place the slices into the slow cooker.

Heat butter in a small skillet over medium heat; add onion and garlic. Cook and stir for 3 minutes or until onion is translucent. Scrape the mixture into the slow cooker, and add stock and thyme.

Cook on Low for 4 to 6 hours or on High for 2 to 3 hours or until fennel is tender. Season with salt and pepper.

Slow Savvy

Although the celerylike stalks are trimmed off the fennel bulb for this dish, don't throw them out. They add a wonderful anise flavor as well as a crisp texture and are used in place of celery in salads and other raw dishes.

Stewed Collard Greens

Prep time: less than 15 minutes   •   Minimum cooking time: 2 hours   •   Makes 4 to 6 servings

2½ lb. collard greens	½ tsp. dried thyme
1 cup vegetable or chicken stock	1 bay leaf
2 garlic cloves, peeled and minced	Salt to taste
¼ cup cider vinegar	Red pepper flakes to taste
¼ cup granulated sugar	

Rinse collard greens well, rubbing the leaves to remove all the grit and sand. Discard stems and cut leaves crosswise into ¹/₂-inch-wide strips.

Bring stock, garlic, vinegar, sugar, and thyme to a boil in a medium saucepan. Add as many greens as will fit into the pan by pushing greens into the boiling liquid. Add more greens as those in the pan wilt. When all greens are wilted, pour the contents of the pan into the slow cooker, then add bay leaf.

Cook on Low for 4 to 6 hours or on High for 2 to 3 hours or until greens are very tender. Discard bay leaf, and season greens with salt and red pepper flakes.

Slow Savvy

Greens were a mainstay of the poor Southern diet, and though the nutritional profile might not have been known at the time, it is certainly impressive. One serving of greens provides more than your daily requirement of vitamins C and A. Greens have a substantial amount of iron and calcium, fiber, and minerals. And they are one of the few good nondairy sources of calcium.

Balsamic Onions

Prep time: less than 15 minutes • Minimum cooking time: 1½ hours • Makes 4 to 6 servings

1 lb. bag frozen pearl onions, thawed and drained

3 TB. butter, cut into small pieces

¼ cup *balsamic vinegar*

¼ cup vegetable or chicken stock

2 TB. granulated sugar

2 tsp. fresh thyme or ½ tsp. dried

Salt and black pepper to taste

Put onions into the slow cooker, and dot the tops with butter pieces. Combine vinegar, stock, sugar, and thyme in a small bowl, and stir to dissolve sugar. Pour this mixture over onions.

Cook on Low for 3 to 5 hours or on High for 1½ to 2 hours or until onions are tender. Stir onions a few times after the liquid starts to simmer. Season with salt and pepper.

Ellen on Edibles

Balsamic vinegar, called *aceto balsamico* in Italian, comes from the Modena region of Italy. It's made by reducing trebbiano and lambrusco grape juice, then aging the vinegar in wooden barrels for several years. It's quite dark in color and is sweet as well. If you don't have any balsamic vinegar, cider vinegar with a bit of sugar or molasses is the best substitution.

Caponata

Prep time: Less than 30 minutes • Minimum cooking time: 2½ hours • Makes 6 to 8 servings

1 (1-lb.) eggplant, peeled and cut into ½-inch cubes

Salt

⅓ cup olive oil (divided use)

2 celery stalks, diced

1 onion, peeled and diced

4 garlic cloves, peeled and minced

¼ cup red wine vinegar

1 tsp. granulated sugar

1 (14½-oz.) can diced tomatoes

1 TB. tomato paste

¼ cup sliced green olives

2 TB. small capers, drained and rinsed

2 TB. anchovy paste (optional)

Salt and black pepper to taste

Put eggplant into a colander, and sprinkle it liberally with salt. Place a plate on top of eggplant cubes, and weight the plate with cans. Place the colander into the sink or on a plate, and allow eggplant to drain for 30 minutes. Rinse eggplant cubes, and pat them dry on paper towels.

> **Crock Tales**
>
> Caponata is a Sicilian vegetable dish that always has eggplant although some of the other ingredients can vary. The name probably comes from the Latin word *caupo,* or "tavern," because this is the sort of robust food that men would eat in taverns.

Heat half the oil in a medium skillet over medium heat; add celery, onion, and garlic. Cook, stirring, for 3 minutes or until onion is translucent. Remove vegetables from the pan with a slotted spoon, and place them into the slow cooker.

Pour remaining oil into the skillet, and raise the heat to medium-high; add eggplant cubes. Cook and stir for 5 minutes or until they are lightly browned. Spoon eggplant into the slow cooker, and add vinegar, sugar, tomatoes, tomato paste, olives, capers, and anchovy paste (if using). Cook on Low for 5 to 6 hours or on High for 2½ to 3 hours or until vegetables are soft. Season with salt and pepper.

Ratatouille

Prep time: less than 20 minutes • Minimum cooking time: 2½ hours • Makes 4 to 6 servings

1 (¾-lb.) eggplant, trimmed and cut into ¾-inch cubes

Salt

⅓ cup olive oil (divided use)

1 onion, peeled and diced

3 garlic cloves, peeled and minced

1 small zucchini, trimmed and cut into ¾-inch cubes

1 small summer squash, trimmed and cut into ¾-inch cubes

1 (14½-oz.) can crushed tomatoes

2 TB. tomato paste

1 TB. herbes de Provence or 1 tsp. dried thyme, 1 tsp. dried oregano, and 1 tsp. dried rosemary

Salt and black pepper to taste

Put eggplant into a colander, and sprinkle it liberally with salt. Place a plate on top of eggplant cubes, and weight the plate with cans. Place the colander into the sink or on a plate, and allow eggplant to drain for 30 minutes. Rinse eggplant cubes, and pat them dry on paper towels.

Heat half the oil in a medium skillet over medium heat; add onion and garlic. Cook and stir for 3 minutes or until onion is translucent. Scrape the mixture into the slow cooker. Add remaining oil to the skillet; then add eggplant cubes. Cook and stir for 3 minutes or until eggplant is starting to soften. Scrape eggplant into the slow cooker, and add zucchini, summer squash, tomatoes, tomato paste, and herbes de Provence. Stir well.

Cook on Low for 5 to 7 hours or on High for 2½ to 3½ hours or until vegetables are tender. Season with salt and pepper. Ratatouille can be served hot, at room temperature, or chilled.

Cooker Caveats

Even though the eggplant is rinsed, it still provides a fair amount of salt to the dish. Taste it carefully before adding additional salt.

Summer Squash Au Gratin

Prep time: less than 15 minutes   •   Minimum cooking time: 2 hours   •   Makes 4 to 6 servings

2 lb. yellow summer squash (or zucchini), trimmed and cut into ½-inch slices

3 TB. butter

1 large onion, peeled and thinly sliced

¾ cup evaporated milk

½ tsp. dried thyme

1 cup grated sharp cheddar cheese

Salt and black pepper to taste

Slow Savvy

Zucchini and yellow squash can be substituted for one another or combined in any dish. These tender summer squash do not need peeling. When selecting squash, choose small ones. They will be sweeter, and the seeds will not be hard.

Place squash slices into a colander, and sprinkle them liberally with salt. Let them sit for 30 minutes. Rinse and set aside.

Heat butter in a medium skillet over medium heat; add onion. Cook and stir for 3 minutes or until onion is translucent. Layer onion and squash into the slow cooker, and add evaporated milk and thyme.

Cook on Low for 4 to 6 hours or on High for 2 to 3 hours or until squash is tender. Stir halfway through the cooking period. Add cheese to the slow cooker, and season mixture with salt and pepper. Cook for an additional 10 to 20 minutes until cheese is melted.

19

Where Have You Bean?

In This Chapter

- ◆ Nutritious vegetarian bean dishes
- ◆ A variety of beans—and a variety of dishes made with beans
- ◆ Many ways to season bean dishes

The world has changed its attitude toward what it once regarded as the lowly bean. Beans are now praised for their nutritional value as well as flavor. Beans are high in fiber and protein, low in fat, and contain no cholesterol. They are also a good source of B vitamins, especially B_6.

Not only are beans good food, but they're also easy to cook in the slow cooker. In fact, before we had a slow cooker, the same shape of cooking device was called a bean pot. That shows you how perfect this machine is for cooking beans. And with a slow cooker, you don't have to worry about beans on the bottom of the pan scorching, even set on High—a pitfall of bean dishes cooked on the stove.

Completing Proteins

Beans are paired with rice or other grains in dishes around the world for more reasons than the flavor. What generations before us knew instinctively—and we now know scientifically—is that the protein in beans is "incomplete." This means that in order to deliver its best nutritional content—to "complete" the protein—beans need to be paired with carbohydrate-rich grains such as rice or corn.

When the beans and grains are eaten together, they supply a quality of protein that's as good as that from eggs or beef. If you're serving any of these dishes as a vegetarian entrée rather than as a side dish, be sure to serve it on top of some rice or polenta.

The Soaking Step

Experienced cooks will tell you to pre-soak dried beans to cut down on the cooking time. The easiest way to soak beans is to cover them with water and let them sit for at least 6 hours. You can do this right in the slow cooker.

> **Slow Savvy**
> When calculating cooking times for bean dishes, you should take into account that if a recipe contains an acid (such as vinegar, tomatoes, lemon juice, or wine) or a sweetener (such as sugar or molasses), the beans will take longer to soften.

The second way is to cover the beans with water and bring them to a boil on top of the stove. Once they've boiled for 1 minute, turn off the heat, cover the pan, and let them soak for 1 hour.

Using either method, drain the beans after they've soaked, discard the soaking water, and cook them very soon after they're drained. Once the beans have been soaked, bacteria can begin to form and the beans will ferment.

Remember, too, that soaking is not necessary for other members of the legume family such as split peas and lentils.

The Least You Need to Know

- Most dried beans should be soaked before cooking. Other members of the legume family, such as split peas and lentils, do not require soaking.
- Salty, acidic, and sweet foods toughen beans so they take longer to cook.
- Beans provide an incomplete protein that becomes complete when the beans are eaten with rice or other grains.
- Beans do not scorch and stick to the bottom of the slow cooker pot—as if you needed another reason to use your slow cooker.
- Canned beans cook for a relatively short time in the slow cooker because they are already cooked and are just reheated so they absorb flavor from the sauce.

Texas Chili Beans

Prep time: less than 15 minutes • Minimum cooking time: 3 hours • Makes 4 to 6 servings

1 lb. dried pinto beans	4 cups water
1 onion, peeled and chopped	1 TB. chili powder
3 garlic cloves, peeled and minced	2 tsp. dried oregano
1 small jalapeño or serrano chili pepper, seeds and ribs removed, and finely chopped	Salt and black pepper to taste

Rinse beans in a colander, place them into a mixing bowl, and cover with cold water. Allow beans to soak overnight. Or place beans into a saucepan, and bring to a boil over high heat. Boil 1 minute. Turn off the heat, cover the pan, and soak beans for 1 hour. Drain. Discard the soaking water. Place beans into the slow cooker.

Add onion, garlic, jalapeño pepper, water, chili powder, and oregano to the slow cooker. Cook on Low for 6 to 8 hours or on High for 3 to 4 hours or until beans are tender. Add salt and pepper prior to the last hour of cooking time.

Slow Savvy

Dried spices and herbs give food more aroma and flavor if they are toasted before they are added to the dishes. Place the herbs and spices into a small, dry skillet and cook them over low heat for 3 minutes or until they're fragrant—that's the key.

Moroccan Chickpea Stew

Prep time: less than 15 minutes • Minimum cooking time: 7 hours • Makes 6 to 8 servings

2 cups dried chickpeas	4 cups vegetable or chicken stock
3 TB. vegetable oil	1 tsp. *turmeric*
2 onions, peeled and diced	½ tsp. ground cinnamon
3 garlic cloves, peeled and minced	Salt and black pepper to taste
1 (28-oz.) can diced tomatoes	

Ellen on Edibles

Turmeric is sometimes called "poor man's saffron." Although it does not have the same fragrance as saffron, it has its own stronger flavor, and it imparts the same rich yellow color in foods. Turmeric is the root of a tropical plant, and it's what gives American mustard its distinctive yellow color.

Rinse chickpeas in a colander, place them into a mixing bowl, and cover with cold water. Allow chickpeas to soak overnight. Or place chickpeas into a saucepan, and bring to a boil over high heat. Boil 1 minute. Turn off the heat, cover the pan, and soak chickpeas for 1 hour. Drain. Discard the soaking water. Place chickpeas into the slow cooker.

Heat oil in a medium skillet over medium heat. Add onions and garlic. Cook and stir for 3 minutes or until onion is translucent. Scrape the mixture into the slow cooker, and add drained chickpeas, tomatoes, stock, turmeric, and cinnamon. Cook on High for 7 to 8 hours or until chickpeas are soft. Season chickpeas with salt and pepper prior to the last hour of cooking time.

Boston Baked Beans

Prep time: less than 15 minutes   •   Minimum cooking time: 4 hours   •   Makes 6 to 8 servings

1 lb. dried navy beans or any small white bean	6 slices cooked bacon, drained and crumbled (optional)
2 TB. vegetable oil or bacon fat	½ cup prepared barbecue sauce
1 red onion, peeled and diced	1 TB. prepared mustard
2½ cups water	½ cup grated mozzarella cheese
½ cup firmly packed dark brown sugar	Salt and black pepper to taste
½ cup cider vinegar	

Rinse beans in a colander, place them into a mixing bowl, and cover with cold water. Allow beans to soak overnight. Or place beans into a saucepan, and bring to a boil over high heat. Boil 1 minute. Turn off the heat, cover the pan, and soak beans for 1 hour. Drain. Discard the soaking water. Place beans into the slow cooker.

Heat oil in a small skillet over medium heat; add onion. Cook and stir for 3 minutes or until onion is translucent. Add onion to the slow cooker.

Add water, brown sugar, vinegar, onion, bacon (if using), barbecue sauce, and mustard to the slow cooker. Cook on Low for 8 to 10 hours or on High for 4 to 5 hours or until beans are tender. Stir in cheese, and season beans with salt and pepper. Cook for an additional 5 to 10 minutes until cheese is melted.

> **Crock Tales**
> Boston baked beans are so interwoven into the city's history that it's still known as "Beantown." During the Colonial era, the Puritans would bake beans on Saturday and serve them for dinner that night and for lunch on Sunday because no cooking was allowed on the Sabbath.

Mexican Mixed-Bean Stew

Prep time: less than 15 minutes • Minimum cooking time: 1½ hours • Makes 4 to 6 servings

3 TB. olive oil

1 onion, peeled and diced

3 garlic cloves, peeled and minced

½ red bell pepper, seeds and ribs removed, and finely chopped

1 TB. chili powder

2 tsp. ground cumin

¾ cup tomato salsa

1 (8-oz.) can tomato sauce

1 medium zucchini, trimmed and cut into ½-inch dice

1 (15-oz.) can red kidney beans, drained and rinsed

1 (15-oz.) can chickpeas, drained and rinsed

Salt and black pepper to taste

Heat oil in a medium skillet over medium heat; add onion, garlic, and red bell pepper. Cook and stir for 3 minutes or until onion is translucent. Stir in chili powder and cumin. Cook for 1 minute, stirring constantly. Scrape the mixture into the slow cooker. Stir in salsa, tomato sauce, zucchini, kidney beans, and chickpeas.

Cook on Low for 3 to 5 hours or on High for 1½ to 2½ hours or until zucchini is tender. Season with salt and pepper.

Cooker Caveats

Different dried beans require varied cooking times, but all canned beans cook at the same rate. They are completely cooked when you take them out of the can and should not be subjected to long cooking times or they will fall apart. Canned beans should be cooked long enough to absorb the flavor of the sauce, but not for more than a few hours.

Savory Lentils with Black-Eyed Peas

Prep time: less than 15 minutes • Minimum cooking time: 4 hours • Makes 4 to 6 servings

1½ cups dried *lentils*

1 onion, peeled and finely chopped

3 garlic cloves, peeled and minced

1½ cups vegetable stock or water

1 (14½-oz.) can crushed tomatoes

2 tsp. ground cumin

1 tsp. ground coriander

1 (15-oz.) can black-eyed peas, drained and rinsed

Salt and black pepper to taste

Place lentils, onion, garlic, stock, tomatoes, cumin, and coriander into the slow cooker. Cook on Low for 8 to 10 hours or on High for 4 to 5 hours or until lentils are tender.

Stir in black-eyed peas, and season with salt and pepper. Cook for an additional 15 to 20 minutes until black-eyed peas are hot.

Ellen on Edibles _____

Lentils are one member of the legume family with the greatest geographic spread. The tiny, lens-shape pulse has been used as a protein source from France to India and all through the Middle East. The lentils we find most often are the common brown ones, but there are also red and yellow lentils. They all cook the same way.

Refried Beans

Prep time: less than 20 minutes • Minimum cooking time: 4½ hours • Makes 6 to 8 servings

1 lb. dried red kidney beans, rinsed

2 quarts water

½ cup vegetable oil or bacon fat

2 large red onions, peeled and diced

6 garlic cloves, peeled and minced

½ (4-oz.) can diced mild green chilies

½ cup refrigerated commercial tomato salsa

Salt and cayenne to taste

Rinse beans in a colander, place them into a mixing bowl, and cover with cold water. Allow beans to soak overnight. Or place beans into a saucepan, and bring to a boil over high heat. Boil 1 minute. Turn off the heat, cover the pan, and soak beans for 1 hour. Drain. Discard the soaking water. Place beans into the slow cooker.

Slow Savvy

This is one dish that can be started up to 2 days ahead of when you want to serve it. Cook the beans, then refrigerate them, tightly covered. The frying and mashing can take place when the beans are cold. It will just take a few more minutes to get them hot.

Add water to the slow cooker, and cook on Low for 8 to 10 hours or on High for 4 to 5 hours or until beans are very tender and beginning to fall apart. Remove beans from the slow cooker with a slotted spoon, and reserve ½ cup cooking liquid.

Heat oil in a large skillet over medium heat; add onions and garlic. Cook and stir for 4 to 5 minutes or until onions are soft. Stir in beans, chilies, reserved bean cooking liquid, and salsa. Mash beans with a potato masher or the back of a heavy spoon until beans are soft but some beans still remain whole. Season with salt and pepper.

Hoppin' John

Prep time: less than 15 minutes • Minimum cooking time: 3 hours • Makes 4 to 6 servings

1 cup dried black-eyed peas

½ lb. smoked pork butt or ham, cut into ½-inch cubes

2 cups chicken or ham stock

½ tsp. dried thyme

1 bay leaf

Salt and black pepper to taste

Rinse black-eyed peas in a colander, place them into a mixing bowl, and cover with cold water. Allow black-eyed peas to soak overnight. Or place black-eyed peas into a saucepan, and bring to a boil over high heat. Boil 1 minute. Turn off the heat, cover the pan, and soak black-eyed peas for 1 hour. Drain. Discard the soaking water. Place black-eyed peas into the slow cooker.

Add pork butt or ham, stock, thyme, and bay leaf to the slow cooker. Cook on Low for 6 to 8 hours or on High for 3 to 4 hours or until black-eyed peas are tender. Discard bay leaf, and season with salt and pepper.

Crock Tales

No self-respecting Southerner would start the New Year without eating a bowl of Hoppin' John. It's the regional good luck charm. The dish probably came from Africa, and it is mentioned in literature long before the Civil War. Some food authorities say the name comes from children hopping around the table on New Year's Day as a prelude to eating the dish.

Italian Cannellini Beans

Prep time: less than 15 minutes • Minimum cooking time: 5 hours • Makes 6 to 8 servings

1 lb. dried cannellini beans or other small white beans

2 TB. olive oil

1 onion, peeled and diced

3 garlic cloves, peeled and minced

½ green or red bell pepper, seeds and ribs removed, and finely chopped

2 cups tomato juice

1 (14½-oz.) can diced tomatoes

1 TB. Italian seasoning

½ cup grated mozzarella cheese

¼ cup grated Parmesan cheese

Salt and black pepper to taste

Rinse beans in a colander, place them into a mixing bowl, and cover with cold water. Allow beans to soak overnight. Or place beans into a saucepan, and bring to a boil over high heat. Boil 1 minute. Turn off the heat, cover the pan, and soak beans for 1 hour. Drain. Discard the soaking water. Place beans into the slow cooker.

Cooker Caveats

Most cheeses, especially ones like Parmesan and feta, have a high natural salt content. When cooking with these cheeses, add them before you add the salt. Then taste and season accordingly.

Heat oil in a medium skillet over medium heat; add onion, garlic, and green or red bell pepper. Cook and stir for 3 minutes or until onion is translucent. Scrape the mixture into the slow cooker. Add tomato juice, tomatoes, and Italian seasoning to the slow cooker. Cook on Low for 10 to 12 hours or on High for 5 to 6 hours or until beans are tender. Stir mozzarella and Parmesan cheeses into beans, and season with salt and pepper.

Black Bean and Papaya Salad

Prep time: less than 20 minutes　•　Minimum cooking time: 2 hours, plus at least 1 hour to chill beans　•　Makes 4 to 6 servings

Salad:

½ lb. dried black beans

1 cinnamon stick

2 cloves garlic, peeled and minced

Salt to taste

1 ripe papaya, peeled, seeded, and cut into a ½-inch dice

1 medium jicama, peeled and cut into a ½-inch dice

Dressing:

3 shallots, peeled and chopped

2 garlic cloves, peeled and minced

½ tsp. ground cumin

⅓ cup orange juice

3 TB. balsamic vinegar

2 TB. lime juice

Salt and cayenne to taste

3 TB. olive oil

Rinse beans in a colander, place them into a mixing bowl, and cover with cold water. Allow beans to soak overnight. Or place beans into a saucepan, and bring to a boil over high heat. Boil 1 minute. Turn off the heat, cover the pan, and soak beans for 1 hour. Drain. Discard the soaking water. Place beans into the slow cooker.

Pour in enough water to cover the beans by 2 inches, and add cinnamon stick and garlic. Cook on Low for 4 to 6 hours or on High for 2 to 3 hours or until beans are tender but still slightly chewy. Add salt prior to the last hour of cooking time. Drain beans, discard cinnamon stick, and chill well.

Combine chilled beans with papaya and jicama in a mixing bowl.

For the dressing, combine shallots, garlic, cumin, orange juice, vinegar, lime juice, salt, and cayenne in a jar with a tight-fitting lid. Shake well, add oil, and shake well again. Pour over salad and toss.

Slow Savvy

Papaya contains an enzyme, papain, which naturally tenderizes meats and poultry. Save the skin when peeling the papaya and add it to a marinade.

White Bean Salad

Prep time: less than 15 minutes • Minimum cooking time: 2 hours, plus at least 1 hour to chill beans • Makes 4 to 6 servings

2 cups dried white navy beans	½ cup finely chopped scallions
2 garlic cloves, peeled and minced	3 TB. lemon juice
Salt to taste	Black pepper to taste
⅓ cup finely chopped fresh parsley	⅓ cup olive oil

Rinse beans in a colander, place them into a mixing bowl, and cover with cold water. Allow beans to soak overnight. Or place beans into a saucepan, and bring to a boil over high heat. Boil 1 minute. Turn off the heat, cover the pan, and soak beans for 1 hour. Drain. Discard the soaking water. Place beans into the slow cooker.

Pour in enough water to cover the beans by 2 inches and add garlic.

Slow Savvy

For a variation on this dish, add 2 (6½-ounce) cans imported tuna packed in olive oil. Break the tuna into chunks, and use the oil from the cans as part of the oil in the dressing.

Cook on Low for 4 to 6 hours or on High for 2 to 3 hours or until beans are tender. Add salt prior to the last hour of cooking time. Drain beans and chill them well.

Combine parsley and scallions in a mixing bowl, and stir in lemon juice, salt, and pepper. Mix well, add oil, and mix well again. Gently stir dressing into beans, season the dish with salt and pepper, and serve chilled.

Chapter 20

Celebrating Spuds and Grains

In This Chapter

- ◆ Dishes showcasing both white and sweet potatoes
- ◆ Recipes to glorify grains
- ◆ Old-fashioned corn puddings

Potatoes, sweet potatoes, and grains are all complex carbohydrates that are increasingly important in maintaining a healthy body. These foods are also versatile, as you'll see in this chapter.

Each food has its own inherent texture and mild flavor, so they take to a wide variety of seasonings.

Glorious Grains

All grains, including rice, are the fruit produced by grasses, and the less processed the grain, the more fiber it adds to our diets. Food historians frequently divide the world's cultures by the predominant grain. Most European cuisines are based are wheat, while the dietary mainstay of equatorial cultures is rice. It all depends on what can grow on the land, and some countries, like Italy, are lucky enough to have them both.

The basic North American grain was corn, and corn puddings have been part of American cooking since before the first Thanksgiving.

Many grain recipes lend themselves well to preparation in the slow cooker because grains need to be cooked slowly in liquid to soften.

Spectacular Spuds

Potatoes, sweet potatoes, and yams are all tubers, a starchy swollen underground root. We eat these tubers, but the same sort of botany applies to dahlias and other flowers that grow from an elongated stem. The three might look similar, but they come from different families. White potatoes are part of the nightshade family, along with tomatoes and eggplant. Sweet potatoes are related to morning glories, and true yams are a tropical vine.

These tubers can all be cooked in the slow cooker, as long as the recipe includes a liquid. (The slow cooker won't produce a crispy potato.)

The Least You Need to Know

- ◆ The slow cooker can be used for any potato or sweet potato recipe that requires liquid during cooking. It will not produce a crisp potato.
- ◆ Yams and sweet potatoes are not identical species of tuber, but they can be used interchangeably in recipes.
- ◆ Grains are the fruits produced by grasses. The less a grain is processed, the more fiber it adds to the diet.
- ◆ Toasting grains such as barley and bulgur enhances their texture and prevents them from becoming mushy when cooked.

Potatoes Provençale

Prep time: less than 15 minutes   •   Minimum cooking time: 3 hours   •   Makes 6 to 8 servings

2½ lb. red-skinned potatoes, scrubbed and thinly sliced

2 onions, peeled and thinly sliced

2 garlic cloves, peeled and minced

3 TB. butter, cut into small pieces

2 TB. parsley

1 TB. herbes de Provence or 1 tsp. dried thyme, 1 tsp. dried oregano, and 1 tsp. dried rosemary

1½ cups vegetable or chicken stock

1 cup grated Swiss or Gruyère cheese

Salt and black pepper to taste

Spray the inside of the slow cooker with vegetable oil spray. Combine potatoes, onion, garlic, butter, parsley, and herbes de Provence in the slow cooker. Pack it down evenly. Pour stock over potatoes.

Cook on Low for 6 to 8 hours or on High for 3 to 4 hours or until potatoes are tender. Stir in cheese, and season potatoes with salt and pepper. Cook for an additional 10 to 15 minutes or until cheese is melted.

Cooker Caveats

If you're cooking potatoes in a slow cooker on Low, they might discolor. A way to avoid this is to submerge the potatoes in a bowl of water to which lemon juice has been added before cooking them. The lemon will not be detected once the dish is cooked, and it will keep the spuds snowy white.

Scalloped Potatoes

Prep time: less than 15 minutes • Minimum cooking time: 3 hours • Makes 4 to 6 servings

2 lb. small red-skinned potatoes, scrubbed and thinly sliced

1 small onion, peeled and finely chopped

2 TB. butter, melted

1 (10¾-oz.) can condensed cheddar cheese soup

1 cup evaporated milk

1 cup grated sharp cheddar cheese

Salt and black pepper to taste

Grease the inside of the slow cooker liberally with vegetable oil spray. Arrange half the potato slices in the slow cooker. Scatter half the onion on top of the potatoes, and drizzle with half the butter. Repeat with remaining potatoes, onion, and butter.

Slow Savvy

If you want to make this dish in a real jiffy, substitute a 2-pound bag of frozen hash brown potatoes for the red-skinned potatoes. There is no need to thaw the hash browns; just add about 30 minutes to the cooking time.

Mix soup and evaporated milk in a small mixing bowl, and pour it over potatoes. Cook on Low for 6 to 8 hours or on High for 3 to 4 hours or until potatoes are tender. Then, if cooking on Low, increase the heat to High. Stir cheese into potatoes, and season with salt and pepper. Cook on High for an additional 10 minutes until cheese is melted.

Leek and Potato Purée

Prep time: less than 20 minutes • Minimum cooking time: 3 hours • Makes 4 to 6 servings

6 TB. (¾ stick) butter

4 cups finely chopped leeks, white parts only, rinsed and well drained

2 garlic cloves, peeled and minced

3 large Russet potatoes, peeled and cut into ½-inch dice

1 cup evaporated milk

Salt and black pepper to taste

Heat butter in a medium skillet over low heat; add leeks and garlic. Toss to coat leeks with butter, and cover the pan. Cook for 10 minutes, stirring occasionally, until leeks are soft. Scrape leeks into the slow cooker, and add potatoes and evaporated milk.

Cook on Low for 6 to 8 hours or on High for 3 to 4 hours or until potatoes are tender. Put the mixture through a food mill, or purée it in a food processor fitted with a steel blade. Don't overprocess, or potatoes will become gluey. Season the mixture with salt and pepper to taste.

Cooker Caveats

Leeks are like Pigpen in the *Peanuts* comic strip because they seem to trail dirt wherever they go. Rinse the leeks before you slice them; then rinse them again for a long time in a sieve before you begin to cook with them.

Hot German Potato Salad

Prep time: less than 15 minutes • Minimum cooking time: 4 hours • Makes 4 to 6 servings

4 medium red-skinned potatoes, scrubbed and thinly sliced

1 onion, peeled and chopped

⅓ cup water

¼ cup distilled white vinegar

2 TB. granulated sugar

1 TB. prepared mustard

Salt and black pepper to taste

¼ cup bacon grease or vegetable oil

3 TB. chopped fresh parsley

6 slices bacon, cooked until crisp, drained, and crumbled (optional)

Arrange half the potato slices in the slow cooker, and top with half the onion. Repeat with remaining potatoes and onion. Combine water, vinegar, sugar, mustard, salt, and pepper in a jar with a tight-fitting lid. Shake well. Add bacon grease, and shake well again. Pour mixture over potatoes.

Cook on Low for 8 to 10 hours or on High for 4 to 5 hours or until potatoes are tender. Stir in parsley and bacon (if using).

Slow Savvy

If you see a potato that has a greenish tinge, it means it was exposed to light. Cut away that portion of the potato because the green flesh can be toxic. Store potatoes in a cool, dry place—but not with onions. Onions give off a natural gas that can cause potatoes to rot more quickly.

Easy Sweet Potatoes and Apples

Prep time: less than 15 minutes   •   Minimum cooking time: 3 hours   •   Makes 6 to 8 servings

3 lb. (about 4 large) sweet potatoes, peeled and thinly sliced

2 Granny Smith apples, peeled, cored, and thinly sliced

1 cup chunky applesauce

½ cup pure maple syrup

6 TB. (¾ stick) butter, melted

¾ tsp. ground cinnamon

Pinch of salt

Grease the inside of the slow cooker liberally with vegetable oil spray. Arrange half the sweet potatoes and apples in the slow cooker. Combine applesauce, maple syrup, melted butter, cinnamon, and salt in a mixing bowl. Pour half the mixture over sweet potatoes and apples, and repeat with the remaining sweet potatoes, apples, and applesauce mixture.

Cook on Low for 6 to 8 hours or on High for 3 to 4 hours or until sweet potatoes are tender.

Slow Savvy _____

Although sweet potatoes and yams are used interchangeably in recipes, they are different tubers. Yams are native to Africa and have a flesh that is lighter in color but sweeter than sweet potatoes. Yams also have a higher moisture content, so cut back slightly on liquids if you are using an authentic yam in a dish.

Citrus-Glazed Yams

Prep time: less than 20 minutes • Minimum cooking time: 3 hours • Makes 6 to 8 servings

3 navel oranges

2 lemons

¼ lb. (1 stick) butter, melted

1½ cups firmly packed dark brown sugar

3 large yams or sweet potatoes (about 3 lb.), peeled and thinly sliced

Trim the peel and white pith off of oranges and lemons. Thinly slice oranges and lemons, saving any juices. Mix melted butter with brown sugar in a small bowl.

Grease the inside of the slow cooker liberally with vegetable oil spray or butter. Layer half the yams in the slow cooker. Arrange half the orange and lemon slices on top of yams, and dot the surface of fruit layer with half the butter mixture. Repeat with the remaining yams, fruit, and butter mixture.

Cook on Low for 6 to 8 hours or on High for 3 to 4 hours or until potatoes are tender.

Slow Savvy

Here's an easy way to peel all citrus fruits: Cut off a slice from the top and bottom so the fruit will sit firmly on a counter. Then take a paring knife or flexible-blade fruit knife and cut down the sides beneath the peel so the flesh is exposed. Turn the fruit over and do the same on the other side. This is quicker and easier than peeling the fruit and then cutting off the white pith.

Corn Pudding

Prep time: less than 15 minutes • Minimum cooking time: 2 hours • Makes 6 to 8 servings

1 egg, lightly beaten

1 (15-oz.) can creamed corn

2 TB. butter, melted

1¼ cups corn muffin mix

⅔ cup sour cream

1 cup grated cheddar cheese

Liberally grease the inside of the slow cooker with vegetable oil spray. Combine egg, creamed corn, melted butter, and muffin mix in a mixing bowl. Stir well. Scrape the mixture into the slow cooker, and level batter with a rubber spatula.

Dot sour cream on surface of batter, and spread gently with a rubber spatula. Sprinkle cheese over sour cream.

Cook the pudding on High for 2 hours or until a toothpick inserted into the center of the pudding comes out clean. Serve immediately.

Cooker Caveats

Although it's never a good idea to peek into the slow cooker because it allows steam to escape, it's an especially bad idea when cooking this recipe. The muffin mix contains baking powder and/or baking soda, and lifting the lid might cause the fluffy pudding to flatten.

Spoonbread

Prep time: less than 15 minutes • Minimum cooking time: 1½ hours • Makes 6 to 8 servings

3 eggs, lightly beaten	1 (8½-oz.) box corn muffin mix
2 cups half-and-half	½ cup yellow cornmeal
6 TB. (¾ stick) butter, melted	Salt and black pepper to taste

Grease the inside of the slow cooker liberally with vegetable oil spray. Whisk eggs, half-and-half, melted butter, muffin mix, cornmeal, salt, and pepper together in a mixing bowl. Pour the batter into the slow cooker.

Cook on Low for 3 to 5 hours or on High for 1½ to 2½ hours or until a toothpick inserted into the center of the spoonbread comes out clean.

Crock Tales

Spoonbread, a form of corn pudding, is one of the oldest American dishes. The Native Americans who greeted the Pilgrims taught them how to dry and grind corn into cornmeal. Spoonbreads are the next generation from "corn pone"—the Native American bread served at the first Thanksgiving.

Wild Rice Pilaf

Prep time: less than 15 minutes   •   Minimum cooking time: 3 hours   •   Makes 4 to 6 servings

3 TB. butter

1 large onion, peeled and finely chopped

1 carrot, peeled and finely chopped

1 cup wild rice, rinsed

¼ cup dried currants

3 cups vegetable or chicken stock

Salt and black pepper to taste

Melt butter in a small skillet over medium heat; stir in onion and carrot. Cook and stir for 3 minutes or until onion is translucent. Scrape mixture into the slow cooker.

Add wild rice, currants, and stock to the slow cooker. Stir well. Cook on Low for 7 to 8 hours or on High for 3 to 4 hours or until rice is fluffed and tender and stock has been absorbed. Season with salt and pepper.

Ellen on Edibles

Pilaf (pronounced *PEE-laf*) is used in our culture for almost any grain dish that includes other ingredients, such as the vegetables and dried currants in this dish. Pilaf originated in the Middle East where it was always made with rice or bulgur wheat, which were browned before any liquid was added.

Risotto-Style Rice

Prep time: less than 15 minutes • Minimum cooking time: 2 hours • Makes 4 to 6 servings

3 TB. butter	2½ cups vegetable or chicken stock
1 medium onion, peeled and finely chopped	½ cup grated Parmesan cheese
1 cup arborio rice	Salt and black pepper to taste
½ cup dry white wine	

Heat butter in a medium saucepan over medium heat; add onion. Cook and stir for 3 minutes or until onion is translucent. Add rice and stir to coat grains. Raise the heat to high and add wine. Stir for 2 minutes or until wine is almost evaporated. Scrape rice into the slow cooker.

Add stock to the slow cooker and stir well. Cook on High for 2 hours or until rice is soft and the liquid has been absorbed. Stir in cheese, and season rice with salt and pepper.

Crock Tales

Risotto is one of Milan's contributions to Italian cuisine, and legend has it that it originated in the sixteenth century. True risotto *alla milanese* is made with saffron, which perfumes the rice and creates a pale yellow dish. Today, almost any creamy rice dish with cheese added is called a risotto, but the authentic dish is made with arborio rice, which, when cooked, releases a starch and creates its own sauce. The traditional dish requires constant stirring—a step happily unnecessary with the slow cooker version.

Toasted Barley with Mushrooms

Prep time: less than 15 minutes   •   Minimum cooking time: 2 hours   •   Makes 4 to 6 servings

1 cup pearl barley	½ lb. white mushrooms, rinsed, trimmed, and sliced
3 TB. butter	2 cups vegetable or chicken stock
1 shallot, peeled and minced	Salt and black pepper to taste

Heat barley in a dry, medium skillet over medium heat. Cook and stir for 3 to 5 minutes or until barley is lightly toasted. Transfer barley to the slow cooker. Add butter to the pan. When butter is melted, add shallot and mushrooms. Cook and stir for 3 to 5 minutes or until mushrooms begin to soften. Scrape the mixture into the slow cooker.

Add stock to the slow cooker, and cook on Low for 4 to 6 hours or on High for 2 to 3 hours or until barley is soft. Season with salt and pepper.

Slow Savvy _____

Toasting grains is an additional step for many recipes, but the results are worth it. Toasting cooks the starch on the exterior of the grain so the dish doesn't become gummy from too much starch when it cooks. Although barley is best toasted dry, any species of rice can be toasted in butter or oil. With rice, the grains just need to become opaque. They don't even have to brown.

Bulgur with Fennel

Prep time: less than 15 minutes • Minimum cooking time: 2 hours • Makes 4 to 6 servings

3 TB. butter	1 cup *bulgur*
½ small onion, peeled and finely chopped	1½ cups vegetable or chicken stock
½ fennel bulb, cored and thinly sliced	½ tsp. dried thyme
½ carrot, peeled and finely chopped	Salt and black pepper to taste

Melt butter in a medium skillet over medium heat; add onion, fennel, and carrot. Cook and stir for 3 minutes or until onion is translucent. Add bulgur and cook for 2 minutes to coat grains. Scrape the mixture into the slow cooker.

Add stock and thyme to the slow cooker. Cook on Low for 4 to 6 hours or on High for 2 to 3 hours or until the liquid is absorbed. Season with salt and pepper.

Ellen on Edibles

Bulgur (pronounced *BULL-gurr*) is a wheat kernel that has been steamed, dried, and crushed. It's similar to cracked wheat and can be used in the same way. It has a chewy texture and comes both coarse and fine. Fine bulgur is best known in this country as the basis for Middle Eastern tabbouleh. Both bulgur and cracked wheat are dietary staples in the Middle East.

Chapter 21

Enhancing Extras

In This Chapter

- ◆ Exotic chutneys to flavor foods
- ◆ Sauces for all occasions
- ◆ Jams and conserves for you and to give as gifts

Sometimes it's the little touches that make a meal memorable. It could be a homemade jam to spread on toast at breakfast or a unique and sensational sauce for topping or dipping.

The slow cooker creates these foods easily. There's no constant stirring; you just follow the recipe and let the slow cooker do the work. Once you've discovered how easy it is to make condiments for yourself—and how the homemade taste is so special—you'll make it part of your cooking rituals.

In addition, all the recipes in this chapter are candidates for canning. That means you can have a batch to enjoy for months to come and you can present your friends with a homemade gift from your kitchen.

Canning with Care

In Grandma's day, this canning process was called "putting up" food. Before freezers, the best way to capture the bounty of each season was to preserve foods at home. Although the process is called *canning*, it's done in glass jars rather than tin cans. All the recipes in this chapter can be refrigerated for up to three weeks without the step of sterilizing the food. If you want a longer shelf life that doesn't require refrigeration—canning—then you need to know the process for sterilizing.

The Right Stuff

You can't just use any old jar for canning. There are special jars made just for canning—and special lids. The lids are really two parts: the round disk center and the metal screw band with a rubber insert. The rubber insert forms a vacuum seal. You'll find the right jars in most supermarkets as well as kitchen specialty stores.

Hot Bath for Health

In preparation for canning, wash the jars and all parts of the lids in hot, soapy water. Place a metal rack into a large pot and place the jars on the rack. The jars should not sit directly on the bottom of the pot, or they might break from the heat.

Add hot water to cover by 1 inch. Bring the water to a boil and boil for 10 minutes. Leave the jars in the hot water. Put the lids and screw bands in another pot and bring the water to a boil. Remove the pan from the heat, and leave the lids submerged until ready to use.

The jars are now ready to fill. If you're expecting to eat the food in a few weeks and don't need to know about further sterilization, skip the next few sections and go right to the recipes.

Second Sterilizing

Drain one jar at a time using tongs and spoon the filling to within $1/4$ inch of the top so that the level is correct to create a vacuum seal. Wipe the rim clean with a damp hot towel, then drain a lid and screw band and seal the jar tightly. Do one jar at a time, so the jars and lids stay submerged in water until they are filled.

Now comes the processing. Put the filled, sealed jars on a rack in a large pot, making sure that the jars do not touch one another. Pour boiling water over them by at least 1 inch, and boil the jars over medium heat for 15 minutes. Remove the jars from the water bath with tongs, and let them cool on a rack.

Testing Time

Once the jars are cool, press down on the button in the center of the lid with your finger. If the button stays down, the jar is sealed and can be stored in a cool place for up to a year. If it pops back up, refrigerate the jar and enjoy the contents within a few weeks.

This last part is also important to know about every jar you buy in a supermarket. If the button in the center of the lid has popped up, the seal is broken. Don't buy it because the contents could be contaminated. Check your pantry frequently to make sure that all the buttons are still down, and discard any food if the button has popped up.

The Least You Need to Know

- ◆ Making your own sauces and condiments is a way to personalize foods to your taste.
- ◆ Strict canning rules must be followed if you wish to store foods in jars at room temperature.
- ◆ Thick condiments like chutneys and conserves are excellent dishes for a slow cooker because there is no fear of scorching the sugar as the mixture thickens.
- ◆ Homemade condiments make delicious gifts.

Herbed Tomato Sauce

Prep time: less than 20 minutes • Minimum cooking time: 4 hours • Makes 2 pints

3 TB. olive oil

1 large onion, peeled and chopped

½ red bell pepper, seeds and ribs removed, and chopped

2 garlic cloves, peeled and minced

1 (28-oz.) can crushed tomatoes

1 (6-oz.) can tomato paste

½ cup dry white wine

½ cup water

2 TB. chopped fresh oregano or 2 tsp. dried

2 TB. chopped fresh basil or 2 tsp. dried

1 TB. chopped fresh rosemary or 1 tsp. dried

1 bay leaf

Salt and black pepper to taste

Slow Savvy

This sauce is one of the most versatile you can have around. Use it to top grilled or broiled foods, or mix it with some browned chopped meat or Italian sausage and you've got a quickie pasta sauce.

Heat oil in a medium skillet over medium heat; add onion, red bell pepper, and garlic. Cook and stir for 3 minutes or until onion is translucent. Scrape the mixture into the slow cooker, and add tomatoes, tomato paste, wine, water, oregano, basil, rosemary, and bay leaf. Stir well.

Cook on Low for 6 to 8 hours or on High for 3 to 4 hours or until vegetables are tender. Then, if cooking on Low, increase the heat to High. Cook sauce, uncovered, for 1 hour, stirring occasionally until slightly thickened. Discard bay leaf, and season tomato sauce with salt and pepper to taste.

My Favorite Barbecue Sauce

Prep time: less than 15 minutes • Minimum cooking time: 2 hours • Makes 4 cups

1 (20-oz.) bottle ketchup	2 TB. dry mustard
1 cup cider vinegar	2 garlic cloves, peeled and minced
½ cup firmly packed dark brown sugar	1 TB. grated fresh ginger
5 TB. Worcestershire sauce	1 lemon, washed and thinly sliced
¼ cup vegetable oil	½ to 1 tsp. hot red pepper sauce or to taste

Combine ketchup, vinegar, brown sugar, Worcestershire sauce, oil, mustard, garlic, ginger, and lemon in the slow cooker. Stir well.

Cook on Low for 4 to 6 hours or on High for 2 to 3 hours or until sauce is bubbly. Add red pepper sauce. Ladle sauce through a strainer, pressing with the back of a spoon to extract as much liquid as possible. Discard the solids. Ladle sauce into containers, cover tightly, and refrigerate.

Cooker Caveats

Even though citrus fruits might look pristine, there's a chance that there is bacteria or insecticide on them. Wash the fruits with mild soap and water before using them. You won't taste the soap, and it doesn't remove any of the essential oils from the skin.

Pineapple Chili Sauce

Prep time: less than 15 minutes • Minimum cooking time: 2 hours • Makes 3 cups

1 ripe pineapple

1 jalapeño or serrano chili pepper, seeds and ribs removed, and finely chopped

½ cup firmly packed light brown sugar

2 TB. chopped fresh cilantro

2 TB. lime juice

Slow Savvy

Fresh pineapple is really best, but you can save time if you use crushed pineapple packed in pineapple juice. You should have about 3 cups, drained. Don't use the pineapple packed in heavy syrup, though. It will make the sauce too sweet.

Cut the top and bottom off pineapple; then cut off the peel. Use a paring knife to remove the woody eyes. Slice pineapple in half, and cut out the core from each half. Cut pineapple into 2-inch chunks, then chop the flesh in a food processor fitted with a steel blade using the on-and-off pulsing action or by hand.

Combine pineapple, jalapeño pepper, and brown sugar in the slow cooker. Cook on Low 4 to 6 hours or on High for 2 to 3 hours or until pineapple is tender. Scrape the sauce into an airtight container, and refrigerate until cold. Stir in cilantro and lime juice just before serving.

Applesauce

Prep time: less than 15 minutes • Minimum cooking time: 2 hours • Makes 4 to 6 servings

3 lb. McIntosh apples, peeled, cored, and sliced

½ cup crème de cassis

Place apples into the slow cooker, and pour crème de cassis over them. Cook on Low for 5 to 6 hours or on High for 2 to 3 hours or until apples are very tender.

For a chunky sauce, mash apples with a potato masher. For a smooth sauce, purée the mixture in a food processor fitted with a steel blade or in a blender. Chill, tightly covered, until ready to serve.

Crock Tales

Although the Jolly Green Giant is just a fantasy, there certainly was a Johnny Appleseed. Born John Chapman in Massachusetts in 1774, he began to trek the countryside around 1800, planting apple trees in what were then the western territories. He's credited with planting thousands of apple trees before his death in 1845.

Apple Butter

Prep time: less than 15 minutes • Minimum cooking time: 8 hours • Makes 2 pints

2 lb. McIntosh apples, unpeeled, cored, and sliced

1 cup firmly packed dark brown sugar

⅔ cup water

⅓ cup rum or additional water

1 tsp. ground cinnamon

Pinch of ground allspice

Slow Savvy

Instead of apples, you can use pears or apricots using the same recipe and quantities of fruit. You don't have to peel either fruit because the long cooking time will dissolve the tender skins.

Combine apples, brown sugar, water, rum, cinnamon, and allspice in the slow cooker. Cook on High for 3 hours or until apples are tender. Stir and reduce the heat to Low. Cook for an additional 5 to 6 hours, stirring occasionally, until the mixture is very thick and dark brown. Ladle apple butter into containers, cover tightly, and refrigerate.

Apple Orange Conserve

Prep time: less than 20 minutes   •   Minimum cooking time: 3½ hours   •   Makes 3 pints

4 Granny Smith apples, peeled, cored, and cut into ¼-inch dice

3 navel oranges, washed and cut into ¼-inch dice

1½ cups granulated sugar

½ cup dried cherries or raisins

½ cup chopped walnuts, toasted in a 350°F oven for 5 minutes

Combine apples, oranges, sugar, and cherries in the slow cooker. Cook on High for 2 hours or until orange peel is almost tender.

Uncover the slow cooker, and cook on High for an additional 1½ to 2 hours or until the mixture is very thick. Stir in walnuts, and ladle *conserve* into jars, cover tightly, and refrigerate.

Ellen on Edibles

Conserve is one of the many families of preserves. What distinguishes it from a marmalade or a jam is that it always includes at least two different fruits, as well as nuts. It's kept fairly chunky, so you can appreciate the different ingredients.

Cranberry Chutney

Prep time: less than 15 minutes • Minimum cooking time: 4 hours • Makes 4 cups

1 lb. fresh cranberries	2 TB. molasses
1½ cups granulated sugar	2 TB. grated fresh ginger
1 cup golden raisins	1 TB. curry powder
½ cup red wine vinegar	1 TB. Worcestershire sauce
½ cup red wine	½ to 1 tsp. hot red pepper sauce or to taste

Ellen on Edibles _____

Chutneys are spicy combinations that are unified by a hot, sweet, sour flavor profile. They can contain fruits or vegetables. Traditionally, chutney was one of the classic condiments to accompany Indian curry dishes. Today, they are eaten with many foods in place of spreads like ketchup. Chutneys were introduced to this country back in Colonial times.

Rinse cranberries, picking out any shriveled ones or twigs. Place cranberries into the slow cooker. Stir in sugar, raisins, vinegar, wine, molasses, ginger, curry powder, and Worcestershire sauce.

Cook on High for 3 to 4 hours or until cranberries have all "popped." Uncover the slow cooker, add red pepper sauce, and cook on High for an additional 1 to 2 hours or until the mixture has thickened. Ladle _chutney_ into containers, cover tightly, and refrigerate.

Smoked Apple Chutney

Prep time: less than 30 minutes   •   Minimum cooking time: 4 hours   •   Makes 4 cups

1 cup hickory or apple wood chips	¾ cup cider vinegar
6 large tomatoes, cut in half	¼ cup golden raisins
1 large onion, cut in half	¼ cup dried currants
4 garlic cloves, peeled	2 TB. grated fresh ginger
2 apples, peeled, cored, and quartered	Salt and cayenne to taste
1 cup granulated sugar	

Light a charcoal or gas grill. Soak wood chips in cold water for 30 minutes. Drain wood chips, and place them on the fire. Cover the grill with a small-holed fish grill, and place tomatoes, onion, garlic, and apples on the grill. Close the grill lid, or cover the grill with a sheet of heavy-duty aluminum foil. *Smoke* the vegetables and apples for 10 minutes.

Remove vegetables and apples from the grill. Peel, core, and seed tomatoes, and place them into the slow cooker. Peel and finely dice onion, and add it to the slow cooker along with garlic, apples, sugar, vinegar, raisins, currants, and ginger.

Cook on High for 3 to 4 hours or until the mixture is thick. Stir after the mixture comes to a boil. Uncover the slow cooker, and cook for an additional hour uncovered. Season with salt and cayenne. Ladle chutney into containers, cover tightly, and refrigerate.

Ellen on Edibles

Smoking is a technique of both flavoring and preserving food by penetrating it with the chemicals in the wood smoke. In the case of this recipe, the smoking is for flavor and the cooking and canning or refrigeration is what actually preserves the food.

Dried Fruit Chutney

Prep time: less than 20 minutes • Minimum cooking time: 4 hours • Makes 3 pints

½ lb. dried peaches, chopped

½ lb. dried apricots, chopped

½ lb. dried pineapple, chopped

½ lb. pitted prunes, chopped

½ lb. pitted dates, chopped

1½ cups cider vinegar

½ cup water

1 cup granulated sugar

2 tsp. curry powder or to taste

1 tsp. ground ginger

½ tsp. salt

Hot red pepper sauce to taste

Slow Savvy

Most of today's dried fruit is moist and pliable, which is why the dried fruits in this recipe are not soaked before cooking. If your dried fruit is hard and brittle, soak it in very hot tap water for 30 minutes before placing it in the slow cooker.

Combine peaches, apricots, pineapple, prunes, dates, vinegar, water, sugar, curry powder, ginger, and salt in the slow cooker. Stir well. Cook on High for 3 to 4 hours or until fruit is soft. Uncover the slow cooker, and cook on High for 1 to 2 hours more or until chutney has thickened. Season with hot red pepper sauce. Ladle chutney into containers, cover tightly, and refrigerate.

Part 7

Grand Finales

If you look at the dessert menu in a restaurant before deciding what will come first, chances are you're looking at this part of the book first. If so, I'm right with you.

I feel the first duty of any dessert is to be luscious, so you'll find a whole chapter of decadent delights. The slow cooker makes wonderful puddings of all types, as well as sweet fondue.

Then there are those times that the meal is rather heavy, so you want a lighter dessert. There is a barrel of apple favorites, plus other fabulous ways to treat fruit. From start to finish, your slow cooker can do it all.

Chapter 22

Sweet Sensations

In This Chapter

- ◆ Creamy bread and rice puddings
- ◆ Steamed puddings
- ◆ Dessert fondues
- ◆ Slow cooked cakes that make their own sauce

Old-fashioned desserts are always in style. Foods such as rice pudding and chocolate cake are the definition of sweet comfort foods.

You probably won't be surprised (by now) to hear that the slow cooker can create a wide variety of delicious desserts that border on the decadent. The recipes in this chapter don't rely on seasonal fruits, so they are easy to make at any time of the year.

Homey, Not Haute

You can't expect that a slow cooker is going to make swans spun out of sugar. It makes foods that need low heat and steam. That's why the categories of slow cooker desserts are limited. Most baked goods need a higher temperature than can be created in a slow cooker, and they need dry heat.

The "cake" recipes in this chapter are not really cakes; they are baked puddings. But that's all fine. The results are delicious, which is all that matters.

The Least You Need to Know

- The slow cooker can be used to make old-fashioned desserts like rice puddings and bread puddings.
- The slow cooker can make cakes that do not need the dry environment of a conventional oven.
- Use your slow cooker as a steamer for molds holding batters for steamed puddings.
- Fondue desserts can be cooked and served from a 1-quart slow cooker.

Classic Creole Bread Pudding with Caramel Sauce

Prep time: less than 15 minutes • Minimum cooking time: 3 hours • Makes 6 to 8 servings

Bread pudding:

3 eggs

1 cup granulated sugar

1¾ cups whole milk

6 TB. butter, melted

1½ tsp. pure vanilla extract

1 tsp. ground cinnamon

Pinch of salt

5 cups cubed French bread

½ cup golden raisins

½ cup chopped pecans

Caramel sauce:

½ cup (1 stick) butter

1½ cups firmly packed dark brown sugar

½ cup heavy cream

Whisk eggs in a large mixing bowl with sugar until thick and lemon-colored. Whisk in milk, melted butter, vanilla, cinnamon, and salt. Add bread cubes, and press down with the back of a spoon so they absorb egg mixture. Stir in raisins and pecans.

Grease the inside of the slow cooker liberally with vegetable oil spray or butter. Spoon the mixture into the slow cooker. Cook on High for 1 hour, then reduce the heat to Low and cook for 2 to 3 hours or until a toothpick inserted into the center comes out clean and an instant-read thermometer inserted into the center of the pudding reads 165°F.

While pudding is cooking, make the sauce. Melt butter in a small saucepan over medium heat; then add sugar. Cook and stir for 3 minutes or until sugar is melted. Whisk in cream, and stir until smooth, about 2 minutes. To serve, reheat the sauce, if necessary, and spoon it over servings of bread pudding.

Crock Tales

Bread pudding is part of the Creole tradition of Louisiana. It was brought over with the first French settlers. Because it's a way to use up stale bread, it was a "peasant dish" until the twentieth century.

White Chocolate Bread Pudding

Prep time: less than 15 minutes • Minimum cooking time: 2 hours • Makes 6 to 8 servings

3 eggs

2 cups whole milk

1½ cups white chocolate baking pieces, melted

6 TB. butter, melted

1 TB. grated orange zest

½ tsp. pure vanilla extract

Pinch of salt

6 cups cubed French bread

½ cup dried cranberries or raisins

Slow Savvy

This recipe can also be made with dark chocolate. Use the same amount as the white chocolate, and use chocolate milk instead of white milk.

Whisk eggs and milk together in a large mixing bowl. Beat in melted white chocolate, melted butter, orange zest, vanilla, and salt. Add bread cubes and dried cranberries, and press down with the back of a spoon so they absorb egg mixture.

Grease the inside of the slow cooker liberally with vegetable oil spray or butter. Spoon the mixture into the slow cooker. Cook on High for 2 to 3 hours or until a toothpick inserted into the center comes out clean and an instant-read thermometer inserted into the center of the pudding reads 165°F.

Thanksgiving Bread Pudding

Prep time: less than 15 minutes • Minimum cooking time: 2 hours • Makes 6 to 8 servings

2 cups solid-pack canned pumpkin

2 eggs, lightly beaten

1 (12-oz.) can evaporated milk

1 (14-oz.) can sweetened condensed milk

4 TB. butter, melted

2 tsp. pumpkin pie spice or 1 tsp. ground cinnamon, ½ tsp. ground allspice, and ½ tsp. grated nutmeg

Pinch salt

6 cups bread cubes

½ cup raisins

Combine pumpkin, eggs, evaporated milk, sweetened condensed milk, melted butter, pumpkin pie spice, and salt in a mixing bowl. Whisk until smooth. Add bread cubes, and press down with the back of a spoon so they absorb egg mixture. Stir in raisins.

Grease the inside of the slow cooker liberally with vegetable oil spray or butter. Spoon the mixture into the slow cooker. Cook on High for 1 hour, then reduce the heat to Low and cook for 2 to 3 hours or until a toothpick inserted into the center comes out clean and an instant-read thermometer inserted into the center of the pudding reads 165°F. Serve warm.

Cooker Caveats

There are two similar forms of canned pumpkin, and you want to make sure what you're buying is just pumpkin and not pumpkin pie filling. The filling is sweetened and already contains spices.

Orange Cranberry Rice Pudding

Prep time: less than 30 minutes   •   Minimum cooking time: 2 hours   •   Makes 4 to 6 servings

Rice:

1 cup converted long-grain rice

3 cups water

½ cup granulated sugar

1 tsp. salt

Pudding:

1½ cups whole milk

½ cup granulated sugar

½ cup orange marmalade

2 eggs, lightly beaten

½ cup dried cranberries

1 cup heavy cream

Place rice in a sieve, and rinse it well under cold water. Place it into a 2-quart saucepan with water, sugar, and salt. Bring to a boil over high heat, and boil for 15 minutes or until rice is tender. Drain rice. Grease the inside of the slow cooker liberally with vegetable oil spray or butter. Spoon rice into the slow cooker. Combine milk, sugar, orange marmalade, and eggs in a mixing bowl. Stir the mixture into rice, and add cranberries. Cook on Low for 4 to 5 hours or on High for 2 to 3 hours or until custard is set.

Remove pudding from the slow cooker, and chill it well. When rice is chilled, place cream in a chilled mixing bowl. Whip cream with an electric mixer on medium until it thickens, then increase the speed to high, and whip cream until stiff peaks form. *Fold* whipped cream into rice.

Ellen on Edibles

Fold is the term used for combining a light mixture, such as whipped cream or beaten egg whites, with a denser mixture. In this case, the dense mixture is the rice pudding. The light mixture goes on top, and you insert a rubber spatula into the center of the bowl and push it across the bottom of the bowl. This brings up the dense mixture. Then, turn the bowl a quarter turn, and repeat the motion. The object is to combine the two mixtures without deflating the lighter one.

Gingered Rice Pudding

Prep time: less than 15 minutes • Minimum cooking time: 2½ hours • Makes 6 to 8 servings

1 cup arborio rice	2 tsp. ground ginger
1 (14-oz.) can unsweetened coconut milk	½ tsp. ground cinnamon
1 (14-oz.) can sweetened condensed milk	½ tsp. salt
2 cups half-and-half	½ cup heavy cream

Combine rice, coconut milk, sweetened condensed milk, half-and-half, ginger, cinnamon, and salt in the slow cooker. Stir well.

Cook on Low for 5 to 7 hours or on High for 2½ to 3 hours or until rice is soft and the liquid is thick. Stir in heavy cream. Serve hot, warm, or chilled.

Cooker Caveats

Frequently coconut milk separates in the can with the liquid on the bottom and a thick layer of coconut on top. Whisk it briskly until the lumps are gone because they will not break up well in the slow cooker and you might end up with islands of hard coconut in your soft pudding.

Indian Pudding

Prep time: less than 30 minutes • Minimum cooking time: 3 hours • Makes 6 to 8 servings

5 cups whole milk	½ tsp. pure vanilla extract
¾ cup firmly packed dark brown sugar	3 TB. finely chopped crystallized ginger
½ cup pure maple syrup	½ tsp. salt
¾ cup yellow cornmeal	Vanilla ice cream or sweetened whipped cream
6 TB. butter, cut into small pieces	

Crock Tales

Because corn was introduced to the Pilgrims by Native Americans, anything made with corn had "Indian" as a prefix at one time or another. The other term for Indian Pudding is Hasty Pudding, and the Hasty Pudding Club at Harvard University was named for the dessert. Recipes for Indian or Hasty pudding go back to the early eighteenth century.

Combine milk, brown sugar, and maple syrup in a 2-quart saucepan, and stir well over low heat. Heat the mixture to a boil, stirring occasionally. Whisk in cornmeal, and simmer the mixture, whisking frequently, for 15 minutes or until it has thickened.

Stir butter and vanilla into the mixture. Whisk until butter is melted. Remove the pan from the heat, and stir in crystallized ginger and salt.

Grease the inside of the slow cooker liberally with vegetable oil spray or butter. Scrape the mixture into the slow cooker. Cook on Low for 3 to 5 hours or until the edges have darkened slightly and the center of pudding is set. Serve warm with vanilla ice cream or whipped cream.

Steamed Chocolate Pudding

Prep time: less than 20 minutes • Minimum cooking time: 3 hours • Makes 6 to 8 servings

1 TB. butter, softened	1 TB. rum or liqueur
½ cup granulated sugar	3 eggs, separated
¼ lb. good-quality bittersweet chocolate, chopped	1 tsp. pure vanilla extract
	¼ tsp. cream of tartar
¼ cup heavy cream	½ cup breadcrumbs

Generously grease a pudding steamer or mold that will fit inside your slow cooker with butter. Sprinkle the inside of the mold with 1 tablespoon sugar and set aside.

Combine chocolate, cream, and rum in a microwave-safe dish. Microwave on medium (50 percent) power for 1 minute. Stir and repeat, if necessary, until chocolate is melted; this can also be done in a small saucepan over low heat. Whisk egg yolks, and stir them into chocolate mixture along with vanilla.

Place egg whites into a mixing bowl, and beat with an electric mixer at medium speed until frothy. Add cream of tartar, increase the speed to high, and beat until stiff peaks form, gradually adding remaining sugar. Fold chocolate into egg whites, then fold in breadcrumbs. Scrape the batter into the prepared mold. Cover the mold with its lid or a double layer of aluminum foil, and crimp the edges of the foil to seal it tightly.

Place the sealed pudding steamer into the slow cooker, and add 2 cups water to the slow cooker. Steam pudding on Low for 6 to 8 hours or on High for 3 to 4 hours or until a toothpick inserted into the center comes out clean. Remove pudding from the slow cooker, and allow it to sit for at least 30 minutes. Unmold pudding onto a serving tray.

Slow Savvy

Dark chocolate is like fine wine. If stored under the right conditions, its flavor improves with age. Store chocolate in a cool place and tightly wrapped because it does absorb flavors from foods around it. Use milk chocolate and white chocolate within a few months, because the milk solids can spoil.

English Christmas Pudding

Prep time: less than 20 minutes • Minimum cooking time: 4 hours • Makes 6 to 8 servings

Pudding:

5 TB. butter (divided use)

1 TB. granulated sugar

½ cup chopped prunes

½ cup chopped dried figs

½ cup golden raisins

¼ cup dried currants

¼ cup chopped candied fruits

1 medium apple, peeled, cored, and finely chopped

¼ cup chopped walnuts

1 cup brandy

2 eggs, lightly beaten

½ cup firmly packed dark brown sugar

½ cup breadcrumbs

¼ cup all-purpose flour

1 tsp. ground cinnamon

½ tsp. grated nutmeg

½ tsp. baking powder

¼ tsp. salt

Hard sauce:

¼ lb. (1 stick) butter, softened to room temperature

1 lb. confectioners' sugar

2 TB. brandy or rum

¼ tsp. pure vanilla extract

Generously grease a 1½-quart pudding steamer or mold that will fit inside your slow cooker with 1 tablespoon butter. Sprinkle the inside of the mold with granulated sugar and set aside. Melt remaining 4 tablespoons butter.

Combine prunes, figs, raisins, currants, candied fruits, apple, walnuts, and ½ cup brandy in a mixing bowl. Stir to combine. Stir in melted butter, eggs, brown sugar, breadcrumbs, flour, cinnamon, nutmeg, baking powder, and salt. Stir well and pack the mixture into the prepared mold. Cover the mold with its lid or a double layer of aluminum foil, and crimp the edges of the foil to seal it tightly.

Place the sealed pudding steamer into the slow cooker, and add 2 cups water to the slow cooker. Steam pudding on Low for 8 to 10 hours or on High for 4 to 5 hours or until a toothpick inserted into the center comes out clean. Remove pudding from the slow cooker, and allow it to sit for at least 30 minutes. Remove the cover, and place a sheet of aluminum foil on the top. Using oven mitts if necessary, place one hand on top of the foil and flip the pudding steamer over with the other hand, so it sits on the foil. Pour the remaining ½ cup brandy over hot pudding, and cover it with the foil to keep warm.

Cooker Caveats

If you don't have a traditional copper or ceramic pudding steamer, you can make steamed puddings in any mold that will fit into your slow cooker. Do *not* use coffee cans or canned vegetable cans. Most of these cans contain lead and are painted with or sealed with materials that can release toxic gasses when heated.

To make hard sauce, combine butter, confectioners' sugar, brandy, and vanilla in a food processor fitted with a steel blade. Process until smooth, scraping down the sides of the bowl. Alternately, combine ingredients in a mixing bowl, and beat with an electric mixer at slow speed until smooth. Pass hard sauce separately.

Chocolate Fondue

Prep time: less than 15 minutes • Minimum cooking time: 45 minutes • Makes 4 to 6 servings

Fondue:

¾ lb. good-quality bittersweet chocolate, chopped

½ cup heavy cream

3 TB. liqueur or rum or 3 TB. additional cream

Dippers:

Hulled strawberries

Banana slices

Apple slices

1-inch cubes pound cake or angel food cake

Marshmallows

Combine chocolate, cream, and liqueur in a 1-quart slow cooker. Cook on Low for 45 to 60 minutes or until chocolate is melted. Stir well and serve with bowls of strawberries, banana slices, apple slices, cake cubes, or marshmallows for dipping.

Slow Savvy

The choice of liqueur, and whether you use one or not, changes the nature of the fondue. Crème de menthe will make it chocolate mint, while Grand Marnier or Triple Sec will add an orange flavor. Crème de cassis will give the dish a berry flavor, and amaretto adds a nutty aroma as well as flavor.

Butterscotch Fondue

Prep time: less than 15 minutes • Minimum cooking time: 40 minutes • Makes 4 to 6 servings

Fondue:

5 TB. butter

1 cup firmly packed dark brown sugar

1 cup heavy cream

¼ tsp. pure vanilla extract

1 TB. cornstarch

1 TB. cold water

Dippers:

Hulled strawberries

Banana slices

Apple slices

1-inch cubes pound cake or angel food cake

Marshmallows

Combine butter and brown sugar in a small saucepan over medium heat. Cook and stir for 3 to 5 minutes or until the mixture is bubbly. Gradually stir in heavy cream, and cook until any lumps of sugar that form have dissolved. Stir in vanilla, and transfer the mixture to a 1-quart slow cooker.

Cook on High for 25 minutes or until bubbly. Mix cornstarch with water, and stir cornstarch mixture into the slow cooker. Cook for 10 to 15 minutes or until bubbly and thickened. Serve with bowls of strawberries, banana slices, apple slices, cake cubes, or marshmallows for dipping.

Cooker Caveats

When cold cream is added to a sugar mixture, the sugar tends to lump again. Make sure the lumps are dissolved before transferring the mixture to the slow cooker. The slow cooker does not heat up hot enough to dissolve sugar.

Mocha Pecan Pudding Cake

Prep time: less than 15 minutes • Minimum cooking time: 2 hours • Makes 6 to 8 servings

1 cup granulated sugar

1 cup all-purpose flour

1 cup chopped pecans

3 TB. plus ¼ cup unsweetened cocoa powder (divided use)

1 TB. instant coffee granules

2 tsp. baking powder

½ tsp. pure vanilla extract

½ cup whole milk

3 TB. butter, melted

¾ cup firmly packed dark brown sugar

1¾ cups boiling water

Slow Savvy

This pudding cake is a slow cooker classic, and it never fails. It can be personalized in a number of ways. You can omit the coffee and add a few tablespoons fruit- or mint-flavored liqueur to the boiling water. You can add peanut butter baking chips or butterscotch baking chips in place of or along with the nuts.

Combine granulated sugar, flour, pecans, 3 tablespoons cocoa powder, coffee, and baking powder in a mixing bowl. Stir in vanilla, milk, and melted butter. Stir until a stiff batter forms. Grease the inside of the slow cooker liberally with vegetable oil spray or butter. Spread the batter into the slow cooker.

Sprinkle brown sugar and remaining ¼ cup cocoa powder over the batter. Pour boiling water over the batter. Cook on High for 2 to 2½ hours or until a toothpick inserted into the top cake layer comes out clean.

Lemon Orange Pudding Cake

Prep time: less than 15 minutes • Minimum cooking time: 2 hours • Makes 6 to 8 servings

1 (18-oz.) box lemon cake mix

1 cup orange marmalade

½ cup whole milk

1 TB. grated lemon zest

2 TB. lemon juice

2 cups boiling water

Ice cream, sorbet, or sweetened whipped cream

Combine lemon cake mix, orange marmalade, milk, and lemon zest in a mixing bowl. Stir until smooth. Grease the inside of the slow cooker liberally with vegetable oil spray or butter. Spread the batter into the slow cooker. Stir lemon juice into boiling water, and pour the mixture evenly over the batter.

Cook the cake on High for 2 to 2½ hours or until a toothpick inserted into the center of the top layer comes out clean. Serve cake with some sauce from the bottom of the pan, along with ice cream, sorbet, or whipped cream.

Slow Savvy

You'll notice that this dessert does not have any "cake mix taste" because lemon juice and other ingredients are added to the mix. This is called "doctoring" cake mixes, and there's a whole world of ways it can be accomplished. In fact, *The Complete Idiot's Guide to Cooking with Mixes* (Alpha Books, 2003) will be your guide.

Chapter 23

Fruity Favorites

In This Chapter

- ◆ Year-round apple desserts
- ◆ Homey American classics
- ◆ Seasonal specialties
- ◆ Winter treats with dried fruit

Fruit desserts are a way to satisfy your sweet tooth while also eating a nutritionally necessary helping of fruits. Most great fruit desserts let the fruit shine as the star, and you'll find that's true of the recipes in this chapter.

Apples are harvested in the fall, but cold storage techniques allow us to enjoy them year-round, and you'll find many options to enjoy them. Other fruits are more closely associated with summer, when they are local and at their lowest cost. But if you want to enjoy blueberries in January, modern transportation has made it possible to find them—it's the new definition of "airline food."

The All-American Apple

There are more than 300 species of apples grown in the United States—and that figure is down from a century ago. In fact, the array of apples can be a bit confusing. In general, you'll find Red Delicious, Golden Delicious, McIntosh, and Granny Smith in the markets at all times of year.

Granny Smith apples are good for pies because they hold their shape. But they are tart. Unless otherwise noted, the apple desserts in this chapter were created for the other three kinds, and the additional sugar listed is relatively low. If you can't find an apple except Granny Smith, increase the sugar by one third.

Discovering Dried Fruits

Historically, drying fruit was the first form of preserving the best of the season. Although many people associate dried fruit only with the ubiquitous raisin, there are now many succulent options from which to choose.

Dried fruits deliver a real flavor punch, and a little goes a long way. In addition to intense flavor, they're always "in season." And especially in winter, they might look like the best bet.

The Least You Need to Know

- There are more than 300 species of apples grown in the United States, and Red Delicious, Golden Delicious, McIntosh, and Granny Smith are the most common ones found in our markets.
- Granny Smith apples are tart, and unless the recipe specifically calls for this variety, extra sugar should be added if you're using them.
- Cobblers, crumbles, dumplings, and brown Bettys are all desserts that date back to Colonial times.
- Dried fruits have a more intense flavor than their fresh counterparts because the water has been removed.

Apple Crumble

Prep time: less than 15 minutes • Minimum cooking time: 1½ hours • Makes 4 to 6 servings

Apples:

2 lb. apples, cored and thinly sliced (and peeled, if desired)

¼ cup granulated sugar

2 TB. all-purpose flour

½ tsp. ground cinnamon

2 TB. butter, cut into small pieces

Topping:

¾ cup quick oats (not instant or old-fashioned)

½ cup firmly packed dark brown sugar

½ tsp. ground cinnamon

6 TB. (¾ stick) butter, melted

Place apples into the slow cooker. Mix sugar, flour, and cinnamon. Toss apples with the mixture; spread apples into an even layer. Dot the top of apples with butter.

Mix oats with brown sugar, cinnamon, and melted butter in a small mixing bowl. Sprinkle topping over apples. Cook on Low for 3 to 4 hours or on High for 1½ to 2 hours or until apples are soft.

Slow Savvy

This is really a master recipe for the crumble, so feel free to personalize it as you like. Add some chopped walnuts or pecans to the topping, include raisins or dried cranberries with the apples, or complement the cinnamon with ground ginger.

Baked Apples

Prep time: less than 15 minutes • Minimum cooking time: 3 hours • Makes 4 servings

4 baking apples, such as Jonathan and Northern Spy

2 TB. pure maple syrup

2 TB. butter, melted

¼ tsp. ground cinnamon

¼ cup chopped walnuts

¼ cup rum

Cooker Caveats

It's important to peel the top half of the apple. If you don't, the steam builds up inside the skin and the apple tends to fall apart.

Core apples and peel the top half only. Place apples into the slow cooker. Combine maple syrup, melted butter, cinnamon, and walnuts in a small bowl. Spoon equal portions of the mixture into cores of apples. Spoon rum over apples.

Cook on Low for 5 to 7 hours or on High for 3 to 4 hours or until apples are tender when pierced with the tip of a knife.

Apple Pudding

Prep time: less than 20 minutes • Minimum cooking time: 2½ hours • Makes 6 to 8 servings

¾ lb. loaf cinnamon raisin bread, broken into 1-inch pieces

1½ lb. apples, peeled, cored, and thinly sliced

4 eggs, lightly beaten

1 (14-oz.) can sweetened condensed milk

4 TB. butter, melted

½ tsp. apple pie spice or ground cinnamon

½ tsp. pure vanilla extract

Vanilla ice cream or sweetened whipped cream

Slow Savvy

If you want to make this pudding with plain white bread, add ½ cup raisins to the slow cooker along with the bread cubes and add an additional ½ teaspoon cinnamon to the egg mixture.

Grease the inside of the slow cooker with butter or spray it with vegetable oil spray. Combine bread cubes and apples in the slow cooker. Combine eggs, condensed milk, melted butter, apple pie spice, and vanilla in a mixing bowl. Beat well. Pour the mixture over bread and apples and stir well.

Cook on Low for 5 to 6 hours or on High for 2½ to 3 hours or until the pudding is set and puffed. Serve pudding with vanilla ice cream or sweetened whipped cream.

Rhubarb Cobbler

Prep time: less than 15 minutes   •   Minimum cooking time: 2½ hours   •   Makes 4 to 6 servings

Rhubarb:

1½ lb. *rhubarb*, rinsed, trimmed, and cut into ½-inch slices

½ cup granulated sugar

½ cup strawberry jam

Topping:

1 cup all-purpose flour

¼ cup granulated sugar

1½ tsp. baking powder

Pinch of salt

½ cup whole milk

3 TB. butter, melted

¼ tsp. pure vanilla extract

Combine rhubarb, sugar, and strawberry jam in a slow cooker. Cook on Low for 4 to 5 hours or on High for 2 to 2½ hours or until rhubarb is almost tender.

Combine flour, sugar, baking powder, and salt in a mixing bowl. Stir in milk, melted butter, and vanilla. Then, if cooking on Low, raise the heat to High. Drop cobbler batter by tablespoons onto the top of simmering rhubarb. Cook on High for 30 to 40 minutes until a toothpick inserted into the center of a dumpling comes out clean.

Ellen on Edibles

Rhubarb is one of the least understood foods. It's actually a vegetable although we eat it along with fruit and most frequently serve it for dessert. If you buy rhubarb at a farm stand, some of the leaves might still be attached. Discard them immediately because the leaves are poisonous.

Blueberry Dumplings

Prep time: less than 15 minutes • Minimum cooking time: 2½ hours • Makes 4 to 6 servings

Blueberries:

2 pints fresh or frozen blueberries

⅓ cup granulated sugar

2 TB. instant tapioca

1 TB. water

1 tsp. grated lemon zest

Topping:

1 cup all-purpose baking mix, such as Bisquick

2 TB. granulated sugar

⅓ cup whole milk

1 tsp. grated lemon zest

Ground cinnamon

Combine blueberries, sugar, tapioca, water, and lemon zest in the slow cooker. Cook on Low for 4 to 6 hours or on High for 2 to 3 hours or until the mixture is boiling and thickened.

Then, if cooking on Low, increase heat to High. Mix baking mix, sugar, milk, and lemon zest in a small bowl. Stir until the mix is moistened. Drop the batter by tablespoons onto hot blueberries. Sprinkle dumplings with ground cinnamon. Cook on High for 20 to 30 minutes until a toothpick inserted into the center of a dumpling comes out clean.

Slow Savvy

One of the pitfalls of baking desserts in the slow cooker is that the tops of cobblers and dumplings do not brown the way they do when they're cooked in a conventional oven. One remedy is the one used here: Sprinkle the batter with ground cinnamon to disguise its pale appearance.

Pear Brown Betty

Prep time: less than 20 minutes • Minimum cooking time: 2 hours • Makes 4 to 6 servings

8 slices white bread

4 TB. butter, softened

¾ cup firmly packed dark brown sugar

½ tsp. ground cinnamon

4 ripe pears, peeled, cored, and cut into 1-inch cubes

Vanilla ice cream or sweetened whipped cream

Preheat the oven to 400°F. Arrange bread slices on a baking sheet. Mix softened butter with sugar and cinnamon. Spread the mixture on bread slices. Bake bread for 5 to 7 minutes until butter has melted. Remove the pan from the oven, and break bread into 1-inch squares.

Arrange half the bread in the slow cooker, and top with pears. Cover pears with remaining bread pieces, and pack the mixture down firmly. Cook on Low for 4 to 6 hours or on High for 2 to 3 hours or until pears are tender. Serve with vanilla ice cream or sweetened whipped cream.

Crock Tales _____

Early American desserts are still part of our repertoire, and the brown Betty is one of them, along with cobblers, crumbles, and dumplings. A brown Betty is any fruit dessert that is made of layers using bread and fruit.

Poached Pears

Prep time: less than 15 minutes • Minimum cooking time: 2 hours • Makes 4 to 6 servings

4 ripe pears, peeled, halved, and cored

1 cup red wine

¼ cup crème de cassis

½ cup granulated sugar

1 cinnamon stick or ½ tsp. ground cinnamon

Slow Savvy

An easy way to core halved pears and apples is with a melon baller. The shape is efficient, and it leaves a neatly formed round hole.

Arrange pears in the slow cooker; cut them into quarters, if necessary, to make them fit. Combine wine, crème de cassis, and sugar in a mixing bowl. Stir well to dissolve sugar, and pour the mixture over pears. Add cinnamon stick to the slow cooker, or stir in ground cinnamon.

Cook on Low for 4 to 5 hours or on High for 2 to 2½ hours or until pears are tender when pierced with the point of a knife. Remove cinnamon stick if using. Serve warm or chilled.

Mincemeat

Prep time: less than 15 minutes • Minimum cooking time: 5 hours • Makes 4 cups, enough for 1 (9-inch) pie

½ cup shredded *beef suet* or 1 stick unsalted butter, cut into small pieces

2 Granny Smith apples, peeled, cored, and finely chopped

¾ cup firmly packed dark brown sugar

½ cup dark raisins

½ cup dried currants

½ cup chopped dried figs

¼ cup chopped dried dates

1 cup apple cider or apple juice

¼ cup brandy

2 TB. lemon juice

½ tsp. ground cinnamon

½ tsp. ground allspice

½ tsp. grated nutmeg

Pinch of salt

Combine suet or butter, apples, brown sugar, raisins, currants, figs, dates, apple cider, brandy, lemon juice, cinnamon, allspice, nutmeg, and salt in the slow cooker. Stir well to dissolve sugar.

Cook on Low for 6 to 8 hours or on High for 3 to 4 hours or until the mixture is bubbly and apples are soft. Then, if cooking on Low, raise the heat to High. Uncover the slow cooker, and cook for an additional 2 hours or until the mixture has thickened. Stir occasionally during the last hour of cooking.

Ellen on Edibles

Beef suet is the hard white beef fat that surrounds many cuts of meat—it's what you usually discard when you're trimming a roast. It's the traditional fat used in mincemeat because the historic recipe also includes chopped meat. You can substitute 1 stick butter, cut into small pieces or grated, for the suet.

Winter Fruit Compote

Prep time: less than 15 minutes • Minimum cooking time: 2 hours • Makes 6 to 8 servings

1 cup cranberry juice

½ cup granulated sugar

½ cup crème de cassis

1 TB. orange zest

2 tsp. grated lemon zest

1 cinnamon stick

2 TB. butter

3 ripe large pears, peeled and cut into 1½-inch dice

½ cup dried apricots, halved

½ cup dried cranberries

Vanilla ice cream

Crock Tales

Hot fruit dishes such as this one are part of Colonial heritage, especially in the South. In communities such as Williamsburg, Virginia, the pineapple was a symbol of welcome and hospitality, and a cauldron of fruit was included at many meals or as a welcome snack when guests arrived.

Combine cranberry juice, sugar, crème de cassis, orange zest, lemon zest, and cinnamon stick in a saucepan. Bring to a boil over medium-high heat, stirring to dissolve sugar. Pour the mixture into the slow cooker. Stir in butter, pears, apricots, and cranberries.

Cook on Low for 4 to 6 hours or on High for 2 to 3 hours or until pears are tender. Remove cinnamon stick. Serve the hot compote over vanilla ice cream.

Glossary

accouterment An accouterment is an accompaniment, trapping, or garnish.

al dente Italian for "against the teeth." Refers to pasta (or other ingredient such as rice) that is neither soft nor hard, but just slightly firm against the teeth. This, according to many pasta aficionados, is the perfect way to cook pasta.

all-purpose flour Flour that contains only the inner part of the wheat grain. Usable for all purposes from cakes to gravies.

allspice Named for its flavor echoes of several spices (cinnamon, cloves, nutmeg), allspice is used in many desserts and in rich marinades and stews.

almonds Mild, sweet, and crunchy nuts that combine nicely with creamy and sweet food items.

amaretto A popular almond liqueur.

anchovies (also **sardines**) Tiny, flavorful preserved fish that typically come in cans. The strong flavor from these salted fish is a critical element in many recipes. Anchovies are a traditional garnish for Caesar salad, the dressing of which contains anchovy paste.

andouille sausage A sausage made with highly seasoned pork chitterlings and tripe, and a standard component of many Cajun dishes. *Andouillette* is a similar sausage, although smaller and usually grilled.

antipasto   A classic Italian-style appetizer plate including an assortment of prepared meats, cheeses, and vegetables such as prosciutto, capicolla, mozzarella, mushrooms, and olives.

arborio rice   A plump Italian rice used, among other purposes, for risotto.

artichoke hearts   The center part of the artichoke flower, often found canned in grocery stores and used as a stand-alone vegetable dish or as a flavorful base for appetizers or main courses.

arugula   A spicy-peppery garden plant with leaves that resemble a dandelion and have a distinctive—and very sharp—flavor.

au gratin   The quick broiling of a dish before serving to brown the top ingredients. The term is often used as part of a recipe name and implies cheese and a creamy sauce.

au jus   French for "with juice," an expression that refers to a dish that is served with juices that result from cooking (as in roast beef).

baba ghanoush   A Middle Eastern–style spread composed of eggplant, lemon juice, garlic, olive oil, and tahini.

baby corn   This small version of corn on the cob, eaten whole, is a popular ingredient in Southeast Asian–style cooking. In the United States, baby corn is often imported preserved and/or pickled from Southeast Asia.

bake   To cook in a dry oven. Baking is one of the most popular methods of cooking and is used for everything from roasts, vegetables, and other main courses to desserts such as cakes and pies. Dry-heat cooking often results in a crisping of the exterior of the food being cooked. Moist-heat cooking, through methods such as steaming, poaching, etc., brings a much different, moist quality to the food.

baking pans   Pans used for baking potatoes to chicken, cookies to croutons.

balsamic vinegar   Vinegar produced primarily in Italy from a specific type of grape and aged in wood barrels. It is heavier, darker, and sweeter than most vinegars.

bamboo shoots   Crunchy, tasty white parts of the growing bamboo plant, often purchased canned.

barbecue   This is a loaded word, with different, zealous definitions in different parts of the country. In some cases it is synonymous with grilling (quick-cooking over high heat); in others, to barbecue is to cook something long and slow in a rich liquid (barbecue sauce).

basil   A flavorful, almost sweet, resinous herb delicious with tomatoes and in all kinds of Italian or Mediterranean-style dishes.

baste   To keep foods moist during cooking by spooning, brushing, or drizzling with a liquid.

beat   To quickly mix substances.

Belgian endive   A plant that resembles a small, elongated, tightly packed head of romaine lettuce. The thick, crunchy leaves can be broken off and used with dips and spreads.

blanch   To place a food in boiling water for about 1 minute (or less) to partially cook the exterior and then submerge in or rinse with cool water to halt the cooking. This is a common method for preparing some vegetables such as asparagus for serving and also for preparing foods for freezing.

blend   To completely mix something, usually with a blender or food processor, more slowly than beating.

boil   To heat a liquid to a point where water is forced to turn into steam, causing the liquid to bubble. To boil something is to insert it into boiling water. A rapid boil is when a lot of bubbles form on the surface of the liquid.

bok choy (also **Chinese cabbage**)   A member of the cabbage family with thick stems, crisp texture, and fresh flavor. It is perfect for stir-frying.

bouillon   Dried essence of stock from chicken, beef, vegetable, or other ingredients. This is a popular starting ingredient for soups as it adds flavor (and often a lot of salt).

bouquet garni   A collection of herbs including bay leaf, parsley, thyme, and others. Traditionally, these herbs are tied in a bunch or packaged in cheesecloth for cooking and subsequent removal. Bouquet garni is often found in the spice section of your grocery store and through specialty spice vendors.

braise   To cook with the introduction of some liquid, usually over an extended period of time.

bread flour   Wheat flour used for bread and other recipes.

breadcrumbs   Tiny pieces of crumbled dry bread. Breadcrumbs are an important component in many recipes and are also used as a coating, for example with breaded chicken breasts.

brie   A creamy cow's milk cheese from France with a soft, edible rind and a mild flavor.

brine A highly salted, often seasoned, liquid that is used to flavor and preserve foods. To brine a food is to soak, or preserve, it by submerging it in brine. The salt in the brine penetrates the fibers of the meat and makes it moist and tender.

broil To cook in a dry oven under the overhead high-heat element.

broth *See* stock.

brown To cook in a skillet, turning, until the surface is brown in color, to lock in the juices.

brown rice Whole-grain rice with a characteristic brown color from the bran coating; more nutritious and flavorful than white rice.

bulgur A wheat kernel that has been steamed, dried, and crushed that is sold in fine and coarse textures.

Cajun cooking A style of cooking that combines French and Southern characteristics and includes many highly seasoned stews and meats.

cake flour A high-starch, soft, and fine flour used primarily for cakes.

Calvados An apple brandy from Normandy.

canapés Bite-size hors d'oeuvres made up of any number of ingredients but prepared individually and usually served on a small piece of bread or toast.

capers Usually sold preserved in jars, capers are the flavorful buds of a Mediterranean plant. The most common size is *nonpareil* (about the size of a small pea); others are larger, including the grape-size caper berries produced in Spain.

capicolla Seasoned, aged pork shoulder; a traditional component of antipasto dishes.

caramelize The term's original meaning is to cook sugar over low heat until it develops a sweet caramel flavor; however, the term is increasingly gaining use to describe cooking vegetables (especially onions) or meat in butter or oil over low heat until they soften, sweeten, and develop a caramel color. Caramelized onions are a popular addition to many recipes, especially as a pizza topping.

caraway A distinctive spicy seed used for bread, pork, cheese, and cabbage dishes. It is known to reduce stomach upset, which is why it is often paired with, for example, sauerkraut.

cardamom An intense, sweet-smelling spice, common to Indian cooking, used in baking and coffee.

casserole dishes   Primarily used in baking, these covered containers hold liquids and solids together and keep moisture around ingredients that might otherwise dry out.

cayenne pepper   A fiery spice made from (hot) chili peppers, especially the Cayenne chili, a slender, red, and very hot pepper.

ceviche   A seafood dish in which fresh fish or seafood is marinated for several hours in highly acidic lemon or lime juice, tomato, onion, and cilantro. The acid "cooks" the seafood.

cheddar   The ubiquitous hard cow's milk cheese with a rich, buttery flavor that ranges from mellow to sharp. Originally produced in England, cheddar is now produced worldwide.

cheese boards or **cheese trays**   A collection of three or four mixed-flavor cheeses arranged on a tray, platter, or even cutting board. One classic example would be at least one cheese made from cow's, sheep's, and goat's milk. Often restaurants will offer a selection of cheeses as a "cheese flight," or course.

chevre   Goat cheese, a typically creamy-salty soft cheese delicious by itself or paired with fruits or chutney. Chevres vary in style from mild and creamy to aged, firm, and flavorful. *Artisanal* chevres are usually more expensive and sold in smaller quantities; these are often delicious by themselves. Other chevres produced in quantity are less expensive and often more appropriate for combining with fruit or herbs.

chickpeas (also **garbanzo beans**)   The base ingredient in hummus, chickpeas are high in fiber and low in fat, making this a delicious and healthful component of many appetizers and main dishes.

chili peppers (also **chile peppers**)   Any one of many different "hot" peppers, ranging in intensity from the relatively mild ancho pepper to the blisteringly hot habanero.

chili powder   A seasoning blend that includes chili pepper, cumin, garlic, and oregano. Proportions vary among different versions, but they all offer a warm, rich flavor.

Chinese five-spice powder   A blend of cinnamon, anise, ginger, fennel, and pepper used in Asian cooking.

chives   A member of the onion family, chives are found at the grocery store as bunches of long leaves that resemble the green tops of onions. They provide an easy onion flavor to any dish. Chives are very easy to grow, and many people have them in their garden.

chop   To cut into pieces, usually qualified by an adverb such as "*coarsely* chopped," or by a size measurement such as "chopped into ½-inch pieces." "Finely chopped" is much closer to mince.

chorizo   A spiced pork sausage eaten alone and as a component in many recipes.

chutney   A thick condiment always served with Indian curries made with fruits and/or vegetables with vinegar, sugar, and spices.

cider vinegar   Vinegar produced from apple cider, popular in North America.

cilantro   A member of the parsley family and used in Mexican cooking and some Asian dishes. Cilantro is what gives some salsas their unique flavor. Use in moderation, as the flavor can overwhelm.

cinnamon   A sweet, rich, aromatic spice commonly used in baking or desserts. Cinnamon can also be used for delicious and interesting entrées.

cloves   A sweet, strong, almost wintergreen-flavor spice used in baking and with meats such as ham.

coat   To cover all sides of a food with a liquid, sauce, or solid.

conserve   A preserve made with at least two types of fruits as well as nuts.

converted rice   White rice that has been subjected to a steam pressure process that keeps the grains separate when cooked.

cookie sheet   A large, thin, flat tray used for baking cookies and other foods.

core   To remove the unappetizing middle membranes and seeds of fruits and vegetables.

coriander   A rich, warm, spicy herb used in all types of recipes, from African to South American, from entrées to desserts.

cottage cheese   A mild, creamy-texture cheese made from curds from fresh cow's milk cheese. Curds vary in size; containers will indicate, for example, "small curd" or "large curd." In its low-fat and nonfat forms, cottage cheese is a useful component of low-fat dips, spreads, and other recipes.

count   On packaging of seafood or other foods that come in small sizes, you'll often see a reference to the count, how many of that item compose 1 pound. For example, 31 to 40 count shrimp are large appetizer shrimp often served with cocktail sauce; 51 to 60 are much smaller.

coulis   A thick paste, often made with vegetables or fruits, used as a sauce for many recipes.

couscous Granular semolina (durum wheat) that is cooked and used in many Mediterranean and North African dishes.

cream To blend an ingredient to get a soft, creamy liquid or substance.

crimini mushrooms A relative of the white button mushroom but brown in color and with a richer flavor. *See also* portobello mushrooms.

crimp To press pastry between your fingers to create a decorative edge such as around a pie crust.

croutons Pieces of bread, usually between ¼ and ½ inch in size, that are sometimes seasoned and baked, broiled, or fried to a crisp texture.

crudités Fresh vegetables served as an appetizer, often all together on one tray.

cuisine A style of cooking, typically reflecting a country or region (such as "Spanish cuisine"), a blending of flavors and cuisines (called "fusion"), or an updated style (such as "New Latin").

cumin A fiery, smoky-tasting spice popular in Middle Eastern and Indian dishes. Cumin is a seed; ground cumin seed is the most common form of the spice used in cooking.

curing A method of preserving uncooked foods, usually meats or fish, by either salting and smoking or pickling.

curry A general term referring to rich, spicy, Indian-style sauces and the dishes prepared with them. Common ingredients include hot pepper, nutmeg, cumin, cinnamon, pepper, and turmeric.

custard A cooked mixture of eggs and milk. Custards are a popular base for desserts.

dash A dash refers to a few drops, usually of a liquid, that is released by a quick shake of, for example, a bottle of hot sauce.

daube A French slow cooked dish of meat, vegetables, and wine.

deglaze To scrape up the bits of meat and seasoning left in a pan or skillet after cooking. Usually done by adding a liquid such as wine or broth and creating a flavorful stock that can be used to create sauces.

dehydrate To remove the natural moisture from a food by drying it at a low temperature with dry heat.

demi-sec French for "half-dry." Refers to wine that contains residual sugar and has noticeable sweetness.

demitasse   French for "half-cup." Refers to a small cup, usually of coffee.

devein   To remove the dark vein from the back of a large shrimp with a sharp knife.

dice   To cut into small cubes about ¼-inch square.

Dijon mustard   Hearty, spicy mustard made in the style of the Dijon region of France.

dill   A slightly sour, unique herb that is perfect for eggs, cheese dishes, and, of course, vegetables (pickles!).

dolce   Italian for "sweet." Refers to desserts as well as styles of a food (*Gorgonzola dolce* is a style of Gorgonzola cheese).

double boiler   A set of two pots designed to nest together, one inside the other, and provide consistent, moist heat for foods that need delicate treatment. The bottom pot holds water (not quite touching the bottom of the top pot); the top pot holds the ingredient you want to heat.

dough   A soft, pliable mixture of liquid and flour that is the intermediate step, prior to cooking, for many bread or baked-goods recipes such as cookies or bread.

dredge   To cover a piece of food with a dry substance such as flour or corn meal.

dressing   A liquid mixture usually containing oil, vinegar, and herbs used for seasoning salads and other foods. Also the solid dish commonly called "stuffing" used to stuff turkey and other foods.

drizzle   To lightly sprinkle drops of a liquid over food. Drizzling is often the finishing touch to a dish.

dust   To sprinkle a dry substance, often a seasoning, over a food or dish.

emulsion   A combination of liquid ingredients that do not normally mix well beaten together to create a thick liquid, such as a fat or oil with water. Classic examples are salad dressings and mayonnaise. Creation of an emulsion must be done carefully and rapidly to ensure that particles of one ingredient are suspended in the other.

entrée   The main dish in a meal.

etouffee   Cajun for "smothered." This savory, rich sauce (often made with crayfish) is served over rice.

extra-virgin olive oil   *See* olive oil.

falafel   Middle Eastern hand food composed of seasoned, ground chickpeas formed into balls, cooked, and often used as a filling for pita bread.

fennel   In seed form, a fragrant, licorice-tasting herb. The bulbs have a much milder flavor and a celerylike crunch and are used as a vegetable in salads or cooked recipes.

feta   This white, crumbly, salty cheese is popular in Greek cooking, on salads, and on its own. Traditional feta is usually made with sheep's milk, but feta-style cheese can be made from sheep's, cow's, or goat's milk. Its sharp flavor is especially nice with bitter, cured black olives.

fillet   A piece of meat or seafood with the bones removed.

fines herbs   A fresh or dried herb blend made from parsley, tarragon, chervil, and chives.

fish basket   A grill-top metal frame that holds a whole fish intact, making it easier to turn.

fish poacher   A long, rectangular pan with a separate metal basket designed to hold a fish either above boiling water for steaming or in simmering liquid for poaching. Fish poachers come in varying sizes up to 24 inches, although an 18-inch version will cover all but the largest meals.

flake   To break into thin sections, as with fish.

floret   The flower or bud end of broccoli or cauliflower.

flour   Grains ground into a meal. Wheat is perhaps the most common flour, an essential component in many breads. Flour is also made from oats, rye, buckwheat, soybeans, etc. Different types of flour serve different purposes. *See also* all-purpose flour; bread flour; cake flour; whole-wheat flour.

foie gras   A goose liver from specially grown geese, foie gras is considered quite a delicacy for many. *Pâté de foie gras* contains mostly goose liver with pork liver or other ingredients added.

fold   To combine a dense and light mixture with a circular action from the middle of the bowl.

fricassee   A dish, usually chicken, cut into pieces and cooked in a liquid or sauce.

fritter   A food such as apples or corn coated or mixed with batter and deep-fried for a crispy, crunchy exterior.

fry   To pan-cook over high heat with butter or oil.

fusion   To blend two or more styles of cooking, such as Chinese and French.

garam masala   A famous Indian seasoning mix, rich with cinnamon, pepper, nutmeg, cardamom, and other spices.

garlic A member of the onion family, a pungent and flavorful element in many savory dishes. A garlic bulb, the form in which garlic is often sold, contains multiple cloves. Each clove, when chopped, provides about 1 teaspoon garlic.

garnish An embellishment not vital to the dish but added to enhance visual appeal.

ginger Available in fresh root or powdered form, ginger adds a pungent, sweet, and spicy quality to a dish. It is a very popular element of many Asian and Indian dishes, among others.

goulash A rich, Hungarian-style meat-and-vegetable stew seasoned with paprika, among other spices.

grate To shave into tiny pieces using a sharp rasp or grater.

grill To cook over high heat, usually over charcoal or gas.

grind To reduce a large, hard substance, often a seasoning such as peppercorns, to the consistency of sand.

grits Coarsely ground grains, usually corn.

Gruyère A rich, sharp cow's milk cheese with a nutty flavor made in Switzerland.

handful An unscientific measurement term that refers to the amount of an ingredient you can hold in your hand.

haute cuisine French for "high cooking." Refers to painstakingly prepared, sometimes exotic, delicious, and complex meals (such as one might find at a high-end traditional French restaurant).

Havarti A creamy, Danish, mild cow's milk cheese perhaps most enjoyed in its herbed versions such as Havarti with dill.

hazelnuts (also **filberts**) A sweet nut popular in desserts and, to a lesser degree, in savory dishes.

hearts of palm Firm, elongated, off-white cylinders from the inside of a palm tree stem tip. They are delicious in many recipes.

herbes de Provence A seasoning mix including basil, fennel, marjoram, rosemary, sage, and thyme.

herbs The leaves of flavorful plants characterized by fresh, pungent aromas and flavors, such as parsley, sage, rosemary, and thyme.

hoisin sauce A sweet Asian condiment similar to ketchup made with soybeans, sesame oil, chili peppers, and sugar.

hors d'oeuvre   French for "outside of work" (the "work" being the main meal). An hors d'oeuvre can be any dish served as a starter before the meal.

horseradish   A sharp, spicy root that forms the flavor base in many condiments from cocktail sauce to sharp mustards. It is a natural match with roast beef. The form generally found in grocery stores is prepared horseradish, which contains vinegar and oil, among other ingredients. If you come across pure horseradish, use it much more sparingly than the prepared version, or try cutting it with sour cream.

hummus   A thick, Middle Eastern spread made of puréed chickpeas (garbanzo beans), lemon juice, olive oil, garlic, and often tahini (sesame seed paste).

infusion   A liquid in which flavorful ingredients such herbs have been soaked or steeped to extract that flavor into the liquid.

Italian breadcrumbs   Breadcrumbs that are seasoned with parsley, other herbs, garlic, and Parmesan cheese.

Italian seasoning (also **spaghetti sauce seasoning**)   The ubiquitous grocery store blend, which includes basil, oregano, rosemary, and thyme, is a useful seasoning for quick flavor that evokes the "old country" in sauces, meatballs, soups, and vegetable dishes.

jicama   A juicy, crunchy, sweet, Central American vegetable that is eaten both raw and cooked. It is available in many large grocery stores as well as from specialty vendors. If you can't find jicama, try substituting sliced water chestnuts.

julienne   To slice into very thin pieces.

kirsch (also **Kirschwasser**)   A clear, tart, cherry-flavored liqueur.

kosher salt   A coarse-grained salt made without any additives or iodine used by many cooks because it does not impart a chemical flavor.

lentils   Tiny lens-shape pulses (beans) used in European, Middle Eastern, and Indian cuisines.

linguiça   A Portuguese sausage spiced with garlic, cumin, and cinnamon.

liver   The nutritious and flavorful organ meat from all types of fowl and animal.

macerate   To mix sugar or another sweetener with fruit. The fruit softens, and its juice is released to mix with the sweetener.

marbling   The fat that is imbedded in less-lean cuts of meat.

marinate   To soak meat, seafood, or other food in a seasoned sauce, called a marinade, which is high in acid content. The acids break down the muscle of the meat, making it tender and adding flavor.

marjoram   A sweet herb, a cousin of and similar to oregano, popular in Greek, Spanish, and Italian dishes.

marmalade   A fruit-and-sugar preserve that contains whole pieces of fruit peel, to achieve simultaneous sweetness (from the sugar) and tartness (from the fruit's natural acids). The most common marmalades are made with citrus fruits such as orange and lemon.

mascarpone   A thick, creamy, spreadable cheese, traditionally from Italy, although versions using the same name are made in the United States. It is perhaps one of the most delicious and decadent dessert toppings for fruit.

medallion   A small round cut, usually of meat or vegetables such as carrots or cucumbers.

meld   A combination of *melt* and *weld*, many cooks use this term to describe how flavors blend and spread over time throughout dips and spreads. Melding is often why recipes call for overnight refrigeration and is also why some dishes taste better as leftovers.

meringue   A baked mixture of sugar and beaten egg whites, often used as a dessert topping.

mesclun   Mixed salad greens, usually containing lettuce and assorted greens such as arugula, cress, endive, and others.

Mexican cheese blend   A grated combination of Monterey Jack, pepper Jack, and cheddar cheese used in Mexican and Southwestern cooking.

mince   To cut into very small pieces smaller than diced pieces, about ⅛ inch or smaller.

mold   A decorative, shaped metal pan in which contents, such as mousse or gelatin, set up and take the shape of the pan.

muhammara   A classic Turkish dip or spread that contains walnuts, onion, garlic, breadcrumbs, and hot peppers.

mull (or **mulled**)   To heat a liquid with the addition of spices and sometimes sweeteners.

mushrooms   Any one of a huge variety of *edible* fungi (note emphasis on "edible"; there are also poisonous mushrooms). *See also* crimini mushrooms, porcini mushrooms, portobello mushrooms, shiitake mushrooms, and white mushrooms.

nouvelle cuisine   *Nouvelle* is French for "new." Refers to a style of cooking that is relatively light in flavor and consistency.

nutmeg   A sweet, fragrant, musky spice used primarily in baking.

nuts   Shell-covered seeds (or fruits) whose meat is rich in flavor and nutrition. A critical component in many dishes, many nuts are tasty on their own as well. *See also* almonds; hazelnuts; pecans; walnuts.

olivada   A simple spread composed of olives, olive oil, and pepper that carries a wealth of flavor.

olive oil   A fragrant liquid produced by crushing or pressing olives. Extra-virgin olive oil is the oil produced from the first pressing of a batch of olives; oil is also produced from other pressings after the first. Extra-virgin olive oil is generally considered the most flavorful and highest quality and is the type you want to use when your focus is on the oil itself. Be sure the bottle label reads "extra-virgin."

olives   The fruit of the olive tree commonly grown on all sides of the Mediterranean. There are many varieties of olives but two general types: green and black. Black olives are also called ripe olives.

oregano   A fragrant, slightly astringent herb used in Greek, Spanish, and Italian dishes.

orzo   A rice-shape pasta used extensively in Greek cooking.

oxidation   The browning of fruit flesh that happens over time and with exposure to air. Although it's best to prepare fresh fruit dishes just before serving, sometimes that's not possible. If you need to cut apples in advance, minimize oxidation by rubbing the cut surfaces with a lemon half.

oyster sauce   A thick Asian sauce made from ground oysters, salt, and water with a slightly sweet taste.

paella   A grand Spanish dish of rice, shellfish, onion, meats, rich broth, and herbs.

pan-broil   To quick-cook over high heat in a skillet with a minimum of butter or oil. (Frying, on the other hand, uses more butter or oil.)

pancetta   Salted, seasoned bacon; an important element in many Italian-style dishes.

paprika   A rich, red, warm, earthy spice that also lends a rich red color to many dishes.

parboil   To partially cook in boiling water or broth. Parboiling is similar to blanching, although blanched foods are quickly cooled with cold water.

pare   To scrape away the skin of a food, usually a vegetable, as part of preparation for serving or cooking.

Parmesan A hard, dry, flavorful cheese primarily used grated or shredded as a seasoning for Italian-style dishes.

parsley A fresh-tasting green leafy herb used to add color and interest to just about any savory dish. Often used as a garnish just before serving.

pâté A savory loaf that contains meats, spices, and often a lot of fat, served cold spread or sliced on crusty bread or crackers.

peanuts The nutritious and high-fat seeds of the peanut plant (a relative of the pea) that are sold shelled or unshelled and in a variety of preparations, including peanut butter and peanut oil. Some people are allergic to peanuts, so be careful about including them in recipes.

pecans Rich, buttery nuts native to North America. Their flavor, a terrific addition to appetizers, is at least partially due to their high unsaturated fat content.

pepper A biting and pungent seasoning, freshly ground pepper is a must for many dishes and adds an extra level of flavor and taste.

peppercorns Large, round, dried berries that are ground to produce pepper.

pesto A thick spread or sauce made with fresh basil leaves, garlic, olive oil, pine nuts, and Parmesan cheese. Other new versions are made with other herbs. Rich and flavorful, pesto can be made at home or purchased in a grocery store and used on anything from appetizers to pasta and other main dishes.

pickle A food, usually a vegetable such as a cucumber, that has been pickled in brine.

pilaf A rice dish in which the rice is browned in butter or oil, then cooked in a flavorful liquid such as a broth, often with the addition of meats or vegetables. The rice absorbs the broth, resulting in a savory dish.

pinch An unscientific measurement term that refers to the amount of an ingredient—typically a dry, granular substance such as an herb or seasoning— you can hold between your finger and thumb.

pine nuts (also **pignoli** or **piñon**) Nuts grown on pine trees, that are rich (read: high fat), flavorful, and, yes, a bit pine-y. Pine nuts are a traditional component of pesto and add a wonderful hearty crunch to many other recipes.

pita bread A flat, hollow wheat bread that can be used for sandwiches or sliced, pizza style, into slices. Pita bread is terrific soft with dips or baked or broiled as a vehicle for other ingredients.

pizza stone Preheated with the oven, a pizza stone cooks a crust to a delicious, crispy, pizza-parlor texture. It also holds heat well, so a pizza removed from the oven on the stone will stay hot for as long as a half-hour at the table. Can also be used for other baking needs, including bread.

plantain   A relative of the banana, a plantain is larger, milder in flavor, and used as a staple in many Latin American dishes.

poach   To cook a food in simmering liquid, such as water, wine, or broth.

porcini mushrooms   Rich and flavorful mushrooms used in rice and Italian-style dishes.

portobello mushrooms   A mature and larger form of the smaller crimini mushroom, portobellos are brownish, chewy, and flavorful. They are trendy served as whole caps, grilled, and as thin sautéed slices. *See also* crimini mushrooms.

preheat   To turn on an oven, broiler, or other cooking appliance in advance of cooking so the temperature will be at the desired level when the assembled dish is ready for cooking.

presentation   The appealing arrangement of a dish or food on the plate.

preserved black beans   Soybeans packed in salt that have an earthy, pungent flavor.

prosciutto   Dry, salt-cured ham, rich and evocative of Italy. Prosciutto is popular in many simple dishes in which its unique flavor is allowed to shine.

purée   To reduce a food to a thick, creamy texture, usually using a blender or food processor.

ragout (pronounced *rag-OO*)   A thick, spicy stew.

red pepper flakes   Hot yet rich, crushed red pepper, used in moderation, brings flavor and interest to many savory dishes.

reduce   To heat a broth or sauce to remove some of the water content, resulting in more concentrated flavor and color.

refried beans (also **refritos**)   Twice-cooked beans—most often pinto beans—softened into a thick paste and often seasoned with peppers and spices. Most refried beans include lard, but many fat-free, lard-free versions are available.

render   To cook a meat to the point where its fat melts and can be removed.

reserve   To hold a specified ingredient for another use later in the recipe.

rice vinegar   Vinegar produced from fermented rice or rice wine, popular in Asian-style dishes.

risotto   A popular Italian rice dish made by browning arborio rice in butter or oil, then slowly adding liquid to cook the rice, resulting in a creamy texture.

roast   To cook something uncovered in an oven.

Rock Cornish game hens   A hybrid of Cornish and White Rock chickens that weigh about two pounds and are between four and six weeks old.

Roquefort   A world-famous (French) creamy but sharp sheep's milk cheese containing blue lines of mold, making it a "blue cheese."

rosemary   A pungent, sweet herb used with chicken, pork, fish, and especially lamb. A little of it goes a long way.

roux   A mixture of butter or another fat source and flour used to thicken liquids such as sauces.

saffron   A famous spice made from stamens of crocus flowers. Saffron lends a dramatic yellow color and distinctive flavor to a dish. Only a tiny amount needs to be used, which is good because saffron is very expensive.

sage   An herb with a musty yet fruity, lemon-rind scent and "sunny" flavor. It is a terrific addition to many dishes.

salsa   A style of mixing fresh vegetables and/or fresh fruit in a coarse chop. Salsa can be spicy or not, fruit-based or not, and served as a starter on its own (with chips, for example) or as a companion to a main course.

sauté   To pan-cook over lower heat than used for frying.

savory   A popular herb with a fresh, woody taste.

scant   A measurement modification that specifies "include no extra," as in 1 scant teaspoon.

Scoville scale   A scale used to measure the "hot" in hot peppers. The lower the Scoville units, the more mild the pepper. Ancho peppers, which are mildly hot, are about 3,000 Scovilles; Thai hot peppers are about 6,000; and some of the more daring peppers such as Tears of Fire and habanero are 30,000 Scovilles or more.

scrapple   A sausagelike mixture of seasoned pork and cornmeal that is formed into loaves and sliced for cooking.

sear   To quickly brown the exterior of a food over high heat to preserve interior moisture (that's why many meat recipes involve searing).

search engine   An Internet tool that, based on keywords you type, helps find related websites on the topic you searched for. A good search engine such as Google or Yahoo! will suggest sites that are close to what you seek.

sesame oil   An oil, made from pressing sesame seeds, that is tasteless if clear and aromatic and flavorful if brown since the seeds are toasted to release flavor.

shallot   A member of the onion family that grows in a bulb somewhat like garlic and has a milder onion flavor. When a recipe calls for shallot, you use the entire bulb. (They might or might not have cloves.)

shellfish   A broad range of seafood, including clams, mussels, oysters, crabs, shrimp, and lobster. Some people are allergic to shellfish, so be careful when including them in recipes.

shiitake mushrooms   Large (up to five inches or more), dark brown mushrooms originally from the Far East with a hearty, meaty flavor that can be grilled or used as a component in other recipes and as a flavoring source for broth. They can be used either fresh or dried.

shred   To cut into many long, thin slices.

silverskin   The almost iridescent membrane surrounding certain parts of a meat tenderloin.

simmer   To boil gently so the liquid barely bubbles.

skewers   Thin wooden or metal sticks, usually about eight inches long, that are perfect for assembling kebabs, dipping food pieces into hot sauces, or serving single-bite food items with a bit of panache.

skillet (also **frying pan**)   A generally heavy, flat metal pan with a handle designed to cook food over heat on a stovetop or campfire.

skim   To remove fat from the top of liquid.

slice   To cut into thin pieces.

slow cooker   An electric countertop device with a lidded container that maintains a low temperature and slowly cooks its contents, often over several hours or a full day.

smoke   An ancient way to flavor and preserve food with the chemicals from wood smoke.

steam   To suspend a food over boiling water and allow the heat of the steam (water vapor) to cook the food. Steaming is a very quick cooking method that preserves the flavor and texture of a food.

stew   To slowly cook pieces of food submerged in a liquid. Also, a dish that has been prepared by this method.

Stilton   The famous English blue cheese, delicious with toasted nuts and renowned for its pairing with Port wine.

stir-fry   To cook food in a wok or skillet over high heat, moving and turning the food quickly to cook all sides.

stock   A flavorful broth made by cooking meats and/or vegetables with seasonings until the liquid absorbs these flavors. This liquid is then strained and the solids discarded. Stock can be eaten by itself or used as a base for soups, stews, sauces, risotto, or many other recipes.

strata   A savory bread pudding made with eggs and cheese.

stripe   To scrape off a fruit's or vegetable's skin in lengthwise strokes, leaving a "stripe" of the skin between each scrape.

succotash   A cooked vegetable dish usually made of corn and peppers.

suet   Hard white beef fat.

sweat   To cook vegetables, covered, over low heat to soften them.

sweetbreads   The thymus gland from common food animals, most popularly from veal. They are prized for their creamy, delicate texture.

Tabasco sauce   A popular brand of Louisiana hot pepper sauce used in usually small portions to season savory food. The name also refers to a type of hot pepper from Tabasco, a state in Mexico, that is used to make this sauce.

tahini   A paste made from sesame seeds that is used to flavor many Middle Eastern recipes, especially baba ghanoush and hummus.

tamarind   A sweet, pungent, flavorful fruit used in Indian-style sauces and curries.

tapenade   A thick, chunky spread made from savory ingredients such as olives, lemon juice, and anchovies. Adventuresome grocery and gourmet stores are likely to have different versions focusing on specific ingredients, from olives to peppers and mushrooms.

tarragon   A sour-sweet, rich-smelling herb perfect with seafood, vegetables (especially asparagus), chicken, and pork.

thyme   A minty, zesty herb whose leaves are used in a wide range of recipes.

toast   To heat something, usually bread, so it is browned and crisp.

toast points (also **toast triangles**)   Pieces of toast with the crusts removed that are then cut on the diagonal from each corner, resulting in four triangle-shape pieces.

tofu   A cheeselike substance made from soybeans and soy milk. Flavorful and nutritious, tofu is an important component of foods across the globe, especially from the Far East.

tomatillo   A small, round fruit with a distinctive spicy flavor reminiscent of its cousin, the tomato. Tomatillos are a traditional component of many south-of-the-border dishes. To use, remove the papery outer skin, rinse off any sticky residue, and chop like a tomato.

tripe   The stomach of a cow.

turmeric   A spicy, pungent yellow root used in many dishes, especially Indian cuisine, for color and flavor. Turmeric is the source of the brilliant yellow color in many prepared mustards.

twist   A twist (as in lemon or other citrus fruit twist) is simply an attractive way to garnish an appetizer or other dish. Cut a thin, about $\frac{1}{8}$-inch-thick cross-section slice of a lemon, for example. Then take that slice and cut from the center out to the edge of the slice on one side. Pick up the piece of lemon and pull apart the two cut ends in opposite directions.

veal   Meat from a calf, generally characterized by mild flavor and tenderness. Certain cuts of veal, such as cutlets and scaloppini, are well suited to quick-cooking.

vegetable steamer   An insert for a large saucepan. Also a special pot with tiny holes in the bottom designed to fit on another pot to hold food to be steamed above boiling water. The insert is generally less expensive and resembles a metal poppy flower that expands to touch the sides of the pot and has small legs. *See also* steam.

vehicle   A food that is used to scoop or dip another ingredient, such as vegetables or pitas with dip.

venison   Meat from deer or other large wild game animals.

vichy   A classic vegetable dish of carrots cooked in water and sugar.

vinegar   An acidic liquid widely used as dressing and seasoning. Many cuisines use vinegars made from different source materials. *See also* balsamic vinegar; cider vinegar; rice vinegar; white vinegar; wine vinegar.

walnuts   Grown worldwide, walnuts bring a rich, slightly woody flavor to all types of food. For the quick cook, walnuts are available chopped and ready to go at your grocery store. They are delicious toasted and make fine accompaniments to cheeses.

water chestnuts   Actually a tuber, water chestnuts are a popular element in many types of Asian-style cooking. The flesh is white, crunchy, and juicy, and the vegetable holds its texture whether cool or hot.

whisk   To rapidly mix, introducing air to the mixture.

white mushrooms Ubiquitous button mushrooms. When fresh, they will have an earthy smell and an appealing "soft crunch." White mushrooms are delicious raw in salads, marinated, sautéed, and as component ingredients in many recipes.

white vinegar The most common type of vinegar found on grocery store shelves. It is produced from grain.

whole-wheat flour Wheat flour that contains the entire grain.

wild rice Actually a grain with a rich, nutty flavor, popular as an unusual and nutritious side dish.

wine vinegar Vinegar produced from red or white wine.

wok A large, round pan perfect for quick-cooking and stir-frying.

Worcestershire sauce Originally developed in India and containing tamarind, this spicy sauce is used as a seasoning for many meats and other dishes.

yeast Tiny fungi that, when mixed with water, sugar, flour, and heat, release carbon dioxide bubbles, which, in turn, raise bread. The yeast also provides that wonderful warm, rich smell and flavor.

zest Small slivers of peel, usually from a citrus fruit such as lemon, lime, or orange.

zester A small kitchen tool used to scrape zest off a fruit. A small grater also works fine.

Metric Conversion Chart

The scientifically precise calculations needed for baking are not necessary when cooking conventionally or in a slow cooker. This chart is designed for general cooking. If making conversions for baking, grab your calculator and compute the exact figure.

Converting Ounces to Grams

The numbers in the following table are approximate. To reach the exact amount of grams, multiply the number of ounces by 28.35.

Ounces	Grams
1 oz.	30 g
2 oz.	60 g
3 oz.	85 g
4 oz.	115 g
5 oz.	140 g
6 oz.	180 g
7 oz.	200 g
8 oz.	225 g
9 oz.	250 g
10 oz.	285 g

continues

continued

Ounces	Grams
11 oz.	300 g
12 oz.	340 g
13 oz.	370 g
14 oz.	400 g
15 oz.	425 g
16 oz.	450 g

Converting Quarts to Liters

The numbers in the following table are approximate. To reach the exact amount of liters, multiply the number of quarts by 0.95.

Quarts	Liter
1 cup (¼ qt.)	¼ L
1 pint (½ qt.)	½ L
1 qt.	1 L
2 qt.	2 L
2½ qt.	2½ L
3 qt.	2³/₄ L
4 qt.	3³/₄ L
5 qt.	4³/₄ L
6 qt.	5½ L
7 qt.	6½ L
8 qt.	7½ L

Converting Pounds to Grams and Kilograms

The numbers in the following table are approximate. To reach the exact amount of kilograms, multiply the number of pounds by 453.6.

Pounds	Grams; Kilograms
1 lb.	450 g
$1^1/_2$ lb.	675 g
2 lb.	900 g
$2^1/_2$ lb.	1,125 g; $1^1/_4$ kg
3 lb.	1,350 g
$3^1/_2$ lb.	1,500 g; $1^1/_2$ kg
4 lb.	1,800 g
$4^1/_2$ lb.	2k g
5 lb.	$2^1/_4$ kg
$5^1/_2$ lb.	$2^1/_2$ kg
6 lb.	$2^3/_4$ kg
$6^1/_2$ lb.	3 kg
7 lb.	$3^1/_4$ kg
$7^1/_2$ lb.	$3^1/_2$ kg
8 lb.	$3^3/_4$ kg

Converting Fahrenheit to Celsius

The numbers in the following table are approximate. To reach the exact temperature, subtract 32 from the Fahrenheit reading, multiply the number by 5, then divide by 9.

Fahrenheit	Celsius
170°F	77°C
180°F	82°C
190°F	88°C
200°F	95°C
225°F	110°C
250°F	120°C
300°F	150°C
325°F	165°C
350°F	180°C
375°F	190°C
400°F	205°C

continues

continued

Fahrenheit	Celsius
425°F	220°C
450°F	230°C
475°F	245°C
500°F	260°C

Converting Inches to Centimeters

The numbers in the following table are approximate. To reach the exact number of centimeters, multiply the number of inches by 2.54.

Inches	Centimeters
$\frac{1}{2}$ in.	1.5 cm
1 in.	2.5 cm
2 in.	5 cm
3 in.	8 cm
4 in.	10 cm
5 in.	13 cm
6 in.	15 cm
7 in.	18 cm
8 in.	20 cm
9 in.	23 cm
10 in.	25 cm
11 in.	28 cm
12 in.	30 cm

Index

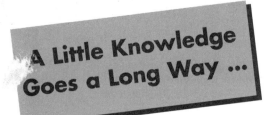
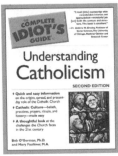

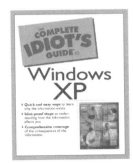